WOMAN ON TRIAL

WOMAN ON TRIAL

Gender and the Accused Woman in Plays from
Ancient Greece to the Contemporary Stage

EDITED BY
Amelia Howe Kritzer and Miriam López-Rodríguez

<teneo> //press
AMHERST, NEW YORK

Copyright 2015 Teneo Press

All rights reserved
Printed in the United States of America

No part of this publication may be reproduced, stored in or introduced into a retrieval system, or transmitted, in any form, or by any means (electronic, mechanical, photocopying, recording, or otherwise), without the prior permission of the publisher.

Requests for permission should be directed to:
permissions@teneopress.com, or mailed to:
Teneo Press
University Corporate Centre
100 Corporate Parkway
Suite 128
Amherst, NY 14226

Library of Congress Control Number: 2015932531
Women on trial: gender and the accused woman in plays from ancient greece to the contemporary stage / edited by Amelia Kritzer and Miriam López-Rodríguez
p. cm.
Includes bibliographical references and index.
ISBN 978-1-934844-59-5 (alk. paper).

TABLE OF CONTENTS

INTRODUCTION
    Amelia Howe Kritzer 1

ANCIENT AND MEDIEVAL DRAMA 23

Chapter 1.: Gender on Trial in Euripides' *Hecuba*
    Chiara Meccariello 25

Chapter 2.: The Confucian View of Woman in *Snow in Midsummer*
    Marta Steiner 45

RENAISSANCE DRAMA 65

Chapter 3.: Woman's Value on Trial in *Troilus and Cressida*
    Lilly J. Goren 67

Chapter 4.: Raping Justice in John Webster's *The White Devil*
    Karol Cooper 87

CROSS-PERIOD COMPARISONS 111

Chapter 5.: Transgressive Women From Shakespeare to Shaw and Bryans
    Dana Di Pardo Léon-Henri 113

Chapter 6.: Why Does Mary Queen of Scots Always Get Her Head Chopped Off?
    Verna A. Foster 137

Chapter 7.: Witchcraft Trials in Arthur Miller's *The Crucible* and Caryl Churchill's *Vinegar Tom*
    Amelia Howe Kritzer 157

MODERN DRAMA 175

Chapter 8.: The Flapper on Trial in *Machinal*
Miriam López-Rodríguez 177

Chapter 9.: Defining Gender and Sexuality in *The Children's Hour*
Araceli González Crespán 199

CONTEMPORARY DRAMA 221

Chapter 10.: Stoning Maries
Valentina Mikluc 223

Chapter 11.: Aileen Wuornos Or, The Heroine of Last Resort
Jules Odendahl-James 239

Chapter 12.: The Trial as Framework in Emily Mann's *Mrs. Packard*
Lisa Hagen 259

Chapter 13.: Race on Trial
Rovie Herrera Medalle 277

Chapter 14.: The Death of Ashley Smith
Amanda Lockitch 293

Index 319

Woman on Trial

INTRODUCTION

Amelia Howe Kritzer

A broad survey of drama since its beginnings in ancient Greece reveals a remarkable figure recurring persistently throughout many centuries: the woman on trial. Considering its frequent appearance across time in Western drama and its presence in non-Western drama as well, this figure deserves attention. The figure of the woman on trial, as played out in dramas of very different social and theatrical contexts, provides a reference point for a trans-historical examination of gender. The plays built around the figure of the woman on trial express awareness of tension between the lives of individual women and the status of women as a class, anxieties regarding the potential power of women, and patterns of gender policing from the early stages of recorded history to the present. The accusations leveled at the women may target actions or behavior, or they may arise from the woman's identity; but in all the plays the accusations against a particular woman point to the artificial and unstable construction of women as a class assigned to a subordinate status in their respective societies. The inherent instability of this class construction is exposed by the unruly woman. The woman deemed unruly by the system of authority governing her society challenges the borders or even the basic structure of her class, displaying a type of power that is seen as a threat to the gendered social order. The trial dramatized in the play reduces the sense of threat by disciplining the unruly woman and reinforcing gender boundaries. Nevertheless, the presence and speech of the unruly woman, especially in the public arena of performed drama, expresses the ongoing and unresolved challenge to gender boundaries and masculine dominance. These dramas—even those that end with the death of the accused woman—celebrate the disruption brought into play by the unruly woman rather than the forces of suppression that restore gender order. Thus, the plays, especially in performance, serve as an ongoing incitement to resist the gender norms through which women are constructed as a class.

Authority, Resistance, Tragedy

Although the dramatist may not intend to incite resistance to gender, in choosing the trial of a woman as a topic, he or she chooses a subject that gives the central female character important action and speech in opposition to male characters. Attesting to historical circumstances, the earlier plays addressed by the essays in this volume are all written by or attributed to men. The standpoint of male privilege in many of the early plays would also have been reinforced, in performances, by the fact that all the characters were played by male actors. As the survey of these plays moves forward chronologically, the mixture of male and female playwrights indicates the emergence of specifically female voices in the ongoing project of articulating the tensions between actual women and the construction of women as a class within male-dominated societies. The most recent plays considered in this volume are all written by women, testifying to a current predominance of female voices in the consideration of issues relating to gender. These plays most often use the woman on trial to illuminate the injustices of male-female power disparities, assuming and addressing a feminist audience.

Trials in themselves provide a rich source of drama, with their clear oppositions, emotionally evocative language, and high stakes, as well as the ceremonious proceedings that enhance the theatricality of the performance when these dramas are presented on stage. Many different kinds of trials have provided the basis for plays, and the questions they address differ accordingly; but when the drama focuses on a woman as defendant within a male-dominated system, the question of gender becomes paramount as oppositions intensify and conflict plays out on multiple levels. This dramatic situation, as observed in works from different time periods and cultures, illuminates gender norms and sanctions for violating those norms, as well as delineating the personalities, motives, and tactics of female characters representing challenges to those norms. The fact that many of the dramas are based on actual people and events enhances their real-life relevance.

As a reflection of the society in which it was created, each play offers a specific perspective on the gendered nature of law as a social institution that has confined, controlled, deprived, and silenced women, as well as on the role of formal and informal systems of law in establishing and maintaining gender as an ideology central to male domination. Historically, the law and the courts enforcing the law have formed one of the strongest bastions of male privilege in the social systems within which they are located. Not until the late 19th century did a handful of women gain admission to the bar in the United States and Europe, and not until the middle of the 20th century did women commonly appear in court as jury members, legal representatives, or judges. Courts have served to affirm the denial of property rights, divorce, custody of children, and bodily autonomy to women. Legal systems have identified certain acts, such as prostitution and contraception, as woman-specific crimes. They have placed special restrictions on women, such as limiting those with whom they could associate or prescribing the wearing of particular clothing. Courts convened by religious bodies or informal courts formed by communities have created even greater disparity between men and women in terms of authority, constraint, and sanctioning: historically, for example, such courts authorized a husband to act as jailor and judge of his wife, giving him the right to assault her as long as he did not kill or maim her. A steady stream of ever more intrusive abortion restrictions at the state level in the United States demolishes the illusion that court regulation of women's bodies is a matter for history books. The recent trial and conviction of the Pussy Riot performance artists in Russia provides further evidence that contemporary courts continue to serve as a means of enforcing social norms based in and related to gender expectations.[1] The dramas of the woman on trial thus take place against the background of patriarchal systems that do not give women the right to define themselves; nevertheless, the dramas represent women through the power manifested in the presence and, in most cases, the speech of the dramatic character.

As a reflection of gender policing, the drama of a woman on trial sets in motion the proverbial clash between an irresistible force and an immovable object. The court or authority presiding at the trial constitutes the immovable object: its very existence implies the maintenance of existing power differentials. The woman on trial is the irresistible force: she resists the governing arrangements, and this resistance constitutes her as a dynamic character who engages the attention and sympathy of audiences. In the social world of the play she may be perceived as a sexual transgressor, a madwoman, an avenger, a witch, or a protestor, but her hallmark consists in expressing a power that is desperate, deviant, anarchic—and dramatic. Her actions mark her as "a renegade from the disciplinary practices which would mold her as a gendered being" (Faith 2). She may be randomly and impulsively rebellious or committed to a "deliberate rejection of the values that sustain existing hierarchical power relations" (Faith 8), but in either case the unruly woman claims autonomy in defiance of the highest authority within her social world. Alone in the nexus of power, the unruly woman's femaleness stands out with particular irony in the public and male-dominated enclave of the court.

The frequent appearance of the unruly woman in drama indicates the broad appeal of this figure, as she invokes freedom and suggests the possibility and even inevitability of resistance against arbitrary authority. Her very presence actualizes the possibility of resistance, and the actions for which she is arraigned demonstrate evasion of or confrontation with established norms. Thus, the unruly woman represents the possibility for individuals to create selves and establish autonomy in defiance of social constraint. The trial, however, is structured and controlled by societal authority, whether presented as a ruler or as rule embodied in law or tradition. When representatives of this power structure bring the unruly woman to trial, the trial itself, regardless of outcome, places her under control and demonstrates her inability to maintain freedom, as it reinstates the unitary power claimed by males in patriarchal societies. While it reinforces traditional power relations, the trial nevertheless almost inevitably functions simultaneously to subvert traditional gender definitions by explicitly enforcing aspects of gender construction that are, in the ideology of patriarchy, posited as natural. Even the statement of charges against the unruly woman exposes the usually hidden mechanisms of control. Furthermore, the trial often gives the unruly woman a voice and a platform for her explanations or justifications of her action. Although the dramatic action may end with loss of life for the central woman character, she has still gained the only kind of victory available to her: a public hearing of her story.

Tragedy most often serves as the dramatic form that expresses and resolves the conflicts inherent in the oppression of women. Tragedy focuses on choice, and thus emphasizes the autonomy of the tragic figure. The tragic woman has, in a sense, achieved tragedy through her exercise of choice. As Aristotle observed, tragedy arouses, intensifies, and ultimately purges fear. Unlike Aristotelian drama's enactment of the fall of powerful men, however, the dramas of women on trial enact the choice to create power that transcends or challenges established patterns through which power is created and exercised, opening up a space in which a woman may exercise choice. The fear aroused by such tragedies goes beyond that associated with disobeying the law; it responds to a threat that boundaries will be dissolved, structures destroyed, and predictable patterns overthrown. Tragedy purges fear not only through the restoration of order, but also through revealing a truth by means of the central character's sacrifice. The tragic woman bears the truth of her choice to rebel, enacting it in the oppositional proceedings of the trial and on the public platform of the stage. While some dramatists—particularly the earlier ones in the chronological survey—use tragic form straightforwardly, modern and contemporary dramatists often invoke the form in order to play against it. Using the Brechtian techniques of interruption, redirection, and theatricalization, they explicitly place choice in the context of existing or historical power relations and prompt audiences to resist those patterns and envision alternatives to them.

Scope of the Essays

This collection of essays considers a diverse range of plays about accused women, from the stages of ancient Greece to those of contemporary societies, identifying the forms through which they expose gender construction and emphasizing the means by which they contest masculine power. Assembled in response to a call for papers, they consider a range of time periods and cultures that is not fully representative geographically or historically, but yet evocative of very different settings. The predominance of plays from Western cultures indicates the centrality of the legal trial in Western culture, while the inclusion of a play from traditional Chinese music theatre provides a glimpse of the ritualistic nature of Eastern processes of justice, in contrast to the adversarial nature of Western court proceedings (see Eyeoyang). Commonalities are striking. The plays present the woman on trial as a representative of an oppressed class, noting that in many cases the social context of the play denies women's rights to their own bodies, their children, and any form of action independent of their husband or other male head of the patriarchal family. The essays illuminate the ways in which the plays interrogate legal authority as an institution that subordinates and controls women through the categories and relationships it constructs, as well as by sanctioning particular actions. In some cases the woman on trial has not committed the offense for which she is being tried; in others she has committed a serious crime, often murder. In some plays, the action hinges on determining innocence versus guilt, while in others, the focus centers on understanding innocence and guilt as qualities that are structured by culture and follow differing parameters for men and women. Many of the plays also highlight additional social factors, especially nationality, race, poverty, or working-class status, as issues that interact with gender to create the persona of the woman on trial. The woman or women on trial may represent dissidents or activists in general rather than women specifically. Finally, the plays often emphasize the failure of the law to protect women—even women who exemplify conventional virtue.

The plays examined in this volume bear a close connection with history. Those from the Western canon testify to the gradual development of the legal trial as a social institution, Thirteen of the twenty-two plays discussed in the essays are based on actual events. Gender definitions and expectations, as "a spectrum, not a binary" (Renzetti 11), vary according to historic norms. Actions considered to be criminal differ from one time period to another, and the scope of choice for women changes as the plays move forward historically. In the earliest play to be considered, Euripides' *Hecuba* (c. 424 BCE), the title character is put on trial because she commits acts of war away from the field of battle, within a domestic space that is the only environment in which Hecuba and the other female slaves with whom she has conspired wield power. Joan, in G.B. Shaw's *Saint Joan* (1923) wages war effectively on the battlefield, but it is her extraordinary leadership in itself that brings accusations, because her youth and gender are considered incompatible with such action except through supernatural force. Hermione in Shakespeare's *The Winter's Tale* (published 1623) finds herself accused of a crime that was defined as such in Tudor England: she, like the unfortunate Anne Boleyn, is accused of adultery, and because she is married to the monarch, is therefore also accused of treason. The women accused of witchcraft in Arthur Miller's *The Crucible* (1953) and Caryl Churchill's *Vinegar Tom* (1976) represent an era spanning the 15th and 16th centuries in which witchcraft was commonly believed to be part of everyday reality and was addressed in law—an area of law primarily directed at the control of women. The title character of Emily Mann's *Mrs. Packard* (2007), a documentary play about a 19th-century legal trial, suffers incarceration in a mental hospital because her opinions on theology differ from those of her husband. Lillian Hellman's *The Children's Hour* (1934) took inspiration from an actual case in 19th-century Scotland, in which two women teachers were accused by a pupil of having a lesbian relationship with each other. Modern plays, reflecting a time period in which women sought greater autonomy and self-expression, as well as contemporary plays set in the present, tend to focus on murder and other acts of aggression, emphasizing questions about responsibility that implicate social conditions for the accused women.

Differences in the nature and outcome of trials reflect the meta-narratives of judgment associated with the historical periods in which they were written. Hecuba's trial is conducted by the legendary military leader Agamemnon, and constitutes just one minor incident in the long and complex narrative of his life. Dou E, the unjustly accused heroine of *Snow in Midsummer*, the 13th-century Chinese music theatre work by Guan Hanqing, receives vindication through supernatural means. Similarly, the supernatural authority consulted in *The Winter's Tale* testifies to Hermoine's innocence. Most of the plays, however, rely on the audience to judge the case presented to them, even if the play deals with a historical incident. The play may create an ironic contrast between the world in which the action took place and the world of the audience, as in John Webster's 1612 play *The White Devil*, Shaw's *St. Joan*, Miller's *The Crucible*, Mann's *Mrs. Packard*, Shelagh Stephenson's *Five Kinds of Silence* (2000), or Debbie Tucker Green's *Stoning Mary* (2005). It may offer a more complete story of the accused woman than that implied by her popular image in literature, as in Shakespeare's *Troilus and Cressida* (c. 1602), the Mary Queen of Scots plays, Joan Bryans' 2006 play *By Some Divine Mistake*, or Carson Kreitzer's *Self Defense, or the Death of Some Salesmen* (2002). It may attempt to present a factual account of the events that produced the accusation, as in Hellman's *The Children's*

Hour. Finally, a number of modern and contemporary plays emphasize the social environment and personal complexities of the accused woman or women, including Sophie Treadwell's *Machinal,*(1928), Churchill's *Vinegar Tom*, Naomi Wallace's *And I and Silence* (2011), Kreitzer's *Self Defense, or the Death of Some Salesmen*, and the two recent plays about the death of a young woman in custody, *The Death of Ashley Smith* (2012) by Leah Jane Esau and *Watching Glory Die* (2012) by Judith Thompson. In all of these plays the accused woman, whether innocent or guilty, presents a narrative that contrasts with or questions the social environment within which she is positioned.

Common Themes

Though these plays have been written over a time period of nearly twenty-four centuries, striking similarities appear in the issues motivating the accusations. These issues highlight the interaction of gender and crime, as described in the *Routledge International Handbook of Crime and Gender Studies*: "Gender is fundamental to our understanding of crime and our response to it. Gender influences whether some actions are defined as crimes, whether someone engages in crime, how and which crimes are committed, and how we respond to crimes" (Renzetti 11).

Two important issues that recur in the plays are the gendered division between public and private spheres, and the question of women's desire. These two issues converge in the term "angel in the house," the title of a poem by Coventry Patmore. Though this poem was first published in 1854 and was first subjected to feminist interrogation in the 1931 essay by Virginia Woolf titled "Killing the Angel in the House," its implications apply to even the earliest plays examined in this volume. All of the plays reveal and, to a greater or lesser extent, challenge the expectation that women's primary role consists in serving a husband or other representative of male authority within the private setting of a household. The 1854 poem, furthermore, expresses confidence that this confinement and service is what women desire. The women on trial, needless to say, bring out the possibility and actuality of very different desires.

The accused women in these plays have, in many cases, responded to the physical violence or psychological oppression of their domestic environment by taking upon themselves the active and oppositional roles associated with the masculine gender. The Young Woman in Treadwell's *Machinal* and Alma in Bryans' *By Some Divine Mistake* remove the primary obstacle to their desires by killing their husbands. The sisters in Stephenson's *Five Kinds of Silence* kill their abusive father. These plays allude to isolated woman forced to seek personal solutions to the social structures in which they are trapped, and women who strike out against the most painfully immediate representative of an oppressive system. Two plays center on revenge killings: in Euripides' *Hecuba,* the title character engineers an attack on the man who killed her son in spite of a pledge to keep him safe; and in Debbie Tucker Green's *Stoning Mary*, the title character kills the boy soldier who has slain her parents. Both of these plays depict women forced to seek personal retribution when the prevailing system of public law does not address their grievance. In addition, several plays show women suspected of killing or plotting to kill their husbands. The central character Vittoria in Webster's *The White Devil,* for example, is falsely accused of murdering her husband. When King Leontes in Shakespeare's *The Winter's Tale* begins to suspect his wife Hermione of infidelity, he adds to that accusation one of plotting to kill him. Finally, suspicions about her involvement in the murder of her husband Darnley contribute to the image created of Mary Queen of Scots as a dangerous woman in the plays based on her life. (Notably, Mary's cousin Elizabeth I, who carefully excluded many markers of femininity from her public identity, legally condemned many men to death.) Accusations that center on murder or threats to murder a husband point to a perception of acute vulnerability and a strong undercurrent of insecurity. While subscribing to the ideas that women naturally desire their husbands and their prescribed roles, the representatives of masculine society in these plays do not fully believe in the loyalty and submission of the women in their intimate circle; thus, the trial represents their attempt to separate the truly feminine woman from the woman who feigns femininity.

Issues related to the gendered division between public and private space play out in a number of trials. Action in the public sphere, which in many historical and cultural contexts is not expected or permitted for women, constitutes the basis of the accusation in several plays. For Joan, in Shaw's *St. Joan*, the action involved taking command of an army and leading it into battle. Mary Queen of Scots engaged in plots and maneuvers aimed at placing her on the throne of England. For the accused women in Churchill's *Vinegar Tom*, merely giving vent to anger in public or seeking relief from domestic pressures in public spaces leads to charges of witchcraft. Mrs. Packard in the play by Emily Mann voices religious opinions that differ from those of her clergyman husband within the church that he leads. The two women at the center of Hellman's *The Children's Hour* have founded a school in which they exercise authority over their pupils, and thus wield influence within the surrounding community. The serial killings carried out by Aileen "Lee" Wuornos in the 1990s, which form the basis of Carson Kreitzer's *Self-Defense, or the Death of Some Salesmen*, generated particular shock and fear because of their public nature, with the bodies of the victims found along interstate highways. Kreitzer's play suggests that Wuornos' lack of access to private space, as an abused and often homeless woman forced to rely on prostitution for survival, created the conditions that led her to kill. The lack of access to private space in itself constitutes a form of trial in several plays. Cressida of Shakespeare's *Troilus and Cressida* finds herself forced cope with the lecherous advances of the Greeks to whom she is sent without the protection of family or friends, and without even the shelter of privacy; her lack of privacy exposes her to the judgment of her lover Troilus in the crucial scene that constitutes her trial. In Naomi Wallace's *And I and Silence*, Dee and Jamie, the two young women who have completed their prison sentences find themselves unable to completely escape the prison environment, because the racism and gender oppression of prison life continue on the outside. The play communicates this blurring of the two worlds of confinement in a public prison and confinement in an oppressive social environment through dramatic action that shifts back and forth in time. The most extreme loss of privacy occurs in *The Death of Ashley Smith* by Leah Jane Esau and *Watching Glory Die* by Judith Thompson: these plays dramatize the case of a mentally ill teenager incarcerated for a minor offense and, because of her unruly behavior in jail, subjected to continuous isolation and surveillance.

Both woman's desire and her desirability constitute disruptive forces that challenge gender relations and lead to accusations and trials. Women who act on their individual desires challenge the system that dictates their role as fulfilling the desires of others. Plays such as John Webster's Jacobean tragedy *The White Devil*, Treadwell's *Machinal*, and Bryans' *By Some Divine Mistake* emphasize the tragic nature of women's desire in the context of patriarchal power. The *White Devil* points to a time period in which the sexual standard for women was absolute: one instance of indulging her own desire marked a woman as evil. The plays by Treadwell and Bryans represent a time period in which women experienced some increase in autonomy but continuing barriers to independence; these plays expose the ways in which a woman who encounters barriers to fulfilling her individual needs and desires may attempt to overthrow the oppressive system by killing her husband, and then pay the price of this crime with her own life. Contemporary plays such as Churchill's *Vinegar Tom,* Liz Lochhead's *Mary Queen of Scots Got Her Head Chopped Off* (1987), and Shelagh Stephenson's *Five Kinds of Silence* offer clear and explicit analyses of the ways in which past and present women are prevented from expressing and acting on their own desires. Women of great beauty, on the other hand, seem to create disruption merely through the desire they arouse, as their desirability accords them a power that challenges masculine dominance. Thus, the beautiful women in Guan Hanqing's *Snow in Midsummer,* Shakespeare's *Troilus and Cressida,* Webster's *The*

White Devil, and the various plays about Mary Queen of Scots find themselves on trial wholly or in part because of the desire they arouse.

Plays that dramatize the trials and convictions of innocent and virtuous women suggest that women are always vulnerable to accusation, regardless of their conformity to gender expectations. Plays in which virtuous women are brought to trial include Guan Hanqing's *Snow in Midsummer*, Shakespeare's *Winter's Tale*, G. B. Shaw's *Saint Joan*, Arthur Miller's *The Crucible*, and Lillian Hellman's *The Children's Hour*. Several of these plays use the trial and conviction of an innocent woman to highlight social injustices, with the virtuous woman acting as a moral agent who exercises her power of action for the sake of principle. Joan of Arc, and the central character Dou E of *Snow in Midsummer*, challenge patriarchal societies that are corrupt and unjust in ways that go beyond their oppression of women. Each of these characters demonstrates a contrary point of view to Aristotle's assertions that "men are good absolutely, women are good for their function" and "women's virtues fit them to be ruled, men's to rule" (Foley 110-111). Even for relatively passive women, conventional virtue does not always protect them from condemnation. Patriarchal power feeds an obsession with absolute control—not only control of action but also of thought and desire. Such an obsession arises from the attempt to defend male vulnerability against women who may conform to the role of a docile and obedient wife but desire to escape from this role. Several of the plays enact the drive for absolute control through a trial aimed at knowing and controlling the woman's desires. When Leontes in *The Winter's Tale* sees that his wife Hermione persuades his friend Polixenes to postpone a scheduled departure, he suspects her of having her own motives for this action, even though he himself commanded it.

The most significant pattern in this broad selection of plays presenting the accusation and trial of women is the degree to which the woman on trial constitutes a metaphor of female subjectivity in patriarchal cultures. On one level, the paradigm of a woman on trial corresponds to the theory of interpellation advanced by Louis Althusser, who in his well-known 1974 essay "Ideology and Ideological State Apparatuses" suggests that subjectivity is formed in response to law. As an example he offers the scenario of being hailed by a policeman: in that call, an individual becomes a social subject in the double sense of being recognized as such by the law and being subjected to the force of the law. The extension of Althusser's simile points to a harsher form of interpellation for female subjects within the apparatus of a patriarchal state. A female becomes a subject in the temporary and fraught space of a trial. She offers a story that is challenged and usually not accepted. She speaks with a voice that is inaudible to the authorities in the world of the play. Female subjectivity resides with the body that is punished and often annihilated in the action of the play. Within the worlds of these dramas, from ancient Greece to the present, female subjectivity most often plays out as tragedy.

Emphasizing the singular and exceptional quality of female subjectivity within patriarchy, the woman on trial is typically isolated. In productions of the plays, the striking spectacle of a lone woman surrounded by men creates visual drama. Furthermore, the social position of these women is usually exceptional: they are queens, members of the aristocracy, women of truly extraordinary ability such as Joan of Arc or even women of extreme desperation such as the character representing Eileen Wuornos in Kreitzer's *Self-Defense, or the Death of Some Salesmen*. The accused woman faces her trial alone, without the support of female family members, friends, or confidantes. In fact, women near the accused bring accusations and collaborate with the persecutors in a number of plays, including *Snow in Midsummer*, the Mary Queen of Scots plays, Miller's *The Crucible*, Hellman's *The Children's Hour*, Churchill's *Vinegar Tom*, and Tucker Green's *Stoning Mary*, pointing to the enforcement of gender ideology by females as well as males within a patriarchal system. When women face accusation together, as in Hellman's *The Children's Hour* and Wallace's *And I and Silence*, the relationship between them constitutes an aspect of the accusation. Notably, the happiest endings occur in plays such as Euripides' *Hecuba* or Shakespeare's *The Winter's Tale*, where women cooperate and conspire among themselves, out of the sight of men, to bring about a conclusion that satisfies their own need for justice, but, notably, does not change their status in relation to the men in their environment. These plays portray the female subject in patriarchy as the unruly woman who ultimately faces the choice between death and submission.

In this group of plays, the women who might be termed ordinary—those who do not assert their individual desires or offer unruly responses to the patriarchal order—form the minority; but they, too, illustrate important aspects of gender construction in patriarchal societies. Cressida in Shakespeare's *Troilus and Cressida* and the accused witches in Miller's *The Crucible* seem to try to conform to the gender expectations of the worlds in which they are located. What they illuminate is the impossibility of gender authenticity in the presence of social stress and instability. While "the angel in the house" serves as a universal prescription for the feminine gender role, to which severe sanctions are attached for women who refuse to conform, its construction does not serve to protect the women within it. When war, as in the situations of Hecuba or Cressida, or extreme anxiety, as in the case of the witch trials, destroys or invades the emblematic house, the woman who knows only the domestic environment finds herself unable to maintain her prescribed role and unable to act in any way that does not expose her to condemnation.

Audience as Jury

It is no accident that the focus on a woman on trial occurs almost exclusively in texts written for theatrical production. As Edith Hall points out, performed drama and court cases share a common origin in classical Athens, having "developed out of the tradition of the aristocratic competition, the *agon*. . . [which] involved a small number of elite individuals competing in front of an audience, often a very large audience, of citizens" (39). In bringing trials to audiences, these plays rely on theatre's special status among the arts as an alternate courtroom. Performed drama, while lacking authority in a society's system of laws and sanctions, does offer audiences the opportunity to critique aspects of that system. In its creation of a tangible, though ephemeral, social reality, live theatre performance involves audiences in a compelling imitation of reality that may also offer enactments of alternatives to the current system. Trials are important in drama not only because of the conflict they present but also because they relate to the central purpose of drama: the discovery of truth. Patriarchy has placed women in an impossible relationship with truth by denying them autonomy; and drama, even when it does not center on gender, often reveals that situation. Jocasta, for example, in Sophocles' *Oedipus Rex*, strives to prevent Oedipus from pursuing the truth about his identity. When he discovers the truth of his birth and subsequent life, this discovery renders Jocasta's relationship to him impossible. Oedipus may go on living, though blinded, but Jocasta must die. The scenario of the woman on trial creates a direct confrontation between the woman and her accusers, rather than the kind of indirect trial observed in *Oedipus Rex*. In doing so, it opens up the possibility of truth. In order to do so, however, it must unravel and expose to the audience aspects of the complex system which has denied women a truthful place in the world. The multiple levels of communication summoned in live theatre performance makes it a particularly effective medium for the "undoing" at the center of feminist storytelling which, as Margaret B. Higgonet describes it, involves "unwinding narratives of gender and the weaving of antistructures" (Dascial vii). Thus, an audience member's understanding of the accusation, process, and outcome of the drama of a woman on trial may allow that audience member not only to sympathize with the accused woman but also observe the way in which her actions challenge the structure of patriarchal ideology that has obstructed the truth of women's lives and power. Plays about historical trials may illuminate conditions that persist into the present, and plays dealing with very recent events may reveal aspects of society unfamiliar to audiences. Some recent plays, notably Carson Kreitzer's *Self Defense* and the two plays about Canadian Ashley Smith's death in prison, *The Death of Ashley Smith* by Lea Jane Esau and *Watching Glory Die* by Judith

Thompson, function like the journalistic exposé, not only presenting subjects ignored or distorted in the journalistic media, but also placing the central character in a dynamic relationship with the audience and giving the audience the opportunity to view the character differently than the media or the actual trial has done. As Jill Dolan and Charlotte Canning have noted, this technique of addressing the audience has the potential to create a sense of community within the audience and in this way both enhance the experience of recognition and generate collective energy toward change.

AIMS OF THE VOLUME

This volume of essays is aimed at active theatre practitioners as well as scholars, critics, and teachers. Though the essays are based on scripts, which are much more accessible than are performances, all of the plays discussed have been staged, and some have been notably successful on stage. It is hoped that the grouping of these plays to highlight a particular theme, as well as the insights offered regarding the particular plays, will interest directors and dramaturgs, especially those who might consider staging a selection of the plays included in this volume together, allowing the works to comment on and illuminate their various meanings in what might be considered a conversation among the playwrights or characters of these plays. One of the most important potentials in staging these works together is the realization that various forms of resistance to gender boundaries have been a corollary of gender construction throughout recorded history.

The range of thinking offered by the essays in this volume is both interdisciplinary and international. Essayists draw upon their knowledge and experience not only in the fields of drama criticism and theatre production, but also in the social sciences. The critical frameworks used by the essayists in their analyses of these dramas build on the knowledge and insights created by feminist scholarship over the past three decades. They offer reexaminations of classic texts as well as analytic readings of new and relatively unknown works. Their understandings of the plays contribute to deconstructing the "appearance of unity and singularity" of law which, as feminist legal scholar Carol Smart asserts, constitutes the basis of its preeminence over other forms of social discourse and its power to "impose its definition of events on everyday life" (4). Therefore, it is hoped that students and scholars outside the areas of drama and theatre might find the insights contained in the essays about these plays helpful in considering the social phenomena with which they are concerned.

This volume, finally, aims to stimulate further consideration of the figure of the accused woman in drama. Though it surveys a wide swath of time and includes many plays, it does not address all the works relevant to this topic. These additional plays thus present an area for further research and analysis. A brief overview begins with the *Antigone* of Sophocles (397-406 BCE); the many later dramas based on the Antigone story also provide material for study. A number of Shakespearean dramas could be examined in light of accusations against women and quasi-trials of those women, including *Hamlet* (1600-01) and *King Lear* (1605-06), as well as *Much Ado about Nothing* (1598-99) and *The Taming of the Shrew* (1593-94). Medieval European drama includes several versions of plays in which a woman referred to as Potiphar's wife is tried for false accusations against the Old-Testament figure Joseph; the best known is by Han von Rűte of Bern (Muir 106). Medieval Chinese drama includes the well-known *Circle of Chalk* written by Li Qianfu during the Yuan Dynasty (1257-1368); this play inspired Brecht's *Caucasian Chalk Circle*. Nineteenth-century plays in which a woman on trial comprises part of the action include Mordecai M. Noah's *She Would Be a Soldier* (1819), in which a young woman escaping an unwanted marriage disguises herself as a man in order to become a soldier, only to be accused of being a spy when captured, and John Nelson Barker's *Superstition* (1826), in which a young woman is accused of blasphemy. Very different in tone, the 1831 play *Sarah Maria Cornell; or, the Fall River Murder*, by Mary Carr Clarke addresses the acquittal of a minister accused of seducing and murdering a young woman by dramatizing the life of the young woman whom the minister had accused of immorality; notably, this case was "tried" before a primarily female audience at a time when women were excluded from juries. In early twentieth-century China, performances of the Peking Opera play *Yu Tang Chun the Courtesan* were debuted by performer Mei Lanfang in 1913; this piece about a woman falsely accused of murdering the man she had involuntarily married, consists of two parts—"Su San Sets Out for Trial" and "The Trial." Modern English-language drama encompasses plays such as Susan Glaspell's one-act "Trifles" (1916), which she later adapted into a story titled "A Jury of Her Peers." In addition to G. B. Shaw's *Saint Joan* (1923), a number of plays, including Bertolt Brecht's *St. Joan of the Stockyards (Die heilige Johanna der Schlachthöfe*, 1929-31), Maxwell Anderson's *Joan of Lorraine* (1946), and Jean Anouilh's *The Lark (L'Alouette*, 1952), dramatize the trial of Joan of Arc. The work of Bertolt Brecht includes two additional plays in which a woman is placed on trial: *The Good Person of Szechwan (Die gute Mensch von Sezuan*, 1939-42) and *The Caucasian Chalk Circle (Der kaukasische Kreidekreis*, 1943-45). The play *Chicago* (1926) by Maureen Dallas Watkins, which formed the basis for the later musical, focuses on the trials of two women on charges of homicide. Two plays based on an actual crime in France, Jean Genet's *The Maids* (1947) and Wendy Kesselmana's *My Sister in this House* (1981) stage the crime with the audience as judges of the motivation involved in the killing of a wealthy woman and her daughter by their maids. Contemporary drama offers several plays centered on the conjunction of gender and political or religious issues. *My Name Is Rachel Corrie*, constructed by Alan Rickman and Katharine Vine using diaries, letters, and other writings of the young American killed by an Israeli tank while attempting to preserve a Palestinian home, follows the example seen in other plays of presenting the central character for judgment by the audience. *You Have Come Back* (1988), by Fatima Gaillaire-Bourega, dramatizes the tragic fate of a young woman who returns to her Algerian village after marrying a Westerner and assimilating to Western culture. *Women's Minyan* (2002) by Naomi Ragen, uses the actual story of an ultra-orthodox Israeli woman deprived of contact with her children by a religious court, to imagine an alternative court composed of women who know the accused mother. *Not Enough Air* (2009) by Masha Obolensky, a reconsideration of the Ruth Snyder trial, attempts to reconstruct the process through which playwright Sophie Treadwell created the play *Machinal* based on her journalistic coverage of the trial. *Photograph 51* (2009) by Anna Ziegler, dramatizes the pioneering work of Rosalind Franklin, appealing to the audience to recognize that she was unjustly denied credit for the discovery of the DNA double helix, for which James Watson and Francis Crick received the Nobel Prize. Similarly, Laura Gunderson's *Emilie the Marquise du Chatelet Defends Her Life Tonight* (2009), challenges the scandal and obscurity that enveloped the eighteenth-century mathematician and physicist, demanding a just recognition of her achievements, as well as understanding of her unconventional love life. These plays and doubtless others not identified here provide a fascinating trove of material for directors and critics interested in the ways gender is and has been constructed and resisted.

Notes

1. Indeed, Vladimir Putin, in a news conference in which he commented on the release of two Pussy Riot performers from prison in December, 2013, revealed the type of judgment to which the young women were subjected, saying, "I feel sorry for Pussy Riot not for the fact that they were jailed, but for its disgraceful behavior that has degraded the image of women" (NBC News, December 19, 2013.)

Works Cited

Althusser, Louis, "Ideology and Ideological State Apparatuses (Notes towards an Investigation)." *Lenin and Philosophy and Other Essays*, trans. Brewster, Ben. New York: Monthly Review Press, 1971. Print.

Canning, Charlotte. "Contiguous Autobiography: Feminist Performances in the 1970s," *Theatre Annual: A Journal of Performance Studies* 49 (1996): 65-75. Print.

Dascial, Reghina. *Episodes from a History of Undoing: The Heritage of Female Subversiveness.* Newcastle on Tyne: Cambridge Scholars Press, 2012. Print.

Dolan, Jill. *Utopia in Performance: Finding Hope at the Theater.* Ann Arbor: University of Michigan Press, 2005. Print.

Eyoyang, Eugene. "Western Agon/Eastern Ritual: Confrontations and Cooptations in Worldviews." *Thresholds of Western Culture: Identity, Postcoloniality, Transnationalism,* ed. Froman, Wayne and John Burt Foster, Jr. London: Bloomsbury Press, 2003: 206-219. Print.

Faith, Karlene. *Unruly Women: The Politics of Confinement and Resistance.* New York: Seven Stories Press, 2011. (Originally published 1993.) Print.

Foley, Helene P. *Female Acts in Greek Tragedy.* Princeton: Princeton University Press, 1991. Print.

Hall, Edith. "Lawcourt Dramas: The Power of Performance in Greek Forensic Oratory." *Bulletin of the Institute of Classical Studies* 40.1 (2010). Online.

Hepperle, Winifred L. and Laura Crites, eds. *Women in the Courts.* Williamsburg, VA: National Center for State Courts, pub. No. R0037 (1978). Print.

Muir, Lynette. *Love and Conflict in Medieval Drama: The Plays and their Legacy.* New York: Cambridge University Press, 2007. Print.

Putin, Vladimir. News conference. NBC News, December 19, 2013. Online.

Renzetti, Claire M., Susan L. Miler and Angela R. Gover, eds. *Routledge International Handbook of Crime and Gender Studies.* London and New York: Routledge, 2013. Print.

Smart, Carol. *Feminism and the Power of Law.* London and New York: Routledge, 1989. Print.

… ANCIENT AND MEDIEVAL DRAMA

CHAPTER 1.

GENDER ON TRIAL IN EURIPIDES' *HECUBA*

Chiara Meccariello

- And how shall women overcome a man?

- There is terror in numbers, numbers joined with guile.

(Euripides *Hecuba* 883-884)

"PUT THIS BARBARIAN IMPULSE FROM YOUR HEART AND SPEAK": FROM SAVAGERY TO DEBATE

As the Greek myth goes, when the Trojan War broke out, the king of Troy Priam and his wife Hecuba entrusted their youngest child Polydorus to the Thracian king Polymestor. After the city was taken and Priam killed, Polymestor murdered Polydorus to get hold of his goods.[1] The second part of Euripides' *Hecuba*, probably performed ca. 425–424 BCE, focuses on the queen's vengeance against Polymestor: old Hecuba, now a prisoner and a widow, deprived of all her children, blinds Polymestor and kills his sons with the help and complicity of her Trojan handmaids. In the final section of the play, Polymestor appears on stage, his eyes bleeding as he chases Hecuba and tries to vent his fury on her (1056-1128). The Greek commander Agamemnon advises him to hold his rage and initiates a formal debate between the two litigants (1129-1131).

The subsequent part of the play (1132-1253), which shows the typical structure of the tragic *agōn* (Lloyd 97-99), has a strong juridical connotation. Agamemnon proposes the debate while ordering Polymestor to dismiss the "barbarian impulse"[2] (*to barbaron*) from his heart, thus marking the shift from a phase of uncontrolled bestiality to an institutional moment, the latter being presented as typically Greek. This shift is emphasized both visually and verbally in the play. When Polymestor appears on stage after Hecuba's vengeance, he is on all fours like a beast (1058-1059: "moving like a four-footed wild beast on my hands"), and he refers to the Trojan women as fiery creatures and "hellish bacchants" (1076). His words portray an irrational and savage scenario, an imaginary mountain setting with its vividness enhanced by Polymestor's visual detachment from the real one.[3]

Agamemnon rushes to the stage roused by the commotion and, taking up the mountain metaphor, describes Polymestor's noise as "shouts" and "no quiet tones" carried by Echo, "child of the rocky cliff" (1109-1113); this inarticulacy is complemented by Polymestor's Bacchic desire to seize, bloody, and tear in pieces Hecuba's body (1125-1126 and 1128). However, after the three lines with which Agamemnon prompts the debate, we see a more self-controlled Polymestor deliver a balanced speech both defending himself and accusing Hecuba, followed by Hecuba's clear-headed reply in a speech of exactly the same length. By exploiting the context and position of the *agōn*, as well as the conventional transition from lyrics to iambic trimeters, Euripides presents the debate as an attempt to overcome savagery through the formal institution of a trial (Gregory 179).

Gender on Trial in Euripides' *Hecuba*

"So that I may judge properly": the trial scene

The trial scene (1129-1295) consists of a brief introduction delivered by Agamemnon (1129-1131), the speeches of the two parties (Polymestor at 1132-1182, Hecuba at 1187-1237), each followed by a two-line comment from the chorus,[4] and Agamemnon's final judgment (1240-1251). After the judge's decision, Polymestor's two-line comment seals his defeat and provides the prelude to a heated debate, in single alternating lines, between the two opponents (stichomythia). Though not part of the trial, the stichomythia, by strongly recalling the tumultuous atmosphere of the preceding section of the play, shows that the trial has not resolved the tensions. The Dyonisiac theme returns in Polymestor's final prophecies about the fate of Hecuba, Agamemnon and Cassandra, which throw a sinister light on post-dramatic time. The trial thus appears as little more than a parenthesis between revenge and retaliation.

The juridical format of the debate is clearly signaled by wording and structure. The frame is provided by the vocabulary of Agamemnon's introduction:

> Hold off: put this barbarian impulse from your heart and speak, so that hearing both you and her in turn I may judge properly why this has been done to you (1129-1131).

The emphasis on orderly speaking and hearing and the phrase "in turn" (*en merei*), which recalls the famous trial scene of Aeschylus' *Eumenides* (436 ff.), create a legal tone. The juridical dimension is further underlined by technical terms such as the verb "judge" (*krinō*, used here and at 1240, in the introduction to the actual judgment) and the words "beaten" (*hēssōmenos*) and "pay the penalty" (*hyphexō dikēn*) in Polymestor's final complaint (1252-1253).

Typical elements of forensic usage can also be found in the two opponents' speeches. The opening words of Polymestor's discourse, "I will speak" (*legoim'an*), are often found at the beginning of formal speeches in Athenian drama and probably reproduce actual contemporary practice.[5]

Both speeches partially reflect the typical articulation of forensic oratory as described in later rhetorical treatises[6]: Polymestor's accusation contains a very detailed *narratio* (1145-1176) and a *peroration* (1176-1182), while Hecuba's discourse starts with an *exordium* (1187-1195) and proceeds through *confutatio* (1196-1232) and *peroration* 1232-1237). It is also worth noting that Polymestor's and Hecuba's speeches have exactly the same length, a detail particularly suitable to the trial atmosphere: in real trials of fifth-century Athens, accusation and defense were given the same amount of time, controlled by special officials.[7]

These formal characteristics assure us that Euripides intended to present this debate as a juridical situation, partially resembling fifth-century judicial life, although in the distant and distancing frame of myth. A trial involving a woman would have been exceptional in contemporary Athens, and the personal delivering of a defense speech on the part of a woman would have been unparalleled.[8] On the one hand, this aspect of the action reflects the nature of tragedy, which typically presents exceptional characters and situations; accordingly, "the women of Greek tragedy... have no precise counterparts among the real women of classical Athens" (Foley "Anodos Drama" 134). On the other hand, as we will see, this is in line with the complex characterisation of Hecuba's gender in the second part of the play.

The function of the trial in the framework of Hecuba is much debated. To what extent can it be considered a credible debate? The main point of controversy lies in its relationship with the scene of the first encounter between Agamemnon and Hecuba, prior to the arrival and punishment of Polymestor (726-904), which I will refer to as the supplication scene. By the end of that scene, Agamemnon, well aware of Polymestor's horrible deed and Hecuba's intention of revenge, has allowed her to act against the Thracian. Therefore, modern scholars have questioned his impartiality as a judge and the credibility of the trial as a whole.[9] However, the real extent to which Agamemnon will assist Hecuba in the final part of the play cannot be inferred from his ambiguous formulations in the supplication scene, and a few elements of both that scene and the trial suggest a non-biased judgement.

First, Agamemnon never states that he will unreservedly support Hecuba's cause. On the contrary, he clearly says that he will help her only as far as his assistance does not affect his reputation among the Greeks (861-863), a statement which raises Hecuba's bitter reflection about human freedom (864-869). It is not by chance that Hecuba plays on this preoccupation in her speech (1233), and that this aspect will be crucial in Agamemnon's final decision (1249): this indicates that Hecuba's choice of arguments is appropriate and effective, not that the trial is prejudiced. Second, the supplication scene leaves us with the feeling that Agamemnon does not believe in Hecuba's ability to actually carry out the revenge, especially in view of her gender (885). His surprise after the revenge (1122-1123) is consistent with this scepticism, and need not be seen as hypocritical.

Third, while Hecuba is preparing her vengeance, the expectation is that Polymestor will be killed. This is what Agamemnon expects at 856 and 877 and the chorus at 1134, and what Hecuba seems to imply when she escorts Polymestor into the tent with the words "you may return with your boys to where you have lodged my son" (1021-1022). Yet her revenge will turn out to be worse than death for her victim, a "calamity too great to bear" according to the chorus (1107): Polymestor himself will lament that the captive women "destroyed me - not destroyed me but more than that" (1121). Hecuba's vendetta is not unquestionable, especially for its fiery connotation and for the inclusion of a typically barbarian practice, the blinding (Hall 25-27). Furthermore, the play emphases the violence at the center of the trial by making the victims clearly visible on stage: the blinded Polymestor and the corpses of innocent children (Taplin 442). In a staged Hecuba this must have been of great impact.[10]

The true anomaly of the trial lies in its position. In the supplication scene Hecuba asks Agamemnon to act on her behalf against Polymestor, and only as a consequence of his refusal does she undertake her own vendetta. Had Agamemnon accepted her request, justice would have been dispensed when expected, with the purpose of establishing guilt and consequent punishment for Polymestor. The commander's cowardly hesitation to support Hecuba has a devastating effect on the dramatic events, and this delayed trial, with its ambiguity between accuser and accused, presents only another symptom of arbitrary power.

"I COULD DO NOTHING BECAUSE OF THE THRONG OF WOMEN": POLYMESTOR, HECUBA, AND GENDER

Polymestor's speech (1133-1182), especially the account of the revenge, is entirely based on an opposition of male and female worlds, through both explicit references and symbolic elements. The vivid description of how Polymestor was deceived, trapped, and defeated by Hecuba and her attendants culminates in a misogynous tirade. The Thracian king depicts the women as a dangerous mass by progressively widening the perspective from Hecuba alone to the Trojan prisoners as a whole, and then to women in general: his view of them "as a cohesive group is part of his attempt to create a parallel fellowship between himself and Agamemnon by contrast with the women" (Mossman 133).

Polymestor tries to establish this gender-based fellowship from the beginning of his speech. At 1137-44, where he justifies Polydorus' murder on the ground of practical considerations, he speaks the male language of war. In Polymestor's view, the murder of Polydorus, which he clearly admits (1136), eliminated a potential enemy for the Greeks, and thus can be seen as a favor[11] to them:

> I was afraid that the boy, left behind as your enemy, might gather Troy together and found it again, and that the Acheans, learning that one of the sons of Priam was alive, would raise another expedition to the land of the Phrygians and then ravage the plains of Thrace in search of plunder, and the Trojans' neighbors would be visited with the very bane with which we were troubled just now, o king[12]. [...] This is what I have endured, for furthering

your interest and killing your enemy Agamemnon (1138-1144 and 1175-1177).

Polymestor, although he especially refers to his own fear of war, emphasizes in the first place that Polydorus, if left alive, would have been Agamemnon's enemy; moreover, the disadvantages of the hypothetical war scenario he portrays are shared with the Greeks, a community underlined by the ambiguous use of the first person plural and the vocative "o king" at 1144. Finally, the last lines of this passage, which take up the initial statements after the description of the guile of the accused female, try to emphasize the relationship between Polymestor and the Greek commander through the polyptoton of the second person singular possessive, leading to the final vocative "Agamemnon."

The longest part of Polymestor's speech is occupied by the account of Hecuba's revenge (1145-1175). This section particularly exploits the opposition between male and female, and the vividness of the account is clearly meant to involve the male addressee, to which the detailed description of how the group of deceitful women managed to disarm and completely destroy a man must have appeared particularly unpleasant. A first indication of the gender contrast explored in this speech comes from the spatial arrangement. Polymestor's entrance into the women's tent, staged in the previous scene and described at the beginning of the account, is more effective if seen against the background of demarcated male and female spaces that characterizes the setting of the play: "the secluded residences of the women" contrast with "the open territory by the shore where men gather from political action" (Zeitlin 174). The dialogue that leads to Polymestor's entrance into the women's tent makes explicit the separateness of male and female spaces:

> HECUBA: I want you to keep safe the money I brought with me from Troy.
>
> POLYMESTOR: Where is it? Have you hidden it in your clothing?

> HECUBA: It is being kept safe in this tent amid the heaps of plunder.
>
> POLYMESTOR: Where? These are the enclosures where the Achean ships are beached.
>
> HECUBA: The captive women have their separate quarters.
>
> POLYMESTOR: It is safe and clear of men within?
>
> HECUBA: Only we women, no Acheans, are inside. But go into the tent... (1012-1019).[13]

This aspect of the situation had previously been emphasized in the supplication scene. At 880, in response to Agamemnon's skepticism about her chances of overcoming Polymestor, Hecuba referred to the "throng of Trojan women" (*Trōiadōn ochlon*) concealed inside the tents. In the following line Agamemnon countered the phrase "throng of Trojan women" with "prey of the Greeks"[14] (*Hellēnōn agran*), effectively located in the same metrical position. The shift from "throng" (the same word used by Hecuba at 868 to indicate the Greek army) to "prey" and from a defining genitive to a possessive one suggests a covert contempt of female initiative and indicates that "Agamemnon is asserting control" (Marshall 130). Nevertheless, Hecuba seems to echo these lines in the passage quoted above, when she explains that the treasure she will show Polymestor "is being kept safe in this tent amid the heaps of plunder" (1014: notice that "heaps" here translates *ochlos*, the same word as "throng" at 880). Hecuba here plays on the ambiguity of the word *skylōn*, which indicates the war booty and so correctly points to the Trojan prisoners, although it is meant to be understood as a 'neutral' reference to the plunder. In linking *ochlos* with a synonym of *agra*, "prey", not only does she prefigure the transformation of the Trojan women from object to agent which will happen inside the tent, but also suggests that their strength derives precisely from the exploitation of their inferior status as both women and slaves.

In Polymestor's speech we now see this separate world from inside, and through his words we experience the dangers hidden there. Initially at ease in the female space, Polymestor sits down on a couch surrounded by the Trojan maidens, "as if I were their friend, some on the left, others on the right" (1151-1152). The women are here seen as a collective corpus acting in accordance with their typical attitudes and interests: they admire Polymestor's clothing, show curiosity about his spears, and take his children in their arms (1153-1159). In this frame, Polymestor cannot suspect the real meaning of their gestures, but soon he will realize that the examination of the weapons is an excuse to strip him of their protection, while the maidens' maternal attitude towards the children will turn out to be a way to remove them far from their father. The women actually deprive Polymestor of his male symbols: the spears on the one hand, a sign of his military power, the sons on the other, his offspring and therefore a symbol of his political power. In this way they prepare his complete humiliation. To attract Polymestor into the tent, Hecuba cleverly exploited a gender-based custom in order to conceal her real feelings toward the Thracian: "Hecuba deceptively plays the woman to him, claiming that she is ashamed to look him in the eyes (968-975)" (Foley 286). In the same way, the maidens exploit to their advantage the separateness of their space and the usual expectations about their behavior.

What happens at this point is described by Polymestor as a sudden change from "peaceful talk" (1160). Again, the guile is hidden in a gender-marked element, the dress (*peplos*)[15]: "all of a sudden from somewhere in their clothing they produced swords and stabbed the children" (1161-1162)[16]. The dress hides swords (*phasgana*), an object of the male world, the weapon about which Agamemnon had earlier expressed doubt that a woman could handle (876). At the same moment, Polymestor is immobilized by other women, who hold him by his arms, legs and hair —the latter element particularly suggesting a reversal of the expected relations of power between men and women, since holding by the hair was usually a means of controlling women (Collard 1991, 193). Polymestor is now impotent: "if I tried to move my hands, unhappy man that I was, I could do nothing because of the throng of women" (1166-1167). This heated description of the mass of women reducing a single man to impotence culminates in the retelling of what the Thracian calls "a terrible thing... woe greater than woe" (1168-1169), the blinding. This act is carried out with the brooches fastening the *peplos* (1170 *porpas*); again, the violence is carried out by means of gender-marked dress.[17]

This description culminates in the general misogynous formulation that concludes the speech:

> To avoid making my speech too long, if any of the ancients spoke ill women, or someone is now speaking or will speak[18], I shall sum up all their words: neither the sea nor land breeds any creature like them. Anyone who has dealings with them know this well (1177-1182).

Polymestor's hyperbolic view is a consequence of the collective dimension of the revenge. Hecuba alone would not have been able to carry out the double deed. It is not by chance that when Hecuba tries to persuade Agamemnon of her capability to overcome Polymestor she refers to mythical exempla involving plural feminine entities, namely the Danaids and the Lemnian women (886-887). The female cohesion described by Polymestor continues the female solidarity that has characterized this tragedy since the first appearance of Hecuba. Unlike other tragic heroines, she does not need to obtain complicity from the women of the chorus before undertaking her action. The captive women will be spontaneously ready to act in support of Hecuba and her attendants in the crucial moment of revenge (1042-1043). Female solidarity and community cross ethnic boundaries in this play: Foley (2001) points out that "as survivors of war who will be forced to adapt to the ways of other cities, the Trojan women in the chorus of Hecuba... imaginatively share the sufferings of a Spartan woman (650–656) or join the women of the Greek cities to which they will come as slaves in ritual (455–474)" (287).

Gender on Trial in Euripides' *Hecuba* 35

Polymestor's representation of women as a unitary corpus and his undifferentiated misogyny emphasizes gender opposition from the point of view of a male character. Agamemnon's reservations about the credibility of female actions are another aspect of the same issue, expressing doubt about "the possibility and legitimacy of female action" (Foley *Female Acts* 286). However, Polymestor's attempt to establish a "male fellowship" with the judge fails, and Hecuba's rhetorical strategies prevail. As during the realization of the revenge plot, when Hecuba and her accomplices were able to take swords in hand and effect a sudden change from their typically female attitude, in the trial the queen manages to deliver an excellently articulated speech in which she embraces male values and uses them to her advantage.

According to Lloyd, "Hecuba's reply is one of Euripides' most sophisticated pieces of forensic rhetoric. [...] Now she seems to be in full command of the latest argumentative devices" (97-98). Lloyd underlines Hecuba's "elaborate concern for taxis" (that is, the disposition of the structural elements of the speech), and shows her use of devices such as *hypophora* and hypothetical syllogism (*ibid.*). Her speech also gains effectiveness from rhetorical questions (1201-1205) and the regal tone of certain passages (especially 1232-1237: see Matthiessen 411). Another important strategy is the reuse of her opponents' words. The ending of 1201 (*speudōn charin*—pursuing a favor), for example, is taken up from Polymestor's 1175 only to show its improper use in his speech; and in telling Agamemnon "you will show yourself to be base" (1233), Hecuba verbally echoes what she told Polymestor at 1217 ("hear now how vile you are shown to be"), thereby emphasizing the analogy between the two characters in case the Greek commander does not judge to her advantage. In addition, the values considered at 1234-1235 (respect of gods and justice, piety) are partially modeled on those embraced by Agamemnon at 852-53.

Besides these formal devices, the unifying ingredient of Hecuba's rhetoric in this speech, and more generally in the whole second part of the play, is the exploitation of male values particularly dear to the characters she tries to persuade. Hecuba attracts the Thracian king into the female space by using a value of his world, the gold, a motive of the murder he committed. This is the same technique she used in the supplication scene, when, as the last resort, she referred to Agamemnon's relationship with Cassandra to win his connivance: it is significant that Cassandra was the commander's motive in the debate about Polyxena's sacrifice according to the chorus' account (120-122). In the same way, in her defense speech Hecuba uses Agamemnon's concern about reputation among the army—the same concern he expressed in the supplication scene (861-863)—to persuade him to judge in her favor. The queen puts the commander on the spot: he cannot help but agree with her, unless he rejects the values to which he has expressed commitment.

"She who outstrips every man, every woman in misfortune": Hecuba across gender

The strong and at the same time unsettling part of Hecuba's character in this section of the play is her ability to master both the male and the female world. The contrast between the Hecuba of the first part of the play and the Hecuba of the second is striking. The former is shown in her female functions: portrayed as a mourning mother since the prologue, whose speaker Polydorus presents himself in the first place as Hecuba's son (3: "I am Polydorus, son of Hecuba"), she experiences the total loss of her children in the course of the dramatic time. When Polyxena's imminent sacrifice is announced, the theme of maternity is especially developed in the lyric lamentation involving the two female characters (177-215), in which the words "mother" and "child" recur obsessively. Hecuba's female functions are emphasized by contrast with Polyxena, who behaves according to the heroic code and receives a reward normally paid to male aristocrats, the *phyllobolia* (573-574; see Battezzato "Ospitalità rituale"). Hecuba's feebleness, on the contrary, is deeply rooted in her gender: she is a slave because she is a woman, and she is in mourning because she is a mother.

After the discovery of Polydorus' corpse, Hecuba is not just a mourning mother. Her suffering now crosses gender boundaries, as the servant who brings her the corpse explicitly declares: "Women, where is Hecuba the utterly wretched, she who outstrips every man, every woman in misfortune? No one will take this crown from her! " (658-660).

From this point onwards, Hecuba will prove to be able to shift from the female to the male world and to exploit both female and male prerogatives in order to obtain all that is left to her, the revenge against Polymestor. The strength she acquires is evident in the contrast with the previous Hecuba, as two examples will show. First, when she reappears after the blinding and infanticide (1044) she is triumphant and proud. She focuses on the imminent appearance of the proofs of her deeds (1047-1053) and underlines her personal success with the effective repetition of the clause "whom I have killed" (*hous ektein'egō*) at 1046 and 1051, and the alliterative *dikēn de moi / dedōke*, "he has paid me satisfaction", at 1052-1053 (notice the powerful position of the first person pronoun *moi* at the end of the line). This entrance is in striking contrast with her first appearance at 53, when a feeble Hecuba arrived, supported by her maidens, former subjects and now fellow slaves. Second, the rhetorical ability she displays in her trial speech counters her rhetorical failure in the debate with Odysseus concerning Polyxena's sacrifice (218-341), a failure she commented upon at 334-35 with the words: "Daughter, my speech pleading against your murder has been cast idly to the winds."

In the treatment of the gender theme which runs through the whole play, and especially in the characterization of Hecuba's gender, the trial appears to be a pivotal moment. As a delayed and indecisive trial, it serves as an expression of the violent and unjust world of which Hecuba and the other women of the play are victims. Furthermore, it highlights the gender opposition on the one hand, and Hecuba's ability to master both genders on the other: the female in the action described in Polymestor's speech, the male in her own defense.

"Beaten by a woman": Polymestor and Euripides

Why is gender so central in Polymestor's speech? What was Euripides' point in representing his misogyny? Tragedy, with its intertwining voices, poses a difficult task to the reader who seeks the playwright's view, and the ending of Hecuba is particularly generous in ambiguities and unresolved tensions.[19] Misogyny is in the mouth of the losing character; the women of the chorus moderate it by introducing distinctions in his hyperbolic formulation, but do not challenge his basic assumption of gender peculiarity. After Agamemnon's judgment, Polymestor's first complaint is about having been defeated by a woman, a bitter and at the same time ironic consideration on the part of a misogynist.

Polymestor's description remains in the mind of the audience in all its vividness, and, as Harris maintains, "the co-operation of a group of violent women must have made the act seem all the more unpalatable to the male audience" (2021), although this does not necessarily affect the moral evaluation of Hecuba's revenge. In the nineteenth century a philologist like Gottfried Hermann still considered gender as an aggravating circumstance of Hecuba's deeds, and his sensitivity may well have been closer to that of the Greek audience than to ours.[20]

Identifying Euripides' strategy, however, requires consideration of the wider context. Women are represented as the main victims of war in this play. The concept of the female as a prey, if not the prey par excellence, is well rooted in traditional ideology, as expressed in the Homeric line "let no man make haste to depart homewards until each have lain with the wife of some Trojan" (Il. 2.355). Euripides stages a problematized version of this aspect of war, by privileging the point of view of the victims even in the visual arrangement: apart from the prologue scene, during which Polydorus is the only visible character,

Gender on Trial in Euripides' *Hecuba*

from Hecuba's first entrance, women are constantly the main presence. Hecuba is almost uninterruptedly on stage, supported by the omnipresent chorus of prisoners and her silent maidens. The movements of the male characters are movements to and from a markedly female space, and there are no dialogues between men only, in the absence of women.

Thus, behind the dissolution of human values and relationships that war entails we see a constant female solidarity, not only among the chorus, Hecuba and her maidens, but also among barbarian prisoners and Greek women. This solidarity, strong both when women are presented as passive victims (like during Hecuba's first entrance) and when they are the guileful mass deceiving Polymestor, runs throughout the play as much as does gender contrast. Polymestor's view of the women serves the double purpose of sharpening the contrast and emphasizing the feminine connotation of the revenge.

Yet against this all-female background, Hecuba emerges as a peculiar character. As we have seen, in the first part of the play she is a typical representative of her gender; in the second, on the contrary, when the loss is total and not balanced by heroism, Hecuba exploits her female prerogatives for the purpose of revenge, and acquires a strength which goes beyond gender. The trial as a whole highlights this overturning of expectations by juxtaposing the misogynous point of view of Polymestor and the representation of a lucid and superior Hecuba, capable of using both female devices and the male values of her opponents in her single-minded plan for revenge, when that becomes all that is left to her. Hecuba is represented as a victim especially inasmuch as she is a mother who has lost all her children—that is, a woman who used to be what a woman is meant to be and is now deprived of that status. When it comes to revenge, Hecuba exceeds the limits of womanhood as a consequence of the dramatic events: since she has no more male kin who could take revenge on Polymestor, and since Agamemnon, despite being her master, has refused to act on her behalf, all she can do is turn from mater dolorosa to a manly woman.

Hecuba is the tragedy of a woman who turns from victim to victimizer, and is both a victim and a victimizer as a result of men's violence and failure to guarantee justice: what is staged in this play, and what the trial scene encapsulates, is an insuperable suffering that induces its victim to violate the boundaries of her gender.

Notes

1. Euripides is our oldest witness to this version of Polydorus' death, and the whole story may well be the playwright's own invention. Polymestor is not mentioned in any source prior to Euripides; moreover, in Homer Polydorus is the son of Priam and Laothoe and is killed in battle by Achilles (Il. 20, 407-422). Euripides might have introduced the genealogical innovation (Hecuba instead of Laothoe) in order to build a double plot centred on Hecuba and explore the effects of a double loss, the traditional sacrifice of her daughter Polyxena and the pitiful death of Polydorus, in the context of her reversal of fortune after the fall of Troy: see Gregory "Intertextuality and Genealogy" 389. Another possible genealogical innovation of this play is the name of Hecuba's father, here Kisseus instead of Dymas as in the Homeric tradition: on the possible reasons of this choice see, again, Gregory. It is worth noting that the Thracian setting of the play entails a significant change in the setting of Polyxena's sacrifice on Achilles' tomb which takes place in the first part of the tragedy: Achilles was traditionally buried in the Troad, while in *Hecuba* the tomb and the sacrifice are located in Thrace.
2. All translations are from Kovacs unless otherwise stated.
3. On the Dionysiac theme in this play see Zeitlin 172-216, and Schleiser.
4. After Polymestor's speech the manuscripts preserve a four-line comment, but the second couplet (1185-1186) is probably spurious: see Matthiessen 405-406 for a detailed discussion.
5. See Fraenkel 386-87, on Aesch. *Ag.* 838.
6. For example Quint. 4.1.
7. On this topic see Rhodes 719-28.
8. Cf. Allen 111-113.
9. See for instance Mastronarde, who labels this scene as a "mock trial" (259). On the contrary, Gregory, in *Euripides: Hecuba* (177-178), argues for a real trial, with a non-granted outcome.
10. The text offers no indications about the removal of the corpses of Polymestor's sons, and it is plausible that they remain on stage until the end of the play, so increasing the final sense of bleakness: see Mossman 68.
11. The Greek word is *charis*, a key-concept in *Hecuba*: see for example Adkins, Stanton, Battezzato "Ospitalità ritual."

12. The vocative "o king", *anax* in the Greek, is absent in Kovacs' translation. In what follows I also place the vocative "Agamemnon" at the end of the sentence as in the Greek text, while Kovacs has it after "endured".
13. The association of women with the indoor space, as opposed to the outdoor space more suitable to men, is frequent in ancient sources and is connected to the division of male and female activities: see, for example, Xen. *Oec.* 7.22.
14. Here the translation is my own: Kovacs' free translation of the line "you mean the captives, those the Greeks have taken?" does not reproduce the imperfect symmetry of the Greek.
15. The word *peplos* in tragedy does not necessarily refer to a female dress (see Finglass 67-68, with further bibliography), but the gender connotation of the dress is here guaranteed by the thematization of female garments in this specific play. In particular, the Trojan prisoners composing the chorus of the play, who were captured and forced to leave their chambers while they were ready for the marriage bed, refer to their own dresses, worn on that occasion and still on them during the dramatic time, as single *peplio* (933-934, where the *hapax monopeplos* is used). The prisoners who assist Hecuba's revenge "are to be imagined dressed like their fellow prisoners" (Battezzato "Dorian Dress" 361). On the role of clothing in this play, see especially Marshall.
16. It is the same place where Polymestor suspected Hecuba was hiding the treasure of Troy at 1113: "Where is it? Have you hidden it in your clothing?"
17. The use of the brooches obviously implies a loosening of the dress; see again Battezzato "Dorian Dress" 362.
18. Kovacs deletes 1179 ("or someone is now speaking or will speak"), but the line is faultless: see Matthiessen 405 for a defense.
19. On the "critical disagreement about the protagonist's moral stature" see Mastronarde 229.
20. Hermann XVII: *Non illa quidem iniuste agit, quum vindictam meditatur, sed quum oculi eruuntur homini scelerato filiique innocentes trucidantur, et a feminis quidem, foedum id facinus est et quod quaevis fera bellua patret.*

Works Cited

Adkins, A.W.H. "Basic Greek Values in Euripides' Hecuba and Hercules." *Furens, CQ* n.s. 16 (1966) 193-219. Print.

Allen, D.S. *The World of Prometheus. The Politics of Punishing in Democratic Athens*, Princeton, NJ: Princeton University Press, 2000. Print.

Battezzato, L. "Dorian Dress in Greek Tragedy." *Euripides and Tragic Theatre*, ed. M. Cropp and K. Lee. (Illinois Classical Studies 24-25), 1999-200: 343-362. Print.

--------. "Ospitalità rituale, amicizia e charis nell'Ecuba." *Ricerche euripidee* 2003: 13-41.

Collard, C., ed. *Euripides: Hecuba*, Salisbury, Wiltshire: The Warminster-Press, 1991. Print.

Finglass. P. J. "A New Fragment of Euripides' *Ino.*" *ZPE* 189 (2014) 65-82. Print.

Foley, H.P. "Anodos Drama: Euripides' *Alcestis* and *Helen*." *Innovations of Antiquity*, ed. Hexter, R. and D. Selden. New York: Routledge, 1992: 133-160. Print.

Foley, H.P. *Female Acts in Greek Tragedy*. Princeton, NJ: Princeton University Press, 2001. Print.

Fraenkel, E., ed. *Aeschylus: Agamemnon*. Oxford: Clarendon Press, 1950. Print.

Gregory, J. "Genealogy and Intertextuality in Hecuba," *AJP* 116 (1995): 389-397. Print.

-------- . *Euripides, Hecuba: Introduction, Text, and Commentary*. Atlanta: Scholars Press, 1999. Print.

Hall, E., *Inventing the Barbarian: Greek Self-Definition through Tragedy*. Oxford: Clarendon Press, 1989. Print.

Harris, W.V. "The Rage of Women." *Ancient Anger. Perspectives from Homer to Galen*, ed. Braund, S. and G. W. Most, G.W. Cambridge: Cambridge University Press, 2004: 121-43. Print.

Hermann, G., ed. *Euripidis Hecuba*, Lipsiae: 1831. Print.

Jenkins, I.D.. "The Ambiguity of Greek Textiles." *Arethusa* 18 (1985) 109-32. Print.

Kovacs, D., ed., *Euripides*, vol. 2, Cambridge, MA: Harvard University press, 1995. Print.

Lloyd, M. *The Agon in Euripides.* Oxford: Clarendon Press, 1992. Print.

Marshall, M.C. "The Costume of Hecuba's Attendants." *Acta Classica* 44 (2001) 127-36. Print.

Mastronarde, D.J. *The Art of Euripides. Dramatic Technique and Social Context.* Cambridge: Cambridge University Press, 2010. Print.

Matthiessen, K., ed. *Euripides: Hekabe.* Berlin, New York: Walter de Gruyter, 2008. Print.

Mossman, J. *Wild Justice: a Study of Euripides' Hecuba.* London: Bloomsbury Academic, 1995. Print.

Rhodes, P.J. *A Commentary on the Aristotelian Athenaion Politeia.* Oxford: Clarendon Press, 1981. Print.

Schlesier, R. "Die Bakchen des Hades. Dionysische Aspekten von Euripides' Hekabe." *Métis* 3 (1988) 111-135. Print.

Segal, C. *Euripides and the* Poetics *of* Sorrow: *Art, Gender, and Commemoration in Alcestis, Hippolytus, and Hecuba.* Durham, NC: Duke University press, 1993. Print.

Stanton, G.R. "Aristocratic Obligation in Euripides' Hekabe." *Mnemosyne* 48 (1995) 11-33. Print.

Taplin, O. *The Stagecraft of Aeschylus. The Dramatic Use of Exits and Entrances in Greek Tragedy.* Oxford: Clarendon Press, 1977. Print.

Zeitlin, F. *Playing the Other. Gender and Society in Classical Greek Literature.* Chicago: University of Chicago Press, 1996. Print.

CHAPTER 2.

THE CONFUCIAN VIEW OF WOMAN IN *SNOW IN MIDSUMMER*

Marta Steiner

SNOW IN MIDSUMMER AND THE CHINESE THEATRICAL TRADITION

Traditional Chinese music theatre is called *xiqu*, which could be translated as "music play" and used to be translated into Occidental languages as "Chinese opera." It is generally a performing, not a literary tradition, but in one historical period, considered the "Golden Age" of Chinese drama, *xiqu* attained the status of a literary art. This period occurred during the reign of the Yuan dynasty, 1279-1368. Guan Hanqing (c.1225-1302),[1] a poet and playwright, is considered one of the greatest dramatists of that epoch. He wrote about sixty-seven dramas (West and Idema 2), of which fourteen survive and are still performed (Crump 18). *Snow in Midsummer* (Dou E yuan) is among the most popular and most often produced of

Guan Hanqing's plays. It is thoroughly familiar to Chinese audiences in its various versions according to local subgenres of *xiqu* in different provinces of China, and the scene between Mr. Dou Tianzhang and the ghost of his wronged daughter is one of the best known and admired ghost scenes in Chinese traditional music drama. Taking all that into consideration, *Snow in Midsummer* can be seen as a paramount example of Chinese theatrical heritage.

People who know many *xiqu* dramas could on that basis easily reconstruct the whole traditional juristic system of imperial China. Scenes that take place in a court of law abound in *xiqu* repertoire, as do tortures and executions. One of the dramatic characters most cherished by audiences is Judge Bao, a just and clever judge who appears in many dramas (see Hayden). As an essentially didactic type of drama, *xiqu* portrays the grim experience of injustice in this world, but at the same time gives the spectators the satisfaction of seeing wrongs made right—usually in the final scene. *Xiqu* strongly engages with ethics; it strives toward re-establishing harmony in the world and exercises a meliorating social function. It does so through employing traditional beliefs concerning "The Rule of Nature" or "The Way," called *dao*.[2] Therefore, the aesthetic of *xiqu* can be considered very pragmatic. The pragmatism of Chinese theatre is best encapsulated in the well-known text by Hu Zhiyu (1227-93) written for a famous courtesan-actress, entitled "Preface for the Poem for Madam Song" (Zeng Songshi xu):

> [M]an seldom knows ease for his heart or rest for his bones. ...In that brief time had he nothing to loosen the toils of the world ... lift his heart, show him some small pleasure with which to banish his burden of bitterness, it were hard to be a man at all!
>
> This is why the Sage used music.... Musicians and players are equally precious to the ruler because the sounds of music match the harmonies of government, and the dramas of players can change to fit the ideals of any age. ...No sentiment exists which

these dramas are incapable of expressing nor is there behaviour which they have not explored (Crump 190-191).

Numerous stories about injustice and abuse have ghosts as their protagonists. These ghosts either return to the world themselves for revenge (assuming a ghostly or a human form) or work through the dreams of mortals. Some drag the living back to the spirit world with them. The Chinese world of ghosts is "much more fair than this one," because in it "the powerless are justified among the spirits": "[i]f you were a scholar cheated out of a deserved official's position in the world of the living, you might find yourself appointed governor of ghosts" (Siu 189). Ghost characters are easily recognizable on the traditional Chinese stage. A unique convention, specifying a white costume and a long strip of white paper suspended from above the ear, indicates that the person is a spectre. White is associated with death and funerals in Chinese culture, and so the theatrical convention is easily understood.

THE PLOT OF SNOW IN MIDSUMMER

Snow in Midsummer (known also as "The Injustice Done to Dou E"[3] or simply as "The Story of Dou E"), a four-act play, tells the story of a girl who lost her mother at the age of three. When Dou E was seven years old, she was sold by her father, a destitute scholar, to cancel his debts and to finance his journey to the capital so that he might try his hand in the exams for a clerical position. She was bought by her future mother-in-law, called Mother Cai, to serve at her house as a domestic helper. Dou E was a dedicated servant. Unfortunately, soon after her marriage to the son of Mother Cai, the seventeen-year-old Dou E became a widow.

The stage action begins after the death of Dou E's husband, when she is living with her mother-in-law who wishes her to remarry. The heroine resists marrying again, and as a result she becomes the victim of revenge taken by the man who has asked for her hand. The man, a local bully, is called Donkey Zhang. He is the son of Old Zhang. Both men are in search of a wife. Widowed Mother Cai seems quite willing to accept remarriage, but Dou E decides to stick to Confucian norms and not to remarry. Donkey Zhang then tries to poison Mother Cai, hoping it will facilitate managing Dou E alone. By accident the poisoned soup is drunk by Old Zhang instead of Mother Cai, and the old man dies promptly. The tricky young man accuses Dou E, and subsequently she is charged with murder and flogged to force a confession. When she does not admit guilt, a corrupt judge orders the widow Cai to be flogged in front of Dou E. The young heroine cannot bear this sight and confesses to the murder. She is sentenced to death. The abused woman swears on the day of her execution that her death will prompt Heaven to send snow in midsummer, and—in a genuine *coup de theatre*—it happens indeed.

The father of Dou E meanwhile sits in his office and investigates the papers. He now holds an administrative post and is responsible for examining the affairs of local courts of law. In a *deus ex machine*, the ghost of Dou E starts its "second life," a purely theatrical life that gives the play an unforgettably theatrical impact. The female ghost cries out her whole tragic story and ends with the following words:

> For resisting seduction I was executed!
>
> I would not disgrace my clan; so I lost my life! ...
>
> You are sent by the emperor to investigate trials;
>
> Consider this case and this man's wickedness;
>
> Though you cut him in pieces, I shall not be satisfied!
>
> (Kuan 1957, 154) [4]

It is clear that *Snow in Midsummer* cannot be considered to be a generic crime story with suspense. There is no need for forensic psychology; the reader knows from the very beginning who is the killer and who will be sentenced to death. Instead, all efforts are made to describe the ethical dimension of the injustice done. Thus, it is important to know the nuances of Confucian ethics in order to understand the dramaturgical conflicts and tension in this play.

THE ROLE OF WOMEN IN SOCIETY ACCORDING TO CONFUCIAN ETHICS

On hearing that her mother-in-law wants to remarry and that she advises her to do the same, Dou E reproaches the old lady and sings an aria about virtuous women of days past:

> Where is the woman whose tears for her husband
>
> Caused the great Wall to crumble?...
>
> Where is she who changed into stone through longing for her husband?
>
> How shameful that women of today are so unfaithful,
>
> So few of them are chaste, so many wanton!
>
> All, all are gone, those virtuous women of old. . . .

There is no doubt that Dou E sees herself as a model Confucian woman. The following quote can draw attention to her reflexive self-creation as such a model. At the execution ground she makes an allusion to legendary women who have also been wrongly accused and sentenced to death. Dou E sings:

> In midsummer, you say, it cannot snow;
>
> Have you ever heard how frost was caused in June?
>
> My blazing hate and fury

> Can make the snow fall thick and white as cotton....

She further predicts: "If injustice has been done, sir, this district will suffer from drought for three whole years." Then she sings again:

> You think Heaven knows no justice, men no pity?
>
> Almighty Heaven will listen to men's prayers.
>
> Once in Tunghai, for three years no rain fell.
>
> Because a good daughter-in-law was unjustly treated.
>
> Now your district's turn has come. (Kuan 1957, 149-150)

Throughout the play Guan Hanqing consistently portrays his heroine as a person of tremendous moral courage who remains true to the virtues of chastity and filial duty, even in the face of torture and humiliation. In my view, however, she adheres to Confucian ideals only to such extent as will not interfere with typical Chinese principles of theatrical aesthetics. I will address that issue later on, but first will indicate who can be called an ideal Confucian woman. The Confucian view of women is well epitomized in *Precepts on Family Life*, a work written by Confucian scholar Sima Guan:

> The husband is Heaven; the wife is earth. The husband is the sun; the wife is the moon. ... Heaven is honoured and occupies the space above. Earth is lowly and occupies the space below. ... Therefore wives take as their virtues gentleness and compliance and do not excel through strength or intellectual discrimination. (Ebrey 24)

Was Dou E's late husband like Heaven to her? The answer would be yes, since she died in the name of fidelity to his memory and to fulfill her Confucian duty of maintaining sacrifices to her husband's deceased family members, which implies not remarrying. But can we draw an inference that Heaven, which Dou E asks for help in her execution scene, has something to do with the husband-Heaven figure? I presume so, because one's agency is always situational and relational to the surrounding social and natural context. Heaven is Dou E's *dao*. Thus Dou E calls Heaven for help; but—one could ask—why doesn't she call on any Chinese goddess? She could look for protection from the Buddhist Guanyin (Goddess of Mercy) or the Taoist Xiwangmu (Queen Mother of the West), who was believed to confer immortality. The answer is, in my opinion, that neither Buddhism nor Taoism glorify society; on the contrary, both advise withdrawal from any social bonds. Confucian ethics regards society as a value in itself, and it was that principle of adjusting the individual to social regulations that Dou E wanted to obey. Dou E's Heaven is a patriarchal society, and the same patriarchal system causes her death.

The play raises the question why a woman so dedicated to patriarchal Confucian codes for female behavior must be sentenced by the court of justice to death? Nevertheless, the theatrical character of this victimized young woman would be too flat if it were the whole story. The drama concerns Confucian ethics, but also employs powerful theatrics. An obedient, pious Confucian woman could never take revenge for her sufferings; therefore, her revenge on the *xiqu* stage takes a purely conventional, suppositional, and theatrically artificial form. It enters an aesthetic domain that makes it an object of theatrical emotions, not those of daily life. I would borrow here a term coined by Haiping Yan in her studies of *xiqu*, and call it an aestheticized ethics of *xiqu* (73).

Having the non-realistic nature of the dramatic action in view, one could ask whether the agency of Dou E has subversive power. She respected and revered the ethical system with no rewards for women, and she took revenge on that system while in her ghostly form. Was it effective? Confucian rational thought despised belief in ghosts, which has always been so popular among Chinese folk. Even though on the *xiqu* stage a ghost of a woman might appear mighty, Confucian scholars would not take it seriously. Yet theatre in China was usually a place for common people, and especially so in Guan Hanqing's time. Although everyday Confucian society excludes female agency, the on-stage world allows it in order to channel the real tensions and transform them into controlled theatrical emotions. It is easy to imagine the audience reaction when Donkey Zhang cries: "A ghost! A ghost! Heaven preserve us! Protect me from evil spirits!" And Dou E's ghost replies:

> Face to face with this scoundrel...
>
> You murdered your own father by mistake;
>
> But you cannot put the blame on me!
>
> (Tou Ngo's spirit beats Donkey)

After the beating she continues:

> I should never have signed a false statement;
>
> But I did it in filial piety,
>
> And thereby caused my own ruin....
>
> And I, a poor, weak woman.... (Kuan 1957, 146-147)

A woman's fidelity, called *jie* or *zhen*, was one of the most important Confucian virtues, equal to filial piety (*xiao*) or patriotism (*zhong*). Dou E is a model Confucian woman when she is alive. But Guan Hanqing was not a preacher or a moralist, he was a dramatist of genius. He knew that in order to make the character vivid, plausible and theatrically effective, he had to make it human-like. And in Chinese lore, ghosts are believed to be troubled with very human emotions. Dou E is both an illustrious Confucian woman, who preserves her chastity on the one hand, and an anti-Confucian, fearless woman, who takes revenge on a treacherous male on the other. Thus, Confucian ethics meets a theatrical adversary.

The Female Protagonist and the Poetics of Xiqu Drama

Dramatists in pre-republic China were almost exclusively male literati trained in Confucian ethics and aesthetics by means of a system of special examinations that allowed them to work in public administration. A natural consequence of that is that the Chinese traditional drama mirrors Confucian ideology and propagates Confucian morals. This fact explains the number of *xiqu* plays dealing with justice and trials. One of the tenets constituting the poetics of Chinese drama is the rule concerning dramatic conflict, which is to be located in the imaginary social world presented on the stage, rather than in the protagonist's psyche. One can presume then that the problem of the construction of gender in traditional Chinese plays focuses on its interest in addressing the question of how a woman should behave in an exemplary Chinese society, rather than how it feels to be a woman as such.

A Chinese woman as the heroine of a *xiqu* drama is a literary construct conceived by the male imagination exclusively, because in the Confucian system there was no room for any form of female agency. Yet, even a brief look at *xiqu* repertoire shows that the majority of its protagonists are active, not passive women. It is female agency that feeds the plot, as is clear in the plot of *Snow in Midsummer*. How should that paradox be understood? One can interpret the play as an indication that the exemplary female character in traditional Chinese drama is a woman who is so ideal, according to Confucian standards, that she could never possibly exist in everyday life. The onstage agency of a female character transcends the social order that prevents women from taking the initiative. It transcends the mundane world and even ventures a view of Heaven. *Xiqu* drama poetically employs the character's gender as a figural, emblematic quality. The aesthetic aim of *xiqu* was based on emotion. The presented stage action should "move Heaven and Earth," evoking very strong feeling in the viewers (Yan 66). However, it could also aim to move the Highest Court of Justice, as Heaven in traditional Chinese religion is imagined as a sort of administration or government with its Emperor and Ministers. One can conclude that the ethical system imbedded in *xiqu* is not of this world.

Why does Guan Hanqing not allow his heroine to live; why does he expunge her from the world of living by presenting the scene of her execution? The answer could be because only in such a way can the female dramatis persona gain her theatrical agency. A woman of flesh and bone on the *xiqu* stage has to change into a theatrical ghost to effectively perform her part. As long as Dou E was a more or less literal theatrical representation of a woman, she was powerless and vulnerable. After she became a ghost, she automatically gained might. The farther away the drama moves from verisimilitude, the more a female character gains her rights. Hence, must a powerful woman be unreal? Haiping Yan argues that the human feelings that are the focus of *xiqu* concern not so much how one feels in a normal world, but "how one feels in the midst of being out of joint with the world" (76). What is to be revealed on the *xiqu* stage is not so much the resolution of what really happened to Dou E, but rather how she feels about what happened to her (76). Theatrical truth on the Chinese traditional stage resonates with and is defined by true feelings. Taking that into consideration, one can conclude that Dou E dies in order to create a powerful ending to the play.

The Female Protagonist in Theatrical Performance

Ironically, real justice starts to operate only after the heroine is dead. Is this justice for nothing, then? To the contrary, only in this way can the stage performance of a *xiqu* drama be fully effective. Only then, according to the poetics of Chinese drama, can the audience be truly moved. The world of the *xiqu* stage is a highly stylized, imaginary, ideal world. If the world is to be changed, the heroine has to mutate to open the metaphysical modus of life. A female character must mutate into a ghost in order to gain its agency.

The Confucian View of Woman 55

A performance on stage is a crucial reference for understanding the construction of gender in any *xiqu* drama.[5] Cross-gender acting has a long[6] tradition in China. As concerns a performance of *Snow in Midsummer*, a subversive dimension emerges when the female protagonist is played by a male actor, as was a common practice in the old Chinese theatre. These circumstances spotlighted gender on the *xiqu* stage. As Elin Diamond rightly notes, "When gender is alienated or foregrounded, the spectator is enabled to see a sign system as a sign system ..." (85). When considering the construction of gender in Chinese traditional plays, one has to bear in mind that the genders on *xiqu* stage are theatrical constructions par excellence. That is, they are stylized to suit specific aesthetic principles and do not struggle to achieve verisimilitude or the illusion of gender in real social contexts. With cross-gender acting functioning as a crucial element of Chinese theatricality, the real sex of a performer was never a decisive factor that could influence a viewer's perception in her/his mental process of constructing the character she/he is watching. On the contrary, a spectator had to read purely theatrical signs, such as the costume and the acting conventions, to learn the gender of a dramatic character. For example, each movement of a female character must be soft, rounded, agile, and delicate. The fingers must never be outstretched. Every digit should be bent in a different manner to form what is called the "flower-bud-hand." The performer does not expose the thumb, but must keep it concealed by the middle finger. A female impersonator should also stay erect but with shoulders pressed down to simulate limpness. While turning, the performer must move the entire body, not only the head. An actor portraying a woman must take short steps, and in the case of a lady shoes ought to be covered by the rim of a long skirt. If a character is young, a performer is supposed to step mincingly. In the old days there was a special device, similar to small stilts, in use to imitate on stage the bound, tiny feet of a "beautiful" Chinese lady.

Dou E is a female prisoner, which is also conventionally shown on the stage. As a rule persons condemned to death are clad in red. A woman additionally has her head wrapped in a blue kerchief to indicate that her hair is not being done because she has been jailed. A long ponytail of black artificial hair hangs from the top of the head of the actor. On the *xiqu* stage such a hair style indicates a person in distress. According to the traditions of Chinese daily life, one should not wear blue hair ornaments or hats, because it brings bad luck; thus, the blue head cover of a woman prisoner stands for her miserable fate in the theatrical code as well. In a sense Dou E is a visual symbol of misery. No less significant are the proxemic conventions. In her execution aria, although she is said to be walking, she doesn't move.

Haiping Yan argues that the style of acting on the *xiqu* stage should be named "suppositional in its overall mode" (67), and that such performance can both "inscribe a specific system of ethics and exceed the limits of the system, thereby activating transformative imaginations" (75). In such a perspective the inhabiting of a theatrical female role becomes for an actor a matter of using a prescribed set of gender construction tools. The gender norms predate the actor or the specific performance by many centuries. Thus "representation installs a gender that it seems to describe" (Jackson 202). Furthermore, theatrical empathy does not function in *xiqu* the way it does in Occidental cultures. For Chinese viewers there is no such question as "how would I feel in Dou E's shoes?" because they cannot possibly identify themselves with the onstage happenings. *Xiqu*'s cultural matrix, consistent with traditional Chinese beliefs and ethical systems, is based on the notion of *dao*, or The Way. Thus, the relevant question would be "what is the *dao* of a woman?"

Arias sung by actors playing the heroines constitute the emotional core of *xiqu* aesthetics and are cherished by traditional Chinese audiences. The mode of acting in *xiqu*, the maneuvers of role playing, openly encourage viewers to scrutinize "[h]ow players feel when they play the effects of social scripts that oppose their character, and how such feelings are compelled and denied by routine events ..." (Yan 76). Such sufferings displayed by actors may have offered varied interpretations in regard to gender. As presented on stage, gender might have appeared unstable,

The Confucian View of Woman 57

as opposed to the unchanging set of norms that was employed in the presentation. It is interesting to note, for example, that when the actor playing the character of Dou E was a female, she may have cried out against her own private position in society as a condemned actress whose sin was to show her face in public, which was considered highly improper and indecent by strict Confucian adherents. When the actor playing Dou E was a male, he might have evinced homosexual emotions and reactions (Tian 83), that can be grasped as eventually creating a sadomasochistic dimension. A man playing a suffering woman for the satisfaction of another man in the audience creates a performed genre construction with multiple layers.

The next step could be to interpret *Snow in Midsummer* from a perspective given by an indigenous Chinese notion of *xiqu* as a "feminine" genre of theatre. This idea has been proposed by theoreticians such as Wang Jide and Xu Wei, who have compared Chinese traditional theatre to an alluring woman (Li 174-175). Given that there were possible situations in which a spectator was not able to guess the biological sex of the performer playing Dou E, it is even more intriguing to examine the embodied aesthetic construction of the gender of that character onstage. The final and extreme implication is that the task might be to explore a phenomenon that is neither the sex of a private performer nor the sex of the actor-in-the-dramatis-persona, but rather a blurred, aesthetic gender. Taking Elin Diamond's approach that "[w]hen gender is alienated or foregrounded ... the gender lexicon becomes so many illusionistic trappings to be put on or shed at will" (195), we can consider the Dou E character played on the stage by an actor/actress as a blurred or multi-faceted gender susceptible to any number of readings by the spectators.

Who Has Been Indicted?

The play's indictments can be many, as it is charged with a profound ethical impetus. Who has been indicted then? It is not nature that is under indictment in *Snow in Midsummer*. In fact nature acts in favor of Dou E.

She asks heaven and earth to do miracles after her death, and her prayer is fulfilled. This outcome accords with traditional Chinese philosophy:

> [M]an is part of the universe, the universe is part of man's being. ... our life and nature are inextricably intertwined and completely involved in each other. This is the theory of the unity of Heaven and man as enunciated by Confucian scholars (Chai xix).

The play obviously raises a point about the patriarchal system of pre-revolutionary China's Confucian society. In my opinion it is not the males who have been indicted, because Dou E's mother-in-law was also responsible for the trouble. Donkey Zhang and his father are portrayed as ridiculous simpletons, not as tyrants. The case of the judge and the legislative system he represents is evident: the unethical rulers must be indicted on charges of corruption. The play obviously condemns the juridical system of the Yuan dynasty and questions its foundations. The institution that is responsible for promoting social order and exercising justice does quite the contrary.

Guan Hanqing wrote his play in the thirteenth century (after the Mongols set up their capital in Cambaluc in 1264), when the Chinese felt discrimination and injustice at the hands of their conquerors. Thus the figure of Dou E can also be seen to represent all Han-Chinese people oppressed under the Yuan regime. Taking the patriotic dimension of the play into consideration, one can perceive the dramatis persona of Dou E as a metonymy. This reading is the most popular interpretation in Chinese literary criticism. It is said that Guan Hanqing was known for his integrity as a Confucian scholar, living under the anti-Chinese Yuan court (Yan 70). What is more, Dou E is just one of many other miserable female leading characters in Guan's theatrical *oeuvre*. Perhaps the figure of a victimized young woman of low social status denoted, in his eyes, the most common and obvious example of a social victim and therefore was to be universally understood by the audience. Our motherland is like that condemned, innocent girl—and we must stop it! Such a slogan could sum up the story told in *Snow in Midsummer*. To go even further, the fate of heroine Dou E can be taken as a symbolic indictment of the feudal system of Imperial China, and this interpretation was popular indeed in all the communist criticism of that drama written in the twentieth century in the People's Republic of China. What is striking is that those anti-feudal as well as patriotic interpretations mentioned above use the female dramatis persona as a tool, an exemplary metonymy, a commonly understood symbol—in other words, as a rhetorical figure known to be characteristic of the traditional Chinese allusive style of narration. The prevailing intra-cultural, indigenous Chinese interpretation thus reads: being a woman stands for being a victim.

The political mechanisms of victimization might be a clue, but *Snow in Midsummer* "seems more than a simple play of social criticism or a satire against the ruling class" (Hwang 172). Unfortunately, we know very little about the life of Guan Hanqing, and all the suppositions about his patriotic preoccupations are therefore ungrounded. We simply do not know whether Guan wanted to accuse the Mongol rulers or not. So little is known about this prolific playwright that some scholars—feeling unease on that account—have even supplied fanciful information about him (Crump 9). The facts are that he was born in Yanjing (later known as Dadu; modern Beijing) and he once visited Lin'an in South China. As Hargett states, "Virtually every other surviving account or anecdote related to his life and career is controversial and thus unreliable" (113). All we have are his plays.

Interestingly, another of Guan Hanqing's plays, *The Riverside Pavilion*, also addresses the question of widowhood. Surprisingly, this time he allows his female lead, Tan Qier, to remarry and to live happily with her second husband. In fact, the description of their romantic love in this drama "is unmatched in Chinese literature" (Hargett 115). Does it mean that Guan Hanqing was not as orthodox a Confucian as some Chinese critics would like him to be? Does it make a good case to conclude that the ethical dimension of *Snow in Midsummer* is subversively articulated according to Confucian values? Under Mongol rule Confucianism was officially condemned (Shih 81). Does that controversy express Guan Hanqing's ambiguous feelings about Confucianism? In search for the answer one also has to bear in mind that the cult of widows' fidelity was not so strong in Guan Hanqing's lifetime, and only gained importance later during the Song dynasty, reaching its apogee in the eighteenth and nineteenth centuries (Elvin 12). Finally, when coming to terms with the ultimate answer about whether Dou E's Confucian firmness is praised or questioned by Guan Hanqing, one can only state that it is unclear. Mark Elvin, who has explored the efforts of the traditional Chinese state to promote widow chastity as a virtue, comes to a similar conclusion:

> These two contrasting conceptions, the Confucian esteem for fidelity and chastity, and the celebration of the satisfaction of physical passion, can also be found—but not together—in plays of the Yuan (or Mongol) dynasty (1279-1367), even in different pieces from the brush of the same author. Unlike the early modern West, there seems never to have been any open dialogue between "virtue" and "vice" (114).

Only one question cannot be put easily to rest: Why does a good character have to suffer such severe punishment? Why is that character a female? To me, the theatrical perspective gives the answer: Chinese theatre is a place that traditionally offers its audience a better alternative to the real word. Dou E is an exemplary figure of those vulnerable to victimization in traditional Chinese society. She is an ideal character shown on the stage in order to prove that theatre can create a world which is more just than this one. The moral implications of the play are achieved in a theatrical way. On the stage the young and just female never dies.

Notes

1. These are traditional dates. Modern research places his birth between 1241 and 1250 and his death between 1320 and 1324 (West and Idema 1).
2. Although *dao* is popularly identified with Daoism, it is by no means confined to it. It is equally crucial for Confucianism. The only difference is that Daoists consider it to be a single system, whereas Confucians believe there are multiple expressions of *dao*.
3. The name Dou E is in Mandarin Chinese. In other Chinese languages it is pronounced differently. For example the Cantonese version is Tou Ngo, so the title of a Cantonese version of that drama is *The Injustice Done to Tou Ngo*. The translators of *Snow in Midsummer*, Yang Hsien-yi and Gladys Yang, used the Tou Ngo version.
4. Cf. (Kuan, 1958). The edition of 1958 differs slightly from the edition of 1957, although the translators are the same: Yang Hsien-yi and Gladys Yang.
5. In the old days Chinese literati did not treat drama as one of the literary genres, because those texts were not meant for reading but for performing exclusively.
6. Some scholars date the beginning of cross-gender acting to the second (see Tian), others to the seventh century (see Chou).

Works Cited

Chai, C. w. C. W. *The Story of Chinese Philosophy.* New York: Washington Square Press, 1961. Print.

Chou, H.-l. "Striking Their Own Poses. The History of Cross-Dressing on the Chinese Stage." *The Drama Review* 14.2 (1997): 130-152. Print.

Crump, J. I. *Chinese Theatre in the Days of Kublai Khan.* Ann Arbor: Center for Chinese Studies, The University of Michigan, 1990. Print.

Diamond, E. "Brechtian Theory/Feminist Theory." *The Drama Review* 32.1 (1988): 82-94. Print.

Ebrey, P. B. *Women and the Family in Chinese History.* London: Routledge, 2002. Print.

Elvin, M. "Female Virtue and the State in China. Past&Present." *Issue* 104 (1984): 111-152. Print.

Hargett, J. M. *The Plays of Guan Hanqing* (Kuan Han-ch'ing). *Great Literature of the Eastern World,* ed. McGreal, I. P.. New York: HarperCollins, 1996: 113-116. Print.

Hayden, G. *Crime and Punishment in Medieval Chinese Drama: Three Judge Pao Plays.* Cambridge, Mass.: Harvard University Press, 1978. Print.

Hwang, M.-s. "The Deaths of Cordelia and Tou O: Morality and Theatricality." *Studies in Chinese-Western Comparative Drama,* ed. Luk, Y. Hong Kong: The Chinese University Press, 1990. Print.

Jackson, S. "Theatricality's proper objects: genealogies of performance and gender theory." *Theatricality.* Cambridge: Cambridge University Press, 2003:187-213. Print.

Kuan, H.-c. *Snow in Midsummer. Chinese Literature* 1 (1957):133-158. Print.

Kuan, H.-c. *Snow in Midsummer. Selected Plays of Kuan Han-ching.* Peking: Foreign Languages Press, 1958: 21-47. Print.

Li, S. L. *Cross-dressing in Chinese Opera.* Hong Kong: Hong Kong University Press, 2003. Print.

Shih, C.-w. *The Golden Age of Chinese Drama: Yuan Tsa-chu.* Princeton, New Jersey: Princeton University Press, 1976. Print.

Siu, W.-N. *Chinese Opera. Images and Stories.* Vancouver: University of British Columbia Press, 1997. Print.

Tian, M. "Male Dan: the Paradox of Sex, Acting, and Perception of Female Impersonation in Traditional Chinese Theatre." *Asian Theatre Journal* 17.1 (2000): 79-97. Print.

West, S. H. and Idema, W. L., eds. "Moving Heaven and Shaking Earth: The Injustice to Dou E." *Monks, Bandits, Lovers, and Immortals: Eleven Early Chinese Plays.* Indianapolis: Hackett Publishing, 2010: 1-37. Print.

Yan, H. "Theatricality in Classical Chinese Drama." *Theatricality.* Cambridge: Cambridge University Press, 2003: 65-89. Print.

RENAISSANCE DRAMA

CHAPTER 3.

WOMAN'S VALUE ON TRIAL IN *TROILUS AND CRESSIDA*

Lilly J. Goren

Recent highly publicized cases in the United States, India, and Pakistan have brought renewed attention to the crime of rape. According to most analyses, far more rapes occur than are ever reported or brought to trial, both because the nature of the crime makes it sometimes difficult to prove in court, and because rape often carries a stigma of lost "honor" for the victim. In the absence of legal sanctions, rape functions as a weapon, a form of power, and as a threat facilitating control. Within stable political regimes, rape involves a demonstration of power over another person, more often a woman dominated by a man whom she may or may not personally know. When social and political institutions break down, rape threatens the majority of women, as reported in this 2004 human rights bulletin:

> [M]ass rape in war has been documented in various countries, including Cambodia, Liberia, Peru, Bosnia, Sierra Leone, Rwanda, the Democratic Republic of Congo, Somalia and Uganda. A European Community fact-finding team estimated that more than 20,000 Muslim women were raped during the war in Bosnia. (*In-depth: Our Bodies-Their Battle Ground*, online.)

In some cultures a significant consequence of rape is the experience of shame by the woman's immediate family. The victim is considered sexually dishonored and accordingly devalued as the result of an assault which she had no power to prevent or terminate. Regardless of how virtuous a woman might be before she is violated, after the fact, she is considered in many cultures to have lost her purity. Thus women often suffer scars from rape that are not visible, in contrast to the way that a physical assault can leave a scar that is seen and may even be a point of pride.

Literature reveals a fascination with rape through a number of legendary rape victims, including Leda, Helen, Lucretia, and Lavinia. Both Lucretia, of Roman legend and numerous literary works, including Shakespeare's poem "The Rape of Lucrece," and Lavinia, of Shakespeare's *Titus Andronicus*, are raped as a form of revenge; in both cases the women reveal the criminal and die soon after the perpetrator is punished. Lavinia is killed by her father after she observes the revenge on her behalf, and Lucretia takes her own life after demanding that her virtue be avenged. Both of these women call upon the power of the patriarch to reestablish their treasured virtue through vengeful acts, thus instituting a form of justice. Rape and the threat of rape play a part in the action of Shakespeare's *Troilus and Cressida*; however, Helen and Cressida, the two female characters at the center of the play, find themselves in much more precarious situations. Both are subjected to evaluation throughout the play, and Cressida is placed on trial by means of a scene in which she is covertly observed interacting with a suitor.

The Context: Seven Years at War

Troilus and Cressida opens mid-Trojan war, as the Prologue comes to the stage, armed for battle and affirming that the armies have been engaged for quite some time. The Prologue explains that the Greek princes, "their high blood chafed," have come to "ransack Troy, within whose strong immures The ravished Helen, Menelaus' queen, With wanton Paris sleeps; and that's the quarrel" (Prologue.ln.2; lns 8-10). The Prologue thus defines the issue of ownership of women as central to the war, which at this point has become frustrating to both sides because of its intransigence. The setting for the action is violent, unstable, and ungoverned by the rule of law. This environment of insecurity encompasses both the Trojans and the Greeks, though it may be even more pronounced on the Greek side because they are away from home, their families, and the restraints of their own culture. The play heightens this insecurity by communicating utter disgust regarding war, ironically disparaging the romanticized system of chivalry and courtly love that has surrounded the tale of Troilus and the Trojan War in general. Heather James notes that the play is "bristling with anger and defenses, one whose competing ideologies are constantly staging their *aristeia*—the stepping forth of a warrior (or idea) to prove itself in battle" (89). Patriarchy, hierarchy, and order are all questioned in the context of the play, most pointedly by Ulysses early in Act I. Kristina Faber, noting the difficulty that many scholars have in categorizing this play and analyzing it contextually, draws upon the observations of Marilyn French and F. H. Langman to note the coterminous nature of usually disparate plot elements, concluding that "in *Troilus and Cressida*, love *is* war"(134).

Women on Trial

Troilus and Cressida, unlike many plays that have more clearly delineated themes or morals, poses questions about the position, power, autonomy, and agency, of women treated as objects of consumption. While it does not present the formal trial of any one woman, the play puts women on trial through its presentation of Cressida, and to a lesser extent, Helen. Its discussions about the value of beauty, or attributing a value to beauty and gauging the extent of its devaluing or debasement, places this trial in the realm of what contemporary courts would term a civil dispute, rather than a criminal complaint. The dilemma highlighted by the play is that the value placed on women's beauty, in a system where men view women as possessions, is constantly threatened by its association with sexuality. Security of ownership depends on reputations that are defined and constructed for women based on a projection of their desire for and enjoyment of sex. Crucially, the woman alone bears responsibility for maintaining her reputation free of corruption. The male pursuit of female beauty, combined with the sexual desire of both men and women, played out in the context of warring societies pursuing martial glory and honor based on the value of a woman (Helen), gives rise to three unique scenes in which both Helen and Cressida—and by extension, all women—are subjected to judgment for the loss of that value accorded their sexual purity.

CRESSIDA AND HELEN

The two female characters who most embody the messy pursuit of the war, Cressida and Helen, have substantially different histories, roles, and places within the play; but they are both accused of corruption and of corrupting men through their beauty, which so inflames desire that it leads to corruption. In concentrating on three particular scenes, this analysis prompts an evaluation of the way in which Shakespeare examines the construction of gender, especially with regard to female beauty and sexuality. The play questions binary thinking about women and sexuality, suggesting that the opposition between women who are virtuous and women who are corrupt is imposed on women by men. It demonstrates the greater insistence on this opposition at times when the standards of the societies rest on fragile and contested foundations, especially when those foundations are defined by martial glory and the pursuit of an elusively defined honor. Mary Beth Rose summarizes the association between women's honor and men's honor in the play:

> That women and eros are depicted as subversive of public action does not score a point for misogyny in the play, nor does it demonstrate the superiority of military heroism. Instead, these representations serve to underscore the delusions of chivalry by emphasizing the evasive emptiness of its predominant sexual ideology, in which women, idealized as themes of honor and renown, in fact play at best a peripheral and at worst an antagonistic role in the chivalric conception of glorious male action (205).

The Prologue gives us some insight into how the characters, as representatives of their respective societies, see the situation. The Greeks have come to "To ransack Troy," because "[t]he ravish'd Helen, Menelaus' queen,/With wanton Paris sleeps" (Prologue, lines 8-11). Helen has been ravished but is not here described as ravishing. Her value has been undermined by this ravishing. Helen, of course, while the center of the quarrel that frames the play, is not the center of the play. That role goes to Cressida—much more, in fact, than it goes to Troilus. In a sense, Helen is a kind of echo or reflection of Cressida: their stories are similar in that they are traded and valued based on the designations of others, especially in regard to their beauty. Though their external beauty is constantly discussed, suggesting a consistent desirability, its value does change or decline based on the way they are perceived by others, especially with regard to their morals. This loss of value forms the crux of their respective trials, trials over which the two women have little control and even less voice or authority.

Troilus and Cressida reveals a form of gender construction that defines —and confines or traps—women through informal but damning processes of judgment. Both women are suspended between and, to some extent, claimed by both the Trojans and the Greeks. Neither woman enjoys the freedom to choose her side or her dwelling place, and neither has the ability to influence or change the evaluation of her worth by one or both sides. Helen and Cressida both find themselves evaluated and subsequently trapped within these evaluations, because they have no agency to challenge or change the basis of these evaluations: the classic virgin/whore binary. James O'Rourke notes the rigid structure that patriarchy imposes on the experiences and perceptions of both the men and the women in the play:

> The legendary defamation of Cressida as a whore is a corrupted version of the metalepsis of Helen's idealization ("Helen must needs be fair,/When with your blood you daily paint her thus" [1.i.93-94]) Just as those who war for a woman will (as they do with Helen) blame the women, those who drive women into prostitution will identify prostitutes as the source of disease ("galled g[ee]se of Winchester" [5.x.54]), when the real source is precisely the patriarchal sexual economy represented by Pandarus and the sexual practices it fosters (141).

The play calls attention to the general devaluing of women in the context of war with its crude language and frequent references to sexually transmitted diseases. In the prevailing system of ownership, a woman's preferences have little impact on whose possession she becomes, as is seen most acutely by Cressida's predicament in the latter part of the play, but it is certainly the tale of Helen as well. In the context of ongoing war, the individual woman cannot depend on her status, family, or previously acknowledged virtue to protect her value. O'Rourke, again, notes:

> The debased nature of this sexual economy shows itself in the interchangeability of the terms "whore" and "woman". The term "whore" is never used in the play to describe women paid for sexual services but refers to those who have been forcibly transferred from one man to another..., and to Patroclus, a man who, for lack of "stomach to the war" (3.3.221), has been made a sort of woman, a "masculine whore (5.1.17) (141).

Woman's Value on Trial in *Troilus and Cressida*

JUDGING HELEN

Three scenes comprise the trial of Helen and two trials of Cressida. The scenes are not constructed as formal trials, and neither Helen nor Cressida has any real foreknowledge of what is at stake, but in them Helen and Cressida face accusation and judgment of their beauty, their moral virtue and constancy, and ultimately their worth to the state. Hector states his valuation of Helen thus: "She is not worth what she doth cost/the holding" (II.ii.1043), as the Trojan princes argue with Priam, their father and King of Troy, about whether they should keep Helen or return her, accepting the Greek offer that all damage done "shall be struck off" (II.ii.7). The discussion pits Paris and Troilus, who want to keep Helen for the sake of the honor of Troy, against Hector, who urges Priam to return her. This scene encapsulates the driving theme of the play, which revolves around the value and role of honor in society. The play shows the absurd circularity of Trojan honor based on the value of Helen, and Helen's value resting in the fact that she is the source of the war between two empires. If the war ends, the cherished item of beauty (already said to be sullied) returned, and the honor of those who died essentially undermined, what is left of Trojan society?

While Helen stands at the crux of this discussion, the ideal of honor is actually on trial. Instead of interrogating the assumed foundation of honor—the glory of Troy and what value that may have for Trojan society—the speakers question Helen's worth in relation to the continued pursuit of the war. Troilus argues, "She is a theme of honour and renown / A spur to valiant and magnanimous deeds / Whose present courage may beat down our foe / And fame in time to come canonize us." (II.ii.199-202) Keeping Helen gives them a reason to continue fighting the Greeks. In a sense, she becomes a stand-in for argument and reason. This truncated conversation highlights the degraded world of both the Trojans and the Greeks—a world in which life is always in jeopardy, but motivation focuses on the value or degradation of beauty, as if this asset, so much more ephemeral than life itself, should subsume life, as opposed to life subsuming beauty.

    Ultimately, Troilus prevails, and thus it would seem that Helen is judged favorably. Her despoiled quality, while taken into consideration in determining her value, drives part of the argument, since her worth would be further reduced should she be returned (passed back and forth between Menelaus and Paris, as it were). Helen herself, as a person, however, is almost erased by this conversation; she has as much particular value as the pearl to which Troilus compares Cressida in his early soliloquy ("Her bed is India; there she lies, a pearl." I.i.96). Helen is a commodity, and this discussion indicates that her value is based on the market, the *demand* for her and the limited supply. As James observes, "The play's interest in the traffic in women partly explains why Helen of Troy, so authoritative elsewhere, is aggressively vacant when she enters into a play in which economics dominate and interpret the action and language" (104-105). Unlike Euripides' Helen, the Helen of Shakespeare speaks little and appears as an object.

CRESSIDA AMONG THE GENERALS

Cressida's trials, which are more complex than this discussion of Helen's value, revolve primarily around her capacity for fidelity, and her representation of women's capacity for fidelity. They begin when she is notified of her impending transfer to the Greek camp. At the beginning of Act IV Aeneas comes to Troilus early in the morning and explains that Cressida, with whom Troilus has just spent the night, has been traded to the Greeks for one of the captured Trojans (Antenor). Once Aeneas apprises Troilus of the trade, Troilus' response is strikingly distinct from his defense of Helen earlier in the play: Troilus merely asks, "Is it concluded so?" (IV.ii.68). He does not defend Cressida or dispute this turn of events. His main concern is to conceal his tryst with Cressida, as he instructs Aeneas not to divulge where he was found. Troilus, Pandarus and Cressida then engage in a dialogue that displays in ironic excess the medieval renderings of Troilus' devotion to Cressida and her sexually debased image within literature. Troilus pleads with Cressida to "be true," outlining the standards by which he will measure her fidelity.

Cressida, on the other hand, expresses worry about going to the Greek camp. Her father, Calchas, who is Trojan, had defected to the Greeks because he had a vision that the Greeks would win the war. While the Greeks liked his vision, they also were wary of him because of his traitorous past. Thus Cressida's father would be of little assistance or protection for her. As Diomedes will escort Cressida in her transfer from the Trojan to the Greek camp, he responds to Cressida's anxiety by way of reference to her value. Diomedes notes, "[t]he lustre in your eye, heaven in your cheek, Pleads your fair usage;" (IV.iv.117-118). Cressida's beauty indicates her value, which calls for "fair usage" as opposed to abuse. Diomedes rebukes Troilus for his excessive entreaties with regard to Cressida (as once again, Troilus acts in a rash and overt manner) while simultaneously implying Cressida's insecure position in the Greek camp: "To her own worth She shall be prized; but that you say 'Be't so', I'll speak it in my spirit and honour: 'No.'" (IV.iv.132-134). This exchange is contextualized by an earlier conversation between Paris and Diomedes regarding Helen's worth—harkening back to the Trojan analysis of her value and reinforcing comments made by the men of the play with regard to women. Paris had asked Diomedes: "who, in your thoughts, merits fair Helen most, myself of Menelaus?" (IV.i.55-56). Helen was judged, along with Paris and Menelaus, in Diomedes' response:

> He merits well to have her that doth seek her,
>
> Not making any scruple of her soilure,
>
> With such a hell of pain and world of charge;
>
> And you as well to keep her that defend her,
>
> Not palating the taste of her dishonour,

> With such a costly loss of wealth and friends...
>
> Both merits poised, each weighs nor less nor more,
>
> But he as he. Which is heavier for a whore?...
>
> For every false drop in her bawdy veins
>
> A Grecian's life hath sunk; for every scruple
>
> Of her contaminated carrion weight
>
> A Trojan hath been slain. (VI.i.57-74)

This prelude to the trial to come of Cressida, when she enters the Greek camp demarcates the comingled relationship between women and war in this play and the way in which all women here are measured against Helen and her estimated worth.

The scene of Cressida's arrival at the Greek camp in Act IV subjects her to a corrupt trial, where biased evidence and threats of punishment force her to come to her own defense in a manner that marks her as an unruly woman. Diomedes enters the Greek camp with Cressida, and Agamemnon welcomes her with a kiss. Nestor notes that Cressida is saluted by "our general" with a kiss (IV.v.20). Ulysses turns this into the trial that will follow by suggesting that it "'Twere better she were kissed in general" (IV.v.22). Nestor then proceeds to kiss Cressida. Thus far Cressida has neither consented nor uttered a word. Achilles and Patroclus follow, amid banter employing double entendres, mostly at Menelaus' expense. Cressida finally replies, in response to Menelaus' demand for his kiss ("I'll have my kiss, --Lady, by your leave." VI.v.36). This becomes an interlocution between Menelaus and Cressida as she and Menelaus banter—apparently lightheartedly, with double entendres throughout—until Cressida's remarks hit "too close to home" in regard to Paris' cuckolding of Menelaus. Ulysses then enters the fray, "begging" for a kiss. Cressida has intellectually engaged the Greek generals, responding to their ironic banter at the same time that she senses little security in this new situation. Diomedes once again enters the dialogue, following the exchange with Ulysses, and offers to take Cressida to her father. But Ulysses has rendered judgment: he is disgusted with Cressida. He conflates her witty responses to the demands for sexual "favors" in the form of kisses with a despoiled nature. Female intelligence or wit must indicate a slatternly disposition. The virginal ideal of the female, a voiceless, beauty locked within protective walls, is at odds with a smart and quick beauty who finds herself in the midst of a war with constantly shifting allegiances and aims.[1] Mary Beth Rose notes that "[l]oved women were better left exalted, remote, and untouched" (21). Once the women become real, tactile, tangible, vocal, they are "set...down for sluttish spoils of opportunity and daughters of the game." (IV.v.62-64)

Cressida could have remained remote and silent, but as she notes when we first meet her, she has always known the need to defend herself—with any means at her disposal—to keep watch, to defend herself, or fight back as she does in this situation. She is unclear as to her position within the Greek camp, and her first introduction to it—with kisses given and begged in a "gamelike" environment—does not provide her with much security. She must be considering whether she belongs to the Greek army as a whole as they approach her in this manner. Cressida replies to the most powerful men among the Greeks in an attempt to demonstrate that she will not simply be diminished by their easy, sexual familiarity with her. She may have, as Nestor suggests, the "quick sense" to respond to these sexual overtures so as to beat them back, but her sense also indicates her understanding of the precariousness of her situation and her lack of power within it.

In this pivotal scene in *Troilus and Cressida*, Ulysses quickly sums up his judgment of Cressida, essentially closing down any further evidence that might indicate Cressida is not a "daughter of the game." Her trial is over and she has been sentenced, by Ulysses, to fulfilling his perception of her—and, by extension, most women.

> Fie, fie upon her!
>
> There's language in her eye, her cheek, her lip,
>
> Nay, her foot speaks; her wanton spirits look out
>
> At every joint and motive of her body. (IV.v.55-58)

Like so many modern defenses of those accused of rape or sexual assault, Ulysses is drawing his conclusions from Cressida's very appearance, how she looks, how she carries herself. By interacting with the generals in a witty manner Cressida's trial is concluded—she has been consigned to whoredom, whether she was aware of this indictment or not, Ulysses blames "the victim" of the kissing game *he* devised.

This scene in Act IV—which G. Wilson Knight terms the "pivotal incident in the play" (47), and which Claire Tylee suggests is "a key to the significance of one of the main questions posed by the play: whether a person's nature or identity is determined by the valuation set on that person by others" (Cambridge Collections online)—subjects Cressida to a type of trial in which the rules and the proceedings have been established by others, particularly by the most powerful men in the Greek camp. Without allies or much preparation, Cressida can only try to defend and, to a degree, define herself and her security against these structures about which she is uninformed. The scene holds up to judgment Cressida's reputation and her conduct in relation to gender expectations, and the conclusion is that she is corrupt, incapable of fidelity.

All the World is Watching—and Judging

Cressida's final trial in the play is a scene that is complexly constructed, providing a number of competing perspectives simultaneously. Act V, scene ii, while certainly not the end of the play, is the last time that the audience sees Cressida. Even though she is, to a degree, the center of the activity in the scene, Cressida herself is obscured by the running commentary from Troilus, who is viewing her actions in the company of Ulysses, while Thersites, from a different position, is also viewing and commenting on Cressida's interactions with Diomedes. Thus, here she has three different external judges and she also judges herself late in this scene. The scene takes place ostensibly in private—in contrast to the public arrival of Cressida in the Greek camp—but obviously not in a securely private environment where her words and actions would not be exposed to observation. Cressida's untenable position of being located within yet not within the private sphere reflects the impossibility she faces of finding a place from which to speak or act in accordance with a unified self or whole-hearted desire.

In understanding the actions and judgments within this scene, it is also necessary to understand the structure of the scene. Diomedes comes to Calchas' tent and asks for Cressida, whom Calchas says will come to him now. If Calchas, as Cressida's father, is able to provide any kind of protection or security for Cressida, this brief exchange suggests that he (perhaps like Pandarus, but with less flourish or sincerity) is willing to give Cressida to whomever requests or wants her. Troilus, as the result of a previous arrangement with Ulysses, is escorted to a place where he can observe and hear Cressida and Diomedes, but where both he and Ulysses cannot be seen by them. Ulysses specifically instructs Troilus to stand "where the torch may not discover us." (V.ii.6) Elsewhere Thersites has positioned himself where he, too, can observe and hear Cressida and Diomedes without being seen or heard.

This scene structurally resembles a modern court hearing where witnesses are questioned, and both defense and prosecuting attorneys approach the validity of the evidence given by the witnesses in attempts to either shore up the integrity of the information given or to undermine both the information presented and the integrity of the witness giving testimony. While Diomedes himself provides at least one approach by his interrogation of Cressida and her affection for him, Troilus,

Ulysses, and Thersites (as well as the audience) also fill the positions of attorneys examining and cross examining the testimony itself as well as the individuals giving testimony (most specifically Cressida, but she is not the only person in the scene who is scrutinized). Her three judges/observers come armed with conclusions they want validated. Troilus wants to see Cressida remain faithful to him; Ulysses has already labeled her a whore and expects to see his opinion verified; and Thersites, who directs his judgmental comments at both Cressida and Troilus, merely seeks further confirmation that the world, and this war, are as corrupt and rotten as he conceives them to be. In this interesting piece of staging, judgment is being passed on a number of different levels.

Diomedes initiates his conversation with Cressida by calling her "my charge"; the term verifies that she is in his care but can also be construed as being his possession. Cressida, in conversation with Diomedes, reflects terms that Pandarus used in his brief conversation with Helen, referring to him as "sweet honey Greek" (V.ii.20).[2] Diomedes, while not occupying precisely the same role as Pandarus, may be of similarly questionable morals and is certainly not valorous—and he, too, tempts Cressida away from one part of her true self to what might be more expedient in terms of her security. Diomedes, like Troilus as Cressida was being taken from him, demands that Cressida keep the oath she made—an oath which she keeps trying not to keep, but ultimately affirms by giving Diomedes Troilus' sleeve as "surety" of her promise, though she also tries to take it back after she has given it to him. Cressida shows uncertainty in her willingness to give herself (her body at least) to Diomedes, but she cannot toy with him or throw him aside because she is fearful of what might follow if she does. Still, she hesitates because of her deep affection for Troilus.

Ultimately Cressida hands over the sleeve that Troilus had given her, though she vacillates not only in giving it over but also in allowing Diomedes to come to see her. She is clearly conflicted, and this conflicted attitude is exploited by Diomedes since he keeps telling her that she should not mock him. Diomedes' success with Cressida gives him an opportunity to display his masculinity and military prowess, as he states that he will wear the sleeve so as to be challenged in the ensuing battle by whomever was Cressida's love. Cressida is tormented by her torn affections, and she has had no word from Troilus since she was taken to the Greek camp. Though he has been able to maneuver into a position from which to observe her interactions with Diomedes, he has not sent her a message or been able to arrange a meeting with her. Cressida does not know very much with regard to Troilus's immediate feelings about her; she knows only what she learned in the course of their evening together and through his entreaties as she was being taken to the Greek camp, which was less about his affection for her and more about demanding her fealty.

Cressida's final speech is a cynical analysis of the position in which women often find themselves, and how they often err, leading themselves towards corrupt or compromised ends.

> Troilus farewell! One eye yet looks on thee,
>
> But with my heart the other eye doth see.
>
> Ah, poor our sex! This fault in us I find:
>
> The error of our eye directs our mind.
>
> What error leads must err. O, then conclude:
>
> Minds swayed by eyes are full of turpitude. (V.ii.113-118)

Cressida has given up. In the untenable situation into which she has been thrust, she cannot "see" her way to an appropriate solution. Powerless to alter this situation, she has experienced potential threat from all of the Greek generals. She has not seen that her father, her uncle or her love, Troilus, are able to provide any kind of protection. Despite the fact that her decision seems to lie in the realm of self-preservation, she casts judgment upon herself (and her sex), noting that the impetus to follow one's eyes will lead to dismal ends, since the mind will follow unless it is compelled by forces in another direction. Thersites notes his analysis of her soliloquy: "A proof of strength she could not publish more, Unless she said, 'My mind is now turned whore'." (V.ii.119-120). Apparently there is no middle ground for Cressida—or for the other women she is meant to represent—in terms of the allocation of affection or attention. If Cressida is torn between two suitors, having followed one and now following another, she is, by default, a whore, according to Thersites' explanation, and certainly according to Ulysses' earlier conclusion. The structure and the content of this scene track quite closely to Act III, scene I of *Hamlet,* where Claudius and Polonius plot to observe Hamlet, and have set up Ophelia to return some 'remembrances" he had given her.

The scene in *Troilus and Cressida* employs a triple observation (Troilus/ Ulysses, Thersites, audience), while the scene in *Hamlet* shows only a double observation in functional terms (Claudius/Polonius, audience), though Ophelia also acts as a kind of observer, since she is confused by and unclear about Hamlet's actions and commentary. The scene in *Hamlet* is not threaded the same way as the *Troilus and Cressida* scene, with the observers commenting on the action as it transpires as opposed to after it has concluded, though the observers of the latter scene also do comment on it after Diomedes has left and Cressida has finished her brief soliloquy. The scenes in both plays center on the actions of a woman who has little choice as to her actions and no control over how they are perceived. Neither Ophelia nor Cressida have much say in how they are used by the men around them, though Ophelia has a bit more protection from her father Polonius—even if he is a bit of a bumbler— and her brother Laertes—though he is absent from Elsinore for much of the play. Just as Thersites casts judgment on Cressida in terms of her femaleness, so too does *Hamlet* cast judgment on Ophelia in a manner that indicts her entire sex.[3]

Troilus' perceptions, ironically, follow the same pattern as Cressida's acknowledgement of her own division, suggesting that the conflicted

Cressida he observes "is and is not Cressida."[4] Troilus has now become Menelaus, with his love, Cressida, now in the the possession of another man, as he has observed himself. This is part of Ulysses' ploy in bringing Troilus to observe the interlude—to present to the Trojans their own cuckold, if not of the same magnitude as Helen, at least of the same kind. Thus Troilus' response is first disbelief that this is the same Cressida he loved—as he says, "this is Diomed's Cressida.... This is and is not Cressid." (V.ii.144/153) He then goes on, not unlike Ulysses in his vast and rather tedious speech about order and hierarchy in Act I, scene iii, to decry disorder and inversion, and ultimately to vow revenge on Diomedes. While judging Cressida and finding her false, Troilus, significantly, never conceives of a means to solve her predicament. He simply sees that she has turned her eye towards Diomedes and thus decides that this is an issue now between himself and Diomedes, to be settled in battle. Though Cressida is condemned by Troilus for breaking her promise to him, she, like Helen, becomes the justification for doing battle.

Thersites' judgment has been woven throughout the play. He finds the whole undertaking, the war, absurd, as he declares in Act II, scene iii:

> All the argument is a whore and a cuckold; a good quarrel to draw emulous factions and bleed to death upon. Now the dry serpigo on the subject, and war and lechery confound all! (II.iii.69-72)

Thersites maintains this attitude towards the actions and discussions he observes in Act V. His judgment barely changes throughout the play: from his standpoint of one above the corruption and stupidity, he is as free with his sexually freighted comments about Cressida as he is about Patroclus. He takes on the role of the fool as truth teller, and not unlike Lear's fool, is often beaten for telling the truth.

Thus this scene, the last one in which we, the audience, see Cressida, provides a forum in which the female protagonist, though not formally tried, has her actions and motivations questioned and her worth determined. Cressida is not presented heroically here, but she is presented in conflict, within herself and in her efforts to stabilize her situation. She is judged by Troilus, by Ulysses (who seems motivated in this scene not by heroism but by a base strategic design to undermine Troilus), and by Thersites. All three cast Cressida as corrupt, to varying degrees, and Cressida herself seems to view her actions as corrupt. The play, however, makes it clear that Cressida's trial takes place in the context of personal dislocation and uncertainty, which should be taken into consideration in the observation of evidence presented and the determination of Cressida's guilt by all concerned parties. Cressida, like the women who have been systematically raped in a number of war zones throughout the world, has found herself displaced from her home, in an environment of insecurity where she and her body are under distinct threat.

Concluding Thoughts

The fact that the war is being waged over a "whore and a cuckold" accentuates the variableness of Cressida's situation. The evaluation of Helen's worth by the Trojans passes judgment on her but keeps her secure and valued—or at least commodified. Cressida's entry into the Greek camp demonstrates that she has no power or real capacity to defend herself, a concern she had expressed early in the play (I.ii.250-255) in what seems to be a very insecure environment. The concluding judgment, voiced by Ulysses after this interlude, is that Cressida is by nature a strumpet. Finally, Cressida is again tried, in a complex scene where she is confronted by Diomedes but observed by Troilus, Ulysses and Thersites. All pass judgment on her, and find that she is a rather cheap commodity, with little value. This circles back to the initial questions posed by the play—what is valuable within the situations presented? The women on trial here, Helen and Cressida, are commodities, summed up with prices on their heads. They have little to contribute to this estimation of their worth, but they must respond to these judgments and valuations, since they live in this uncertain world, one dependent on the value of the beauty of Helen's face.

Notes

1. This conflicted ideal (voiceless, virgin beauty vs. intelligent, engaged sexuality) remains a constant within today's society as well.
2. In Act III, scene I, Pandarus has a brief conversation with Helen and Paris, repeatedly referring to Helen as "my sweet queen" before he serenades them in an effort to deflect them from finding out where Troilus is at that point (since he is with Cressida). Helen responds by calling Pandarus "My Lord Pandarus, honey-sweet lord – " (III.i.63) and the dialogue continues along these same lines for much of this brief scene.
3. I would argue that Shakespeare is pursuing some similar themes in these scenes and these discussions. The way in which women are indicted in both situations—based on their sex and their sexuality—is parallel in many respects and the commentators, in these sequences, are not fully reliable or trusted. It may be that Shakespeare is actually acknowledging the constraining situations in which most women find themselves, the dichotomy between virgin and whore, and the limited capacity that women have to redefine either their positions or their reputations.
4. The different approaches to reason, to intellectual understanding, and to being are demonstrated in this scene. Cressida's whole being is torn by her quandary, and she curses herself and her sex for her inability to find a satisfactory way out of this morally compromised situation. Troilus, in a kind of fun-house mirror inverse reflection, waxes on about the gods (one of the few times they are mentioned in the play), the bifurcation of Cressida, and what she represents. He offers histrionics and excess but no acknowledgement of Cressida's particular situation or his lack of capacity to do anything *for* Cressida or her situation.

Works Cited

Faber, Kristina. "Shakespeare's Troilus & Cressida: Of War and Lechery." *Colby Quarterly* 26. 2 (June 1990). Print.

In-depth: Our Bodies - Their Battle Ground: Gender-based Violence in Conflict Zones: AFRICA-ASIA: Rape as a tool of war, humanitarian news and analysis: a service of the UN Office for the Coordination of Humanitarian Affairs, September 1, 2004. Online

James, Heather. *Shakespeare's Troy: Drama, Politics, and the Translation of Empire.* Cambridge: Cambridge University Press, 1997. Print.

Knight, G. Wilson. *The Wheel of Fire.* London: revised edition, 1949. Print.

O'Rourke, James. "Rule in Unity" and Otherwise: Love and Sex in "Troilus and Cressida." *Shakespeare Quarterly* 43.2 (Summer 1992): 139-158. Print.

Rose, Mary Beth. *The Expense of Spirit: Love and Sexuality in English Renaissance Drama.* Ithaca, NY: Cornell University Press, 1988. Print.

Tylee, Claire M. "The Text of Cressida and Every Ticklish Reader: Troilus and Cressida, The Greek Camp Scene." *Shakespeare Survey* 41: Shakespearian Stages and Staging, ed. Wells, Stanley. Cambridge: Cambridge University Press, 1989. Cambridge Collections Online.

Chapter 4.

Raping Justice in John Webster's *The White Devil*

Karol Cooper

Double Trial

In John Webster's revenge tragedy, *The White Devil* (1612), the audience witnesses a trial of the play's heroine, Vittoria Corombona, as well as a trial of the literary and performance traditions that use the female figure to signify opposed concepts of purity and corruption within masculine-dominated societies. In the character of Vittoria, the two extremes coexist as accusation and defense: the powerful men who surround her accuse her of being a debased whore willing to commit any act for material gain, and she defends herself by identifying with the whore's antithesis—the majestic and incorruptible figure of justice who weighs evidence and judges crime, but whose truth has been brutally manipulated by a metaphorical rape. Vittoria's accusers claim they want to punish her for conspiring with her lover, the Duke of Brachiano, to murder both their spouses. However, in the scene Webster titled "The arraignment of Vittoria," the rhetorical strategies of both accusers and accused indicate a deeper frustration with using a single female figure to stand alternately for men's most cherished ideals, and their most rapacious desires. As they argue over which female figure will take precedence, the root causes of the desires, and the circumstances that set them in violent motion, remain unconsidered.

The play was based on a sex and murder scandal that took place among the Italian nobility in the late 1500s, and its title, an accusatory epithet for the character of Vittoria, conveys the hazardous co-existence of the white allure of her beauty and the devil that allegedly lurks inside her. At the arraignment, the presiding examiner Cardinal Monticelso establishes the key figure of indictment: "Shall I expound whore to you? They are those brittle evidences of law / Which forfeit all a wretched man's estate / For leaving out one syllable" (3.2.90-92). It was men who made and prosecuted the laws relating to property and finances, but Monticelso's example forces the normally masculine agent of the law to don women's clothes, so he can avoid admitting his own responsibility for fraternal betrayals among men. Through the expository enlargement of metaphor, Vittoria can be made responsible for disseminating the contagion of whoring itself, infecting the patriarchal brotherhood and causing one man to cheat another out of his birthright, based only on a linguistic technicality, just as a greedily vindictive and rebellious whore would do. In the eyes of Monticelso and the all-male panel of ambassador onlookers, a woman's exchange of sex for material benefits stands as the font of all criminality, becoming metaphorically interchangeable with the crimes men commit against one another. Webster uses the arraignment to stage a battle of gendered figuring, a folly in which the problems men have dealing with one another are enacted as if they are problems stemming from their dealings with women.

The events leading up to the arraignment scene make the audience privy to the lovers' machinations. Spurred on by some hints that Vittoria conveyed to him from a "foolish idle dream," Brachiano hired a doctor to kill his wife Isabella (she kisses a poisoned picture of her husband), and ordered his secretary and procurer Flamineo, who is Vittoria's brother, to murder Vittoria's comically ineffectual husband Camillo. The deaths of their spouses freed Brachiano to pursue his passion for Vittoria, and Flamineo's assistance afforded him a foothold toward recovering his family's former wealth. These scenes, together with the edge of embittered experience that can be heard in Vittoria's replies to her accusers, do little to suggest she is any better than what they claim her to be, and her demeanor as a witness is negatively impacted. In the English court system of Webster's day, demeanor included piety, "moral status and reputation," "social and economic status" as well as gender, and "became a standard element in the evidentiary tradition" (Shapiro *Culture of Fact* 17). Another major factor in demeanor was the style of narrating events. Too much or too little attention to "circumstances" could make the testimony appear questionable (Shapiro *Culture of Fact* 17).

Vittoria makes some allusion to the circumstances that brought on her plight, but she fails to rise above the typical gender binary of the discourse because of her reliance on the counter-claim of wounded chastity to combat the men's sexual slurs. Even so, she succeeds in satirizing their tactics. Their tropes, already weak as mere language, become even more insubstantial when re-situated within Vittoria's own figuring, which shows her unafraid to rely on her strengths, which can be found in the materiality of her body and the pleasures it holds for those who know how to extract them. She boasts that the words of the accusers—"all your strict combined heads"—are as ineffectual as "glassen hammers" attempting to break her "mine of diamonds" (3.2.143-145). She taunts them for the self-incriminating evasiveness of their speech, full of nothing but "painted devils, / . . . for your names / Of Whore and Murd'ress, they proceed from you, / As if a man should spit against the wind, / The filth returns in's face" (3.2.147-151). Finally, Vittoria accuses the men of distorting her character, an abuse tantamount to raping justice herself —the feminine ideal they should uphold instead of vainly attempting to scapegoat her as a whore. Upon hearing her sentence, that she will be exiled to "A house / Of penitent whores," she cries, "A rape, a rape!...you have ravished Justice / Forced her to do your pleasure" (3.2.267-275). The men's lust for authority over the negative material potentialities of the sign of whore has led them to overpower and debase justice itself, as well as its feminine embodiment in Vittoria. Even as "women's sexual passivity was assumed" in Webster's day, "men's sexual appetites were imagined to be inherently aggressive; as a result, the elision of sex and violence in both legal and popular discourses was routine" (Solga 35).

Feminine Gender and Metaphor

Although Vittoria's rebuttal gives pause to the proceedings, the use of feminine metaphors to depict men's struggles, as well as women's oppression amidst those struggles, ultimately deflects responsibility for that strife onto the female, whether in the form of savior-justice or scourge-whore. Furthermore, embedded in both figures is the presumption that female sexuality is a definitive property, both for female figures and the women they reference. In her reading of gender in Renaissance tragedy, Dympna Callaghan observes:

> The entire realm of sexuality is displaced onto woman who becomes at once the site of instability and at the same time the fulfilling other. The result is a polarization in the concept of woman in tragedy and culture.... The path of woman in tragedy extends through a range of discontinuities from the instigation of the tragic situation by means of an initial transgression, to her sanctification as the chief corpse of the denouement. (65-67)

Vittoria's defense, while savvy, offers no more proof of deeper causes than Monticelso's, for "she is not a chaste woman defending herself from slander; she is an unchaste woman defending herself with clever rhetorical tricks" (Leggatt 126). Her metaphor and other "literary and artistic representations [of rape] contribute to the social positioning of women and men and shape the cognitive systems that make rape thinkable" (Higgins and Silver 3). The scenario Vittoria depicts compares to the story of the rape of Lucretia, in that it does not serve as testimony about a historical act, but rather presents an allegorical literary representation instrumentalizing anti-female violence in the service of justifying some other self-interested action. In her study of the Lucretia narrative's foundational position in the agenda of humanism, Stephanie Jed finds that it acts both as a cathartic exposé of and a delusional cover for placing women in the double bind of chaste exemplar/inevitable victim of sexual violence. The woman becomes the seeming agent for both her own chastity and her rape, so that the cultural processes and psychosocial relations that produce rape go unexamined. Each deployment of the story, instead of prompting critical questioning, arouses hypocritical outrage over what is both accepted and expected. The story performs "as a literary *topos,* isolated from other kinds of writing and alienated from the historical conditions in which this *topos* is, each time, reproduced" (Jed 4). Like the figure of Lucretia, the figure of justice invoked by Vittoria "is inscribed in a language that invites sexual violence" (Jed 7), but which manages to efface the same sort of sexual violence that's being materialized in the here and now of the scene taking place before us—a here-and-now situation to which Vittoria can only allude through the conjoined mediations of gendered metaphor and the cross-dressing male youth performer. Oddly, the exaggerated femininity of the metaphor-cum-actor prevents her character from appearing to live through, or personally witness as a real woman of historical circumstance her own ravishment by men's justice.

In Webster's *Appius and Virginia*, based on another classical story of a virgin's rape resulting in her sacrificial death, a faulty justice is embodied in the character of Appius, a judge who uses his authority to rig the incarceration of Virginia. Because she resists his attempts at seduction, the judge (who is figured as the rapist of his own people: "The high

Colossus that bestrides us all" [3.1]) devises a mock trial in which false proofs are given by his accomplice to show that Virginia was born a slave. No one is fooled by the trial, or by Appius's earlier promise that he would conduct himself as a fair and impartial judge:

> Justice should have
>
> No kindred, friends, nor foes, nor hate, nor love;
>
> As free from passion as the gods above. (1.1)

True to his words, Appius's sense that he holds rights of sexual access to his inferiors is on par with that of the gods, and he carries out his plans to rape Virginia while she is in his custody. Her father Virginius intervenes, slaying his own daughter: "see, proud Appius, see, / Although not justly, I have made her free" (4.1). In Virginius's act, Karen Bamford reads a deft portrayal of the real circumstances behind Virginia's plight, not as a signifier, but as a real body, and a piece of owned property:

> [T]he story provides a paradigm for the ancient legal definition of rape—that is, theft of a woman. . . . Appius is attempting to cheat Virginius of his bride-money. . . The hero's proprietorial stake in the heroine's death, effectively cloaked in *The Rape of Lucrece*, becomes transparent here (79).

There is a similar battle taking place in *The White Devil*, to determine which man can purchase a proprietorial stake in Vittoria, not as a virgin, but as a whore. Meanwhile, she attempts to push beyond the bounds of her materiality by associating herself with justice, an abstract notion under siege.

Nonetheless, it would be vain for Vittoria to hope she could draw strength from a figure whose ravishment was the condition for its coming into existence. Like justice, Vittoria will pay the price of playing the victim in order to elicit the faux-sympathy of her judges. In the final act, her brother Flamineo mocks the insufficiency of her rhetoric. Meanwhile,

Raping Justice in John Webster's *The White Devil*

by a previous order of the now-murdered Brachiano, he prepares himself to become his sister's executioner:

> VITTORIA: O the cursed devil,
>
> Which doth present us with all other sins
>
> Thrice candied o'er . . .
>
> Makes us forsake that which was made for man,
>
> The world, to sink to that was made for devils,
>
> Eternal darkness. . . .
>
> FLAMINEO: Leave your prating,
>
> For these are but grammatical laments,
>
> Feminine arguments. . . . (5.6.56-67)

Elsewhere, in the *Duchess of Malfi*, for example, justice is not figured with a gender-specific pronoun, which allows it to be characterized as a righteously aggressive, masculine force capable of executing a "just revenge" (5.2.340). When Bosola entertains counter-plots against the Cardinal to assist Antonio, he would like to think that his subordinate position in a hierarchy of violent intrigue, rather than subjecting him to rape, as in a feminized concept justice, will empower him to succeed:

> The weakest arm is strong enough that strikes
>
> With the sword of justice. (5.2.341-342)

Vittoria's expression, by contrast, invites a nostalgic projection back to an originary moment when the feminine justice was once an austere mean of pure truth, elevated above the material pressures of the world. Once justice had been embodied as a woman through the process of figuration, it was already too late to save her. Once "it" became a "she," her status as perfect exemplar of a pure ideal was already ravished. The moment she was made a part of the human circuit of sexual transactions, she was no more privileged than any other she in that system, including Vittoria.

CORRUPTION OF JUSTICE

Monticelso's violation is just one more in a series, and he and his ally Duke Francisco have particular reasons for indicting Vittoria with the crime. Francisco wants to punish Vittoria as a way to revenge his sister's death, and to torment Vittoria's lover and his former brother-in-law, the Duke of Brachiano. Monticelso is motivated somewhat to revenge his cousin Camillo's death, but is more motivated by Francisco's promises of political support in Monticelso's quest for the papacy. Ultimately, Francisco hires assassins to execute Brachiano, Vittoria and her brother, but his first strategy is to influence public sentiment against Vittoria. Monticelso convenes a church-run court held before an audience of European ambassadors to try Vittoria for the killing. He admits it can only be linguistically performative, since "we have nought but circumstances / To charge her with . . ./ therefore to the proofs / Of her black lust, shall make her infamous / To all our neighbouring kingdoms" (3.1.4-8).

Monticelso glosses over circumstances in favor of a spoken dumb show of rote accusations. In trying to prove that Vittoria lusted for another woman's husband as well as the gifts he lavished on her, the men overlook the circumstances that led to the crime—the masculine systems of nation, property, social rank, religion and organized violence that created the unequal distribution of benefits and impediments that fostered her frustrations and desires.

Although the actions of his characters indicate a general disinterest in the exploration of the circumstances that produce criminal acts, Webster does on several occasions subvert the tendency toward prejudicial over-simplification of the issues of gender that define and lead to criminality. From time to time characters enumerate the circumstances that dictate the linkage of gender and crime, putting them in the form of an outline of prejudices, or list of salient social factors that no one (including the speaker) is able to look at full-on, due to the distracting theatricality of the male-female, self-other, god-devil dichotomy of difference that controls the putative ethos of the play.

For example, Vittoria's brother Flamineo complains to his mother that it was the circumstances of his upbringing that pushed him into the role of pander for Brachiano:

> My father prov'd himself a gentleman,
>
> Sold all's land, and like a fortunate fellow
>
> Died ere the money was spent. You brought me up
>
> At Padua I confess, where I protest,
>
> For want of means (the university judge me)
>
> I have been fain to heel my tutor's stockings,
>
> At least seven years. Conspiring with a beard
>
> Made me a graduate, then to this Duke's service;
>
> I visited the court, whence I return'd—
>
> More courteous, more lecherous by far,
>
> But not a suit the richer—and shall I,
>
> Having a path so open and so free
>
> To my preferment, still retain your milk
>
> In my pale forehead? No, this face of mine
>
> I'll arm and fortify with lusty wine

'Gainst shame and blushing. (1.2.299-314)

From this passage we can infer that Flamineo learned to be a white devil —fair on the outside, but possessed with an infectious mischief—due to a combination of forces: a lack of inherited wealth, the humiliating drudgery of his schooling, and the corrupt practices of the court. There is no supernatural temptation mentioned, for these lures are all man-made. Save his mother, none of his accusers will ever reflect on the meaning of these circumstances when evaluating Flamineo's crimes.

During Vittoria's arraignment, Monticelso likewise takes poetic flight in portraying a spectrum of natural and social circumstances that both terrify and disgust him in the anarchic blights they visit on men's endeavors. As stated earlier, he believes they can all be laid at the feet of the whore Vittoria. Believing he's found a culprit allows him passionately to list the ills without considering the full breadth of their meaning, or how he and his fellow male authorities are also contributors to the crimes and disasters, and not simply their victims:

> Shall I expound whore to you? sure I shall;
>
> I'll give their perfect character. They are first
>
> Sweetmeats which rot the eater: in man's nostril
>
> Poisoned perfumes. They are coz'ning alchemy,
>
> Shipwrecks in calmest weather! What are whores?
>
> Cold Russian winters, that appear so barren
>
> As if that nature had forgot the spring.
>
> They are the true material fire of hell,
>
> Worse than those tributes i'th' Low Countries paid,

Exactions upon meat, drink, garments, sleep;

...

They are those flattering bells have all one tune,

At weddings, and at funerals. . . . (3.2.79-94)

For Ina Habermann, the battle between Monticelso and Vittoria is "a battle over language and meaning; it becomes clear that neither 'plain speech' nor bodily signs signify in a stable way or secure access to 'the truth', but that the truth is a function of power" (109). The power, and even the humor, of Monticelso's list lies in the contrast between its vast scope, and the narrowness of the human vessel into which he attempts to cram it: a single woman, who appears to be less the agent (or even the sign) of these blights than just another whore among whores.

Elsewhere, both circumstances and the self-serving use of the female figure intersect with arguments regarding the justice of revenge. After Vittoria's trial, Francisco scans a list of criminals to select the man he will hire to murder Brachiano, Vittoria and Flamineo. He chooses Lodovico, who had opened the play complaining of his banishment under suspicion of being a murderer. Both Francisco and Lodovico claim to be motivated for revenge due to their love of Brachiano's wife Isabella. Lodovico confesses to Monticelso that he "did love Brachiano's Duchess dearly; / Or rather I pursued her with hot lust" (4.3.111-112). Francisco, in order to provide himself with the emotional intensity required for plotting such a cold-blooded "massacre" (as the slayings are referred to in the final scene), finds he must conjure up the figure of his dead sister:

To fashion my revenge more seriously,

Let me remember my dead sister's face:

Call for her picture: no; I'll close mine eyes,

> And in a melancholic thought I'll frame
>
> Her figure 'fore me. Now I ha't—d'foot! How strong
>
> Imagination works! How she can frame
>
> Things which are not! (4.1.97-103)

No specific memories of their unique brother-sister relationship are recalled, and no backstory about what talks or activities they may have shared in their youth is provided. Again, the feminine figure, in this case, the imagination, provides the grounds for man's violence. The real motivator of his mind's figural framing, Brachiano, is not invoked, and the erotic dynamic that underlay their mutual rancor is mediated by the insertion of Isabella, as it was during their initial argument at the play's outset.

In the final act, Lodovico and Francisco, who is disguised as a Moor in order to infiltrate the household of Brachiano and Vittoria, draw forth a confirmation from Vittoria's maid Zanche that their two spouses were indeed murdered. Only Flamineo's name is given as the killer of Vittoria's husband, and neither Vittoria nor Brachiano is named explicitly in Zanche's statement. Even so, Francisco calls it a "strange discovery! Why till now we knew not / The circumstance of either of their deaths" (5.3.262-263). Lodovico, who had experienced some small pangs of conscience at having turned assassin, considers the revelation of those circumstances, meager as they are, to be cause for celebration. "Why, now our action's justified," Lodovico exclaims. "Tush for justice," replies Francisco: "the fame / Shall crown the enterprise and quit the shame" (5.3.264-268). Here, the idea of circumstances is confined only to the facts of how the two spouses were killed, facts blithely related by Zanche (Isabella was "empoisoned" and "Camillo's neck / Was broke by damned Flamineo" [5.3.242-244]). Without a true understanding of how Flamineo himself is circumstanced ("For want of means . . . / I have been fain to heel my tutor's stockings, / At least seven years"), there's no chance Lodovico and Francisco would arrive at anything other than a superficial figuration of justice. Fame will make their executions worthy of pride, regardless of whether or not a fully-circumstanced view of justice require them to kill.

Barbara Shapiro, in her discussion of the kind of reading materials that made up the typical Renaissance law curriculum, notes that humanist authors were mixed with the classical style of rhetoric:

> By the late sixteenth century the works of Cicero and Quintilian and the *Rhetorica ad Herennium* were available, and educational reforms had resuscitated rhetorical texts in the new grammar schools. Erasmus' widely disseminated textbook *De Copia* . . . explains that "circumstances" relating to "things" involved cause, place, time, occasion, antecedents to the affair, collateral circumstances, consequences, opportunity, instruments, and methods. Circumstances relating to "persons" included considerations of family, race, country, sex, age, physical appearance, inclinations, previous acts and sayings, passion and so on. ("Rhetoric" 62)

In spite of this exhaustive exploration of what circumstances could and should mean in a law case, all of Webster's plays indicate a marked tension between a cursory view of circumstances that provides just enough motivation for violent revenge, and a fuller exploration into the murkier depths of cause and effect. The contrast is set out to comic effect in the mock trial at the center of Webster's tragi-comedy, *The Devil's Law-Case*, where the personated judge Crispiano begs the prolix lawyer Contilupo to leave off his frivolous rhetoric of circumstances (heavy on poetics, and light on facts), and get to the point:

> CONTILUPO. There stands one,
>
> Romelio the merchant; I will name him to you
>
> Without either title or addition:

> For those false beams of his supposed honour,
>
> As void of true heat, as are all painted fires
>
> Or glow-worms in the dark, suit him all basely
>
> As if he had bought his gentry from the herald
>
> With money got by extortion: I will first
>
> Produce this Æsop's crow, as he stands forfeit
>
> For the long use of his gay borrowed plumes,
>
> And then let him hop naked. . . .
>
> ...
>
> CRISPIANO. Signior Contilupo, the court holds it fit,
>
> You leave this stale declaiming 'gainst the person,
>
> And come to the matter.
>
> . . .
>
> CONTILUPO. I will leave all circumstance, and come to th' purpose:
>
> This Romelio is a bastard. (4.2.100-150)

As R.S.White observes of the several contrasting trials and judgments in *King Lear*, it's possible that "the 'cause' of evil lies not in nature or the human heart, but potentially in 'office' or institutional authority. Not nature, but vested power, creates these hard hearts" of Lear's "unnatural" daughters (191). *Lear* pits the values of natural law ("humanitarian, communitarian") versus positive law ("individualistic, corrupt, and self-seeking") (185). Ignoring circumstances will keep the conscience from rousing, and maintain a system of judgment and action based solely on feelings of fear and desire, which, when conscience is set aside, can result in everything from exploitative insincerity to retributive acts of deadly violence. White explains that the "Christian version" of natural law theory that prevailed in Webster's day:

> [M]aintains that God established a universe governed by reason, and he imprinted conscience on the human mind to enable us actively to choose virtue and reject vice. . . . By implication it also informs our very powerful feelings about the moral pressures resolved or conspicuously not resolved at the end of works of fiction, particularly Renaissance ones, backed up as they are by a theory of didacticism, and some kind of 'poetic justice' which is the literary work's analogy of Natural Law. (2-3).

Subha Mukherji agrees to some extent with White, and states that, in *The White Devil*, "A self-aware analogy with law allows Webster's play to assert its similarities with law's fictions," while demonstrating "its superiority over law's semiotics" (173). Rather than making the stage a version of the court, Webster is "flouting what White calls a 'model' at the heart of literary theory of the times":

> Theatrical reality is ultimately the evidence of images; images that are, in this play, foregrounded, deployed and manipulated, as triumphantly as Vittoria's rhetoric, to leave the audience seeing double, 'with parted eye'. . . . [I]inscribing such an awareness of the fluidity of signs would run counter to the positivism of the institutional discourse of law. . . . The irony of dramatic trials is often the way they relativise 'truth', complicate arbitration or even make it impossible, while the business of law was to arrive at judgment. (172)

The Devil Trope

Webster, like other Jacobean dramatists, both relied on and satirized the intense devil troping that saturated much of the era's literature. For instance, in her study of Webster's works, Muriel West finds a myriad of satanic references in almost every speech, so that no character is exempt from devilish associations. At the same time, the playwright readily subverted such over-reliance on outside forces as an excuse for human evils. Like Ben Jonson, Webster "makes comedy of the theme that men are worse devils than the devils of hell" (West 81). In spite of this sophisticated understanding of men's over-reliance on witchcraft and devilry as a source for their ills, few people were altogether capable of dismissing belief in a supernatural realm of spirits (both good and bad) who could and did influence the lives of people. As King James stated, in his book *Daemonologie* published in 1597, those "who denyeth the power of the Deuill, woulde likewise denie the power of God":

> For since the Deuill is the verie contrarie opposite to God, there can be no better way to know God, then by the contrarie; as by the ones power (though a creature) to admire the power of the great Creator: by the falshood of the one to consider the trueth of the other, by the injustice of the one, to consider the Iustice of the other: And by the cruelty of the one, to consider the mercifulnesse of the other: And so foorth in all the rest of the essence of God, and qualities of the Deuill. (44; bk. 2, ch. 7)

Because it remained an essential mystery just how and when the supernatural interventions occurred, the plays used the resulting confusion over the nature and extent of human agency and responsibility as the basis for the interpersonal conflicts and emotional plagues experienced by their characters.

By ignoring circumstances (in spite of the paradox of being able so eloquently to enumerate them), instead of probing into the circumstances of the murders instigated by Vittoria, circumstances that, if thoroughly considered, might lead them to incriminate themselves as self-interested whores rather than trustworthy judges, Vittoria's accusers rely on poetic rhetoric to transform the plastic surface of her body into a sign of evil. "If the devil / Did ever take good shape behold his picture," says the soon-to-be Pope, Cardinal Monticelso, pointing to Vittoria. At his suggestion, the boy actor, whose costume and accoutrements had initially transformed him into a beautiful woman, is re-rendered into nothing more than the picture of a devil who has taken on the shape of a woman. If the devil can be pictured as a man in the guise of a female temptress, then real women are not solely culpable for the crime of being temptresses, for the one thing even more duplicitous than a devil who has taken on the shape of an alluring woman is a man impersonating a devil who has taken on the shape of an alluring woman.

FEMININITY AND BOY ACTORS

In his discussion of the cultural rationale for the use of young male actors to play female roles, Stephen Orgel finds that England's unique, all-male theatrical tradition allowed the plays to concentrate on men's "fear of losing control over women's chastity" (40) as well as their fears of being sexually imposed upon themselves by other men in a masculine hierarchy that both modeled itself on, and sometimes literally enacted, a sodomitical system of homosocial relationships. The symbolic value of the female impersonator onstage, as negatively feminine as it may be, nonetheless authenticates the absence of the woman herself from the proceedings that are meant to decide what she stands for, and thereby, who she really is. Christina Luckyj notes that "the women of *The White Devil* embrace theatricality, offering extraordinarily self-conscious performances" (xxi) but in her critique, she presumes that the self and its consciousness are supposed to be essentially female. It is true that the men and women characters partake equally of the modes of histrionic empowerment, but the self whom the cross-dressing male performers are trying to bring to the audience's consciousness is being choked off by the rapacious paradox of gendered metaphors.

In the men's exegetical framework of gendered metaphors, there can be no one-for-one system of signification in which the thing can be trusted to stand for itself. In the Christian version of Platonic philosophy, a reified form isn't just a potentially misleading, degraded copy of the ideal forms cognized by the mind; they are in themselves a thing of evil, sinfully manipulative of humanity's excessive dependence on the material world. If a woman looks good, then she must by definition be bad. Justice becomes an exegesis of an individual's gender performance rather than an examination of an individual's real-world actions.

The utter provisionality of Monticelso's proposal ("*If* the devil / *Did* ever take good shape," *then* you could "behold his picture") weakens his accusation against the female, as it unintentionally strengthens the disparagement of masculine dissembling. The man-devil's transformation into the good shape of a woman isn't provisional at all, but a *fait accompli*. We are indeed beholding "his" picture, a picture of a man-devil in the act of possessing the good shape of an innocent woman. Here, the play satirizes the arrogance of relying on the female figure to symbolize masculine evil. Monticelso's authority is destabilized by its placement within the self-referential gesture towards the cross-dressing actor, who is either the picture of a woman possessed by the devil (the misogynistic view), or a picture of the devil himself (the view encouraged by reading the scene as a parody of the authoritative discourse of misogyny).

Revenge and Justice

The revenge tragedy, where the personally instigated murder of one's enemies is deemed the fittest way to secure status and peace of mind, offers an exposé of the destructive nature of that masculine style of justice. It also banishes the delusion that men never practice a feminine style of justice—a more indirect, mediated style that relies on insinuation and temptation to achieve desires, and bring down those who would impede the individual's path to those desires.

The figure of whore is interjected to bring a seeming heteronormativity to the homosocial structures that prescribe and enforce the ways and means of property distribution from man to man. Ideally, the feminine element would harmonize masculine dealings, bringing them into a balanced state of reciprocity. Where each walks away from a transaction relatively satisfied with his lot, the placement of the feminine ideal allows the men to pride themselves on their gentlemanly restraint in not taking justice into their own hands, as it were, and forcing her to comply with their desires. The fact that her will and their desires are commensurate means that in essence, there is no justice that is more powerful than, or that could ever diverge from, their desires. The thought that there could still be an overarching achievement of the ends of justice where one man is left lacking access to what he believes belongs to him is unthinkable without the introduction of the opposing figure of the whore. The brotherhood of men is not corrupt, but rather it has been corrupted by the incendiary allure of the whore, who pits men against one another. As the female figure of justice was an ideal the men had previously established to act as a curb to hyper-masculine tyranny, Vittoria knows she is lost if, in their pursuit of revenge against the whore, men such as dukes and cardinals are willing to rape justice as well. Feminine metaphors—both in the language and the bodily signifier of femininity on stage, the boy actor— rather than serving as inviolable limits of moral meaning, are subject to the same overwhelming violence as real women (and real boys). "[T]he rapable body [is] one which is socially constructed as 'female' and in a position of weakness or ambiguity, able to be taken by force and objectified by those in power" (Robertson and Rose 4). Both language and the bodies that are supposed to convey its transcendent ideals may be compelled to submit to the lusts of powerful men.

Early modern English drama makes occasional self-reflexive references to the fact that female parts were acted by young men and boys. In the final act of Shakespeare's *Antony and Cleopatra*, for example, Cleopatra ruefully predicts that her fall will be completed by its being enacted by "comedians [who]/Extemporally will stage us." Humiliated by watching her once-awesome power burlesqued, she "shall see/Some squeaking Cleopatra boy my greatness/I' the posture of a whore" (5.2.216-221). She worries that the performance will focus so much on deriving meaning from her femininity, that its reductionism must necessarily omit the circumstances of both her accomplishments and her downfall.

Female characters on the Jacobean stage are typically stigmatized for possessing an innate wantonness, by which they pose a devilish threat to masculine potency and status. The anti-female literature of the time, from Swetnam and others, is well-documented. Further, "in the years 1615-21 . . . major scandals saw three men holding high public office brought down through what were widely perceived as unscrupulous and domineering wives and a fourth made a laughing-stock" (Gunby 9). At the same time, James's queen, Anne of Denmark, was noted for her literary patronage (she oversaw Jonson's *Masque of Blackness*) and "never wholly refrained from political behavior" (Barroll 207). Yet the English system of using male actors to embody "depictions of women . . . we consider degrading" cannot be explained simply by "declaring them to be male fantasies" (Orgel 11). The drama must please not only the men in the audience, but the women as well, and occasionally the plays present women as an upstart rank of social climbers, invading male dominions of authority. In Webster's *The Devil's Law-Case*, for example, Crispiano says the Spanish king has hired him to investigate "What mad tricks has been played of late by ladies" who "use their lords as if they were their wards":

> Withal what sway they bear I'th' viceroy's court
>
> You'd wonder at it:
>
> 'Twill do well shortly, can we keep them off
>
> From being of our council of war. (3.1.9-25)

As Orgel says, "The depictions must at the very least represent cultural fantasies" (11), which would include fantasies of women being more thoroughly, if not unproblematically, integrated into public life.

The lawyer prosecuting Vittoria's case defends himself against her critique of his poor rhetorical style by questioning her facility with legal Latin. He scoffs, "the woman / Knows not her tropes nor figures" (3.2.39-40), and he is correct. Vittoria's death in the final scene stands as the enactment of the punishment for woman's refusal to exist as the embodiment of the tropes and figures that establish the extremes of femininity. At the same time, because it is acted by a young male actor who is problematically situated within a similarly restrictive figural structure of masculinity, her death can stand as a masculine protest against the lack of more holistic modes of representing gendered subjects.

In his excellent study, Luke Wilson is sensitive to Webster's warring inclinations to satirize flawed systems while still employing most of their traditional modes of representation: "Insofar as we are able to recognize the inadequacy of the ecclesiastical law, or of revenge, it is because the play is enabling us to make judgments from within a different, if not necessarily superior, system of evaluation. But to what extent does the play in fact permit us such recognitions?" If a feminized justice is raped both by the institutional law of the church and by the personal law of revenge, where do we turn for an alternative way of judging the proceedings and criminalizing the real wrongdoers? If not one of the characters has gotten what he or she deserves, then the justice/whore dichotomy must be set aside, but in its wake Webster has no new, post-gender system of representation or evaluation to offer. The play "refuses to help by refusing a supplemental relation to the law" (Wilson 233).

Through the extremes of figuration, Webster "manages to convey ... a world without a centre" (Boklund 179). The feminized pairs of god/wolf, whore/justice are less allegories of the basic self/other binary, than they are representative of the two most prevalent options for escaping from responsibility, and indicative of the extent of the ambivalence about using beliefs in supernatural intervention in human affairs the basis for making judgments about crimes. Yet, the morally dual female figure becomes a more easily understood overlay for the devil/God binary, since neither of those supernatural beings is likely to appear in their true shapes, whatever those might be. The center Boklund speaks of as being absent is indeed present, in the form of references to circumstances, and of course, in the form of the play itself, which if nothing else shows how people are linked in a network of material circumstance. While the drama is the most apt of literary forms for the three-dimensional portrayal of circumstanced human existence, the format of the revenge tragedy, with its pat affirmation of existing practices and standard moral truths (albeit satirically subverted), is inadequate for a truly substantive, and possibly revolutionary, inquiry into the origin and meaning of those circumstances. Thus, the main contributor to the ineluctability of the tragic machinery is the characters' limited understanding of what circumstances really are—that they are conditions that have a meaning in and of themselves. They are more than the evidences and proofs of personal responsibility for crime. Circumstances encircle the whole of society, and are what establishes or destabilizes the grounds and reasons of human relations. They could, if studied as such, reveal the *meaning*, and not just the facts, of personal responsibility. The tragedy lies in circumstances left unread as texts of social meaning.

WORKS CITED

Bamford, Karen. *Sexual Violence on the Jacobean Stage*. New York: St. Martin's Press, 2000. Print.

Barroll, Leeds. "The Court of the First Stuart Queen." *The Mental World of the Jacobean Court*, ed. Levy Peck, Linda. Cambridge, UK: Cambridge University Press, 1991: 191-208. Print.

Boklund, Gunnar. *The Sources of The White Devil*. New York: Haskell House, 1966. Print.

Callaghan, Dympna. *Woman and Gender in Renaissance Tragedy: a Study of King Lear, Othello, The Duchess of Malfi, and The White Devil*. Atlantic Highlands, NJ: Humanities Press International, 1989. Print.

Gunby, David. "Critical Introduction." *The Devils-Law Case. The Works of John Webster.* Vol. 2. Cambridge: Cambridge University Press, 2007. Print.

Habermann, Ina. "'She has that in her belly will dry up your ink': Femininity as Challenge in the 'Equitable Drama' of John Webster." *Literature, Politics, and Law in Renaissance England,* ed. Sheen, Erica and Lorna Hutson. New York: Palgrave Macmillan, 2005: 100-120. Print.

Higgins, Lynn A. and Brenda R. Silver. "Introduction: Rereading Rape." *Rape and Representation*. New York: Columbia University Press, 1991: 1-11. Print.

James VI, King of Scotland. *Daemonologie, in Forme of a Dialogue.* Edinburgh, 1597. Online.

Jed, Stephanie H. *Chaste Thinking: The Rape of Lucretia and the Birth of Humanism.* Bloomington: Indiana University Press, 1989. Print.

Luckyj, Christina. Introduction. *The White Devil,* John Webster. London: A & C Black Publishers, Limited, 2008. Print.

Mukherji, Subha. *Law and Representation in Early Modern Drama.* Cambridge: Cambridge University Press, 2006. Print.

Orgel, Stephen. *Impersonations.* Cambridge, UK: Cambridge University Press, 1996. Print.

Robertson, Elizabeth and Christine M. Rose. Introduction. *Representing Rape in Medieval and Early Modern Literature*. New York: Palgrave, 2001: 1-17. Print.

Shakespeare, William. *Antony and Cleopatra. The Riverside Shakespeare*. 2nd ed. Boston: Houghton Mifflin, 1997: 1391-1439. Print.

Shapiro, Barbara J. *A Culture of Fact: England, 1550-1720*. Ithaca, NY : Cornell University Press, 2000. Print.

--------. "Rhetoric and the English Law of Evidence." *Rhetoric and Law in Early Modern Europe*, ed. Kahn, Victoria and Lorna Hutson. New Haven: Yale University Press, 2001. Print.

Solga, Kim. *Violence Against Women in Early Modern Performance: Invisible Acts*. New York: Palgrave Macmillan, 2009. Print.

Webster, John. *Appius and Virginia. Dramatic Works of John Webster*. Vol. 3. London: Reeves & Turner, 1897: 123-224. Print.

--------. *The Devil's Law-Case*. London: Ernest Benn Ltd., 1975. Print.

--------. *The Duchess of Malfi. John Webster, Three Plays*. New York: Penguin, 1972: 169-292. Print.

--------. *The White Devil*. London: A & C Black Publishers, Limited, 2008. Print.

West, Muriel. *The Devil and John Webster*. Salzburg: Institut für Englische Sprache und Literatur, Universität Salzburg, 1974. Print.

White, R. S. *Natural Law in English Renaissance Literature*. Cambridge: Cambridge University Press, 1996. Print.

Wilson, Luke. "*The White Devil* and the Law." *Early Modern English Drama, a Companion*. Oxford University Press, 2006. Print.

CROSS-PERIOD COMPARISONS

CHAPTER 5.

TRANSGRESSIVE WOMEN FROM SHAKESPEARE TO SHAW AND BRYANS

ELIZABETHAN WIFE, MARTYRED SAINT, AND MODERN FEMME FATALE

Dana Di Pardo Léon-Henri

This essay aims to trace changes in gender construction by examining three specific women accused of crime in theatrical representations from the Elizabethan period, modern British drama, and contemporary North America. Each of these women transgresses the gender norms of her time and place, and these plays testify to an enduring fascination with the complexity and resilience of such women. One of the three is simply the literary creation of a well-known author, while the other two were actual persons who lived larger-than-life lives and pursued their dreams at very high costs. All three bravely confronted male juries and, according to the times, the outrage and wrath of those in the public world surrounding them. The outcomes of their trials are all tragic to various degrees, but with significant differences. Since all three playwrights present tragic stories involving women on trial, changes can be noted by focusing on the situations and images of these three women.

The trio of remarkable women accused of crime in theatrical representations from the Elizabethan Period to modern day include Hermione, Joan of Arc, and Alma Pakenham Rattenbury. Hermione, the virtuous and beautiful Queen of Sicilia, is falsely accused of infidelity by her husband, Leontes, in William Shakespeare's tragicomedy *The Winter's Tale*, first performed in 1610 or 1611, and published in the First Folio of 1623. George Bernard Shaw, a nonreligious author, gives a second theatrical example of the romanticized woman on trial in his 1923 play, *Saint Joan*, which is based on the life and trial of Joan of Arc. In his preface, Shaw openly criticizes the depiction[1] of Joan as a villainous and cunning witch-like character in Shakespeare's *Henry VI*, accusing Shakespeare of not dealing with the larger forces of the law, or with issues of religion and patriotism which fueled her devout passion. For Shaw, *Saint Joan* provides an opportunity to distill his views on politics, religion and societal evolution, illustrating "the reaction against Christian fundamentalism that characterized the post- Darwinian era" (Searle 139). Finally, the contemporary Vancouver playwright and director Joan Bryans presents a femme fatale version of the woman on trial using the infamous true story of Alma Pakenham Rattenbury, the alleged murderer of her husband Francis Rattenbury, as the protagonist in her 2006 play *By Some Divine Mistake*. The perceived nature of "woman" in terms of gender construction and the deviation of the drama's main character from prescribed gender norms form an important theme in each of the three plays. From adultery and murder to redemption and martyrdom, woman is perceived as both diabolical and saintly in her appearances inside and outside of the courtroom. In two cases, it is only through divine intervention that the woman finds redemption, pointing to the playwright's insistence on an otherworldly judgment that differs from the worldly one.

As each of the three women is subjected to various judicial auditions, she is explicitly and implicitly judged not only by law, but also by her peers and society in general. Despite the nocuous nature of the accusations they faced, they were all viewed as martyrs of some kind. In all three theatrical works, the line between poetic justice and injustice is often blurred by the playwrights who make an attempt at portraying the intricacies of these delicate but fierce protagonists, often by placing them in the context of their most loyal companions and immediate entourage.

Gender Construction in Historical Perspective

Gender construction can be simplified and defined as the classification of the biological sexes in terms of a codified system of thought and behavior. Becoming evident as individuals interact within their social structures and society in general, it has a profound influence on the creation of individual identity. Women and men tend to conform their expectations and behavior to its social and cultural meanings at every level, from the subconscious to legal and even political levels (Castaneda and Burns-Glover 69-91). Gender construction may be seen as a product of psychological imprinting, social learning and language (see Perry). Only recently has there been questioning and reconsideration of traditional theories of the psychology of women and men that have labeled certain characteristics masculine and others feminine and labeled as deviant those whose behavior did not match the gendered expectations for their sex. Feminine gender, in the traditional view, consisted in a negative quality framed by the absence of those characteristics considered masculine; only within the last thirty years has women's development been seen from the perspective of a different developmental path resulting in "primary" or positive femininity (see Gilligan, Horner). Despite changes, even today gender construction remains a powerful force in our culturally diverse societies, from advertisements and the media to film and literature.

The roles attributed to and the images created of women in literature have seen remarkable evolution, and nowhere is that clearer than in drama. In fact, dramatic challenges to gender construction are not new. They are evident even in the ancient Greek playwrights, such as Sophocles, who emphasized the bravery of and self-sacrifice of Antigone and Electra, and Euripides, who dramatized the tragedy of Helen. Nevertheless, the representation of women has changed quite significantly from one era to the next. It is interesting to note that audiences bring more to a theatrical performance than their mere presence. According to Wilson (13-23), they bring a background of personal knowledge and experience which helps them to interpret the impressions they receive during a performance. Their knowledge of the social, political and philosophical world in which the play was written or produced is their link between theatre (the play) and society. Equipped with their personal structure of memories and experience, audience members have ever-changing expectations of the theatre experience, including the presentation of gender, as one aspect of drama's reflection of society.

Historical studies of English life from the 17th to the 20th century (see Shoemaker, Kent, King) identify gender as an important factor in social organization. Long-held views about the particular strengths, weaknesses and appropriate responsibilities of each sex shaped everyday lives, patterns of crime, and responses to crime. Based on concepts of gender difference derived from classical thought, Christian ideology, and contemporary science and medicine, men and women were believed to possess different physical attributes and therefore fundamentally different qualities and virtues. Men were considered the stronger sex, possessing such qualities as intelligence, courage, and determination. Women, by contrast, were thought to be much more ruled by their emotions; their values or virtues were expected to be chastity, modesty, compassion, and piety. Clear examples of this are presented in the research of Beattie, Palk, and Walker, who explain that men and women were thought to be prone to differing faults. According to the authors, men were more prone to violence, obstinacy and selfishness, while female sins included excessive passion, lust, ill-tempered nagging, and laziness.

The Elizabethan period gave rise to an expansiveness of characters and action, though women playwrights and performers were nonexistent (Wilson 26). [2] Gender in theatre was defined by male playwrights, and the various female roles were always interpreted by young boys on stage. A strong contrast between masculine and feminine gender is very evident and almost tangible. While the comedies of Shakespeare play with this contrast by offering numerous examples of cross-dressed young women passing in society as young men, the tragedies tend to emphasize the contrast between powerful, if troubled, men and powerless women. The romances, which are among the final group of plays written by Shakespeare (1603-1613), address women's social position. Typically, they present female characters who suffer from a relative lack of power in their social situations, but who nevertheless transcend or circumvent gender restrictions—sometimes through the aid of magic or otherworldly intervention.

HERMIONE IN SHAKESPEARE'S *THE WINTER'S TALE*

The Winter's Tale provides a clear example of the social position of women in the Elizabethan era refracted through the lens of Shakespearean romance. As the play opens, Hermione, the honorable and charming (and pregnant) Queen of Sicilia, plays the role of gracious hostess to King Polixenes of Bohemia, a childhood friend of her husband Leontes. Using his unquestioned prerogative as the husband, Leontes asks Hermione to take Polixenes aside and persuade him to further extend his already lengthy visit. When the power of Hermione's charm accomplishes what Leontes' entreaties had failed to do—changing Polixenes' mind—Leontes cannot perceive that anything other than sexual attachment underlies Polixines' decision to stay. Overwhelmed by jealousy and suspicion, Leontes publicly accuses Hermione of infidelity. Over the protests of Polixenes, the members of their court, and especially Hermione's handmaid Paulina, Leontes sends Hermione to prison, where she gives birth to a daughter, Perdita. Again disregarding the pleas of those around him, Leontes declares the child illegitimate and condemns her to be taken away and abandoned.

The accusation, imprisonment, and trial of Hermione—compounded by the presumed death of Perdita—constitute acts of raw violence done to the innocent woman and her child. Leontes' power, based on his position as husband and king, to thus mistreat his wife and child emphasizes the powerlessness of a woman—even one with the status of queen. Certain that his suspicions will be confirmed, Leontes brings in an outside authority—the Delphic oracle, an otherworldly means relied on for establishing the truth. When messengers from the oracle arrive, Leontes announces that they will be consulted in "a just and open trial" (II. iii. 204). For this trial scene, Hermione is brought, fresh from her childbed, to the court, where she is "accused and arraigned of high treason, in committing adultery with Polixenes, King of Bohemia, and conspiring with Camillo to take away the life of our sovereign lord the king" (III. ii. 15-16). The trial scene gives Hermione a long speech in which she denies the accusations and defends her innocence eloquently, even while acknowledging that she will not be believed. Shakespeare integrates a dimension of bittersweet and dramatically dark humor when, in a direct exchange with Leontes in which he threatens her with death, Hermione laughs in a cynical manner while declaring that given her suffering thus far, death would be a blessed release.

In the climax of the trial scene, the message from the oracle is unsealed and read aloud: it pronounces Hermione innocent, the child Perdita legitimate, and Leontes a tyrant. It even predicts that Leontes will die without an heir "if that which is lost be not found" (III. ii. 133). Asserting his own power in defiance of this verdict, Leontes insists on the falsehood of the oracle; however, a servant immediately brings news that Mamillus, Leontes' son, has died. Amid the general uproar, Hermione collapses and is taken away. Paulina subsequently reports that she has died. Belatedly, Leontes realizes the wrongs he has committed and pledges to spend the rest of his life doing penance for his sins. Much of the remainder of the play focuses on Perdita as she grows to maturity in a foreign land and falls in love with a young man who, as it happens, is the son of Polixenes. The play's final scene, engineered by the faithful Paulina, reveals that Hermione still lives. In this scene, Hermione's virtue is elevated to a quasi-divine status, as Paulina unveils a "statue" commissioned by Leontes to honor Hermione, and the statue proves to be the woman herself. Perdita's return, along with her affianced husband and his father, completes the reconciliation. The ending thus suggests a benevolent force greater than the power of kings or husbands that will vindicate the innocent and restore harmony in disrupted families. Interestingly, the benevolent force seems to be aided by the women who gain power without losing their traditional feminine virtue, when separated from the men who, according to traditional gender notions, protect them.

What is most striking about the trial in *The Winter's Tale* is that the audience, along with the entirety of the onstage court, is on Hermione's side, and this fact dramatically highlights the madness of her husband. The tyrannical King attracts no sympathy. At this tragic climax of the play and just before her collapse, Hermione gives her final speech, a magnum opus of suffering and persecuted innocence listing all of the dreadful things that have transpired. She questions herself about the reasons for living and eventually gives in to death. With all of Hermione's sadness and suffering, Shakespeare does manage to instill hope through the words of the Oracle; however, at this point, it would appear to the audience that the tragic turn of events is final. Burdened with and perturbed by the vicious persecution of such an admired female and her innocent daughter, the audience is far from imaging the resurrection of Hermione and the child at the end of the play. Within the romantic world of the play, Hermione and Perdita are, of course, reunited at the end with their husband and father Leontes, who has been purged of his madness through suffering and repentance. This restoration, however, brings a notable shift in the power dynamics of the court. Paulina, who has been marginalized through her status as a widowed female servant, takes center stage as she engineers the dramatic unveiling. The newly revealed

Hermione has, through this startling apparent resurrection, gained moral stature and now stands completely above reproach. She is not a man's creation, as in the myth of Pygmalion, but rather, the creation of the unseen relationship between herself and Paulina that has developed in the intervening years not represented in the play. The lost Perdita has found not only her own power but also her own prince, with whom she has established a relatively egalitarian relationship. She restores herself, along with her intended husband and his father, to their rightful places in her home and kingdom. Women, if not completely dominant, seem to occupy a place of enhanced power in this imagined new order. Shakespeare's play, of course, leaves many questions unanswered, and its optimism, from the standpoint of women's social status and power, may be tempered by the title, which seems to refer to the traditionally feminine world of vegetation (ruled in classical myth by Persephone), which disappears during the winter but returns in spring.

JOAN IN SHAW'S *ST. JOAN*

Shaw presents a romanticized version of an actual woman in his play *Saint Joan* (1923), which is described by many critics as Shaw's only tragedy, and is believed to have led to his Nobel Prize in Literature (Martin 484). Shaw based the play on the life and trial of Joan of Arc, who was born into a French peasant family in 1412. As the result of hearing voices which she claimed to be those of Saint Margaret, Saint Catherine and the Archangel Michael, Joan came to believe she had a divinely inspired mission to save her country and its populace from the grips of warring hostilities and injustice. She began her astonishing military career at the age of sixteen, after gaining the support of Charles VII and being pronounced virtuous and pure by the clerics Charles assigned to inquire into her background and motives. When only eighteen years old, she led the French army to victory over the British and their French sympathizers through the use of boldly aggressive tactics. She was, however, captured, and subjected to a trial engineered by Bishop Pierre

Cauchon of Beauvais, who represented political interests aligned with the British and opposed to those of Charles VII. Though political intrigue played a part in her arrest and trial, Joan's very overt transgression of gender norms and success at doing so prompted suspicions that she was receiving supernatural assistance. She was convicted of heresy and burned at the stake. Subsequently Joan of Arc ascended to the status of legendary icon. As Spoto points out, since her death in 1431, Joan of Arc has fascinated people in many lands, since she was subjected to "one of history's most egregious miscarriages of justice" (xii). Authenticated documentation of her remarkable trial, which was recorded fully and in detail, can be found at the Bibliothèque Nationale in Paris and the Bibliothèque Municipale of Orléans.

Clearly, the public's fascination with Joan of Arc in the centuries since her trial and death arises from the startling ways in which she defied the gender role expectations for women in medieval France. Spoto describes some of the ways Joan of Arc violated the gender norms of her time: she repudiated her parents' wishes and refused to marry; she embraced a vow of chastity (an act which ultimately fused with her identity); and she was not intimidated by kings, soldiers or bishops (31-32). With extraordinary confidence, she defended her mission when the vast majority believed she was chasing after quixotic goals. She dressed like a man, cut her hair short, and kept company with and managed hundreds of soldiers, sharing her faith with them and teaching them to respect women and choose the values of marriage instead of the shameful pleasure of prostitution. Throughout her trial she adopted a strong degree of defiance and persistently maintained that every decision was linked to her divine mission. Although Joan of Arc only lived to nineteen years of age, she had an immeasurable impact on her own time, as well as on her home country. For the French, she represents an extraordinary role model who not only traverses boundaries, nations and history, but also incarnates an eternal charisma and beauty of life (Senzig and Gay 279-280).

The publicity surrounding Joan of Arc's canonization by the Roman Catholic Church in 1920 served as a source of inspiration for Shaw, who studied the substantial records and transcripts of her trial. Shaw presents his version of her trial after a close scientific and psychological analysis (Searle 103) of the authenticated judicial documents. His approach to this play, however, eschews historical trappings and instead presents what Shaw himself describes as a modern trial (see Holroyd), with Joan of Arc presented as a victim of the Inquisition. She appears in the play as a young, feminine heroine who faces unscrupulous and villainous accusers. The dramatization of Joan may have been influenced by Shaw's admiration of a contemporary icon, the audacious and courageous Sylvia Pankhurst (1882-1960), a leader of the Suffragist movement in England. According to Shaw, Pankhurst was like Joan of Arc in terms of political lobbying, because she lectured, talked, won over and over-ruled statesmen, while possessing an unbounded and unconcealed contempt for official opinion, judgment and authority (www.sylviapankhurst.com). This Shavian fascination was duly noted in some reviews of the play. After its first London production had been running for six months, in October 1924, a commentary written by "Crites" (T. S. Eliot) in *The Criterion* stated:

> Saint Joan seems to illustrate Mr. Shaw's mind more clearly than anything he has written before...he manipulates every idea so brilliantly that he blinds us when we attempt to look for the ideas *with which he works*...His Joan of Arc is perhaps the greatest sacrilege of all Joans: for instead of the saint or the strumpet of the legends to which he objects, he has turned her into a great middle-class reformer, and her place is a little higher than Mrs. Pankhurst. ("A Commentary" 4-5.)

Shaw not only pays tribute to the desire for power evident in both Saint Joan and Sylvia Pankhurst, but also employs Joan as a point of contrast to a society suffering from malaise and in great need of the spirit, energy, and intelligence Joan manifests in abundance. The playwright often includes revealing remarks about society, such as in Scene 1, when he states, "we want a few mad people now. See where the sane ones have landed us!" (Poulengey, in Saint Joan, sc. 1). Shaw's play represents Joan as triumphing over the men who place her on trial, even as she faces condemnation and a horrifying death. In Joan's trial, the violation of social norms and gender expectations were manifested in explicitly theological terms, as she is charged with insubordination and heterodoxy. Her replies also use theological language: "I hear voices telling me what to do. They come from God," says Joan in Scene 1. When asked if they come from her imagination, however, she gives a reply that implicates the divine in the human and, perhaps specifically, in the female: rather naïvely, she responds, "of course. That is how the messages of God come to us." In her time, the judges only recognized the universal Church and not national boundaries; therefore she was tried not as a traitor, but as a heretic against God and His Church, though it was the pro-English church in Rouen that could not tolerate her rebelliousness and insubordination. A good illustration of the tenacity expressed by the historical Joan is her reaction to the usual admonitions and exhortations, when she states:

> If you tore my limbs and threatened me so far as death, I would never say anything other than what I have already. And if I did so, I would later claim that you drew it out of me by force. (Spoto 174)

Both a devout leader and dedicated warrior, Joan of Arc may have been young in age, but her audacious character and feistiness appears in her every word and contributes to her larger-than-life image.

Canonized by the Catholic Church in 1920, Joan of Arc was, like many saints, literally whitewashed by history. Canonization tends to erase all un-Christian attributes such as rebelliousness, pride and intolerance. Despite having been described as stubborn, haughty, naïve and even foolish, Joan has been remembered for most of history as a pious martyr and a young woman of remarkable composure (Spoto 22). In the play's epilogue, Shaw suggests that it is difficult to distinguish between a saint and a heretic. Joan of Arc's final judgment, in which she is deemed a saint by the same church under whose authority she was burned at the stake, is linked to a divine intervention. However, as Searle (102) explains, Shaw, a nonreligious man, rejected the Catholic view that Joan was endowed with supernatural powers. This line of thought was reflected in one of the most famous lines of the play: "A miracle, my friend, is an event which creates faith" (II. 340). In the epilogue, situated some twenty-five years after her execution, Joan reappears before the king (the former dauphin) and her chief accusers. They have now been condemned by a subsequent court, which has proclaimed Joan innocent of all charges and her judges guilty of a number of crimes. The play then shifts to 1920 and her canonization, offering the premise that she now has the power to return as a living woman. Consequently, she asks everyone who is present whether or not she should return. Horrified, they all confess that their wish is for her to remain dead. Joan then asks of God, "O, Lord, how long before the world will be ready to accept its saints." Herein lays another example of Shaw's critical assessment of society. At this point in the Epilogue, the playwright underscores Joan's innocence; while at the same time criticizing the hypocrisy of society, as each of the people who once praised Joan for her actions during her life now desert her when she offers to return to earth. In the end, Shaw implies that the world will never be ready to accept its saints—or, in Shaw's terms, its geniuses.

ALMA PAKENHAM RATTENBURY IN BRYANS' *BY SOME DIVINE MISTAKE*

In her recent play, the Vancouver playwright Joan Bryans presents a woman on trial whose transgression consists in appropriating for herself many of the personal sexual freedoms regularly accorded to men of her era. Based on a true story, which was also dramatized by Terence Rattigan in 1975, this play is centered on the infamous Alma Pakenham Rattenbury, who was accused of conspiring with her teenaged lover to murder her husband, Francis Rattenbury. This exotic and talented woman, born in British Columbia, became an accomplished songwriter and musician, as well as a widow, decorated army volunteer during

World War 1, mother, and divorcée—all before the age of 29. She acquired the reputation of a femme fatale during her two-year, quite public seduction of Francis Rattenbury, a prominent Vancouver architect and a married man. After openly cheating on his first wife and children, Francis eventually demanded a divorce and married the boisterous and intriguing Alma. Their marriage took place in 1925 in British Columbia; but eventually, giving in to social pressure and negative public opinion, the couple moved to Bournemouth, England, where Alma became tired of her aging, depressed, and alcoholic husband and took as her lover the young handyman, George Stoner. Stoner bludgeoned Francis to death with a mallet on the night of March 24, 1935, after having taken a double dose of cocaine. Bryans' play takes us from the initial love-at-first sight meeting between Alma and Francis, to her relationship with the increasingly possessive Stoner, into the courtroom of England's Old Bailey for her trial and acquittal, and finally to her subsequent suicide. Bryans presents Alma as a gifted individual who, consumed with personal guilt in the wake of the death sentence pronounced on her lover,[3] took her life only four days after the verdict by stabbing herself through the heart and falling into the River Avon.

Despite the sensational events it encompasses, the Rattenbury case offers a glimpse into the beliefs and attitudes of the 1920s, a time period known for rapid change in social mores, especially for women. Both Alma and Francis flaunted the social and sexual conventions of their time; yet, the trial places them within the tightly drawn set of expectations for people in their situation. Consider for example, when Alma Rattenbury, accused of adultery and murder, is probed about her marital 'duty' towards her husband: "If he (the husband) wanted his rights as a husband, would you be ready to grant them to him?" (Bryans 26) In a very nonchalant manner, she initially responds, "If he wanted...what? Oh no. I do not think so," and then adds, "Decidedly not." This line of questioning reveals the fact that, from the perspective of the questioner and the Court, Alma, a married woman, is obligated to satisfy her husband's sexual desire upon demand. Her response explicitly demonstrates that she defends her individual right to decline. Unfortunately, the capricious Alma is at times disserved by her duplicitous identity and coy character when the questioning takes on serious undertones. One example of this occurs when she is asked, "Are you in the habit if deceiving your husband in order to get what you regard as sufficient money for your needs?" (Bryans 29) to which Alma curtly responds, "Absolutely." Alma's credibility further deteriorates when her claim to maternal responsibility is undermined by her admission that her "innocent six year old child" sleeps in the same bedroom where she has extramarital sexual relations with her lover. Her defense is a simple, "but little John is always asleep… and I do not consider that dreadful." (Bryans 30)

Bryans highlights the interaction of modern reality, as transmitted by the media, with traditional forms of community judgment. When the murder hits the headlines, the media swiftly summarizes her character traits and labels her a twentieth-century Circe[4] (Bryans 40):

> [A] picture of an eccentric architectural genius falling under the spell of a talented but self-seeking enchantress and sacrificing home, friends and reputation at her bidding. Alma Rattenbury, the alleged mallet murderess, is seen as a twentieth century Circe, who changed her victims not into swine but into the slaves of her ambition. …Today our source said 'Rattenbury was an elderly man and a strange man, like many geniuses. She had plenty of physical attractiveness, was talented. She had no depth though, no innate refinement – vulgar.

The trial scene gives the audience a sense of the way public opinion develops by presenting the comments of the townsfolk both inside and outside of the courtroom. As gossip-craving townswomen queue to watch the court trial, reporters relay its progress by telephone to their newspapers. Headlines and trial reports are read aloud as the trial unfolds, integrating the role of the media into the developing weight of public judgment. Each time, innuendo in the reports leads to more gossip. As the public struggles to comprehend the facts of the trial, they formulate various suppositions with regards to Alma's motivations, actions, and feelings. When the not-guilty verdict is declared, one townswoman reads aloud from a newspaper: "...as her defense argued: 'She has been punished enough. Wherever she walks she will be a figure of shame'" (Bryans 61). Bryans uses stage directions specifying nonverbal communication to reinforce and emphasize public reaction: "[Townsfolk look knowingly at each other. Exit.]" (61). Should they come across Alma Rattenbury in public, the townsfolk know and understand what kind of behavior is expected from them.

Alma herself, the woman on trial, changes markedly and almost gets lost in the frenzy of these proceedings. As the wife of a very successful architect and member of upper-class society, she attempts to affirm her social status and identity throughout her trial. She appears to put substantial distance between herself and the court proceedings by reflecting on past actions and words. She often appears nostalgic and disconnected with reality, as if she has led a double life. In a touching monologue given in a meeting with her counselor a few days before appearing before the Court, Alma expresses her sadness and remorse for having been separated from everything she has ever loved. As she reflects on the past, she realizes that her life has changed forever. In Court, while subjected to harsh judgment by the jury and the gossipy townsfolk and onlookers, she hesitantly responds to the incisive and damaging questions of the prosecution, aimed at developing her profile as a manipulating charlatan and seducer without scruples. When the questioning takes on moralizing tones with the objective of making Alma feel guilty and ashamed, she enters a fragile state of psychological defenselessness. While murmuring to herself, she relives her past through numerous flashbacks to various pivotal moments of her life. Desperately Alma clings to reality in order to respond appropriately to the questions asked of her and at the same time appear competent and sane. In court she appears frail, uncertain and weak, with little resemblance to the vibrant personality she once was. Her short, curt responses stand in complete contrast to the prosecution's lengthy lists of accusations and factual details.

Though the play incorporates the actual murder trial into its action, its structure suggests that Alma was on trial throughout her life. The narrative is carried, in part, by characters designated as Questioner and Accusers. In accordance with the opening stage directions, scenes of the play should flow one into the other with minimal transitions and no blackouts. The romantic songs that Alma wrote and performed are juxtaposed with the gossip and sordid scandal that, in many ways, defined her life. The climactic event of her suicide can be seen as a response to understanding that the two sets of attitudes evident in the romantic music and the harsh judgments of society could never be reconciled. Throughout the early part of the play, before meeting her lover, she is represented as a dynamic woman and considerate mother who thoroughly enjoys being the center of attention. As she listens to the judge and the final verdict, she is in apparent mental anguish and complete denial. In the last scene of the play Alma provides her most poignant and dramatic soliloquy when she explains her repeated and failed suicide attempts after her lover was convicted and sentenced to death. While observing the pastoral scenes around her, near the river bank at Christchurch, she begs forgiveness and bids adieu. Her last thoughts and words are dedicated to her lover as she recites the lyrics of the song he inspired. She stabs herself five times and falls to her death into the river. The voice-over speech at the very end of the play evokes justice of a higher order, when, reading from the headlines of a newspaper, it declares that "it seems that we have witnessed one instance of where God's justice was more swift and unerring and terrible than even that of England." Even following her untimely death, the media and public opinion render judgment against her. The play, however, draws sympathy to the tormented Alma who succumbed to the pressure of the media, the townsfolk and her own growing guilt for having failed her lover. In the form of song, her last words, "I seem to climb to heaven in loving you" (Bryans 62) endow her with the hope and comfort she needs as she precedes him in death.

CONCLUSION

In terms of the women on trial in these three plays, as extraordinary as their accusations may appear, with each play, we are witness to the changing roles, image and identity of women over the course of four centuries. Each of the three has taken on a self-definition that stands at the center of the accusations brought against her in the trial. The Shakespearean interpretation of female values and virtue focuses on wifely and maternal roles, controlled by the husband, while the modern women presented in the plays by Shaw and Bryans base their identities on individual ideas, capabilities, and desires. In *The Winter's Tale*, Hermione defines herself as a wife. The insinuation of adultery through mere conversation and monologues places her entire identity, purpose, and status at risk; when her virtue is questioned in public, this identity, purpose, and status are destroyed, leading to her apparent—and symbolic—death. Joan of Arc identifies herself outside the gender system, as a unique servant of God. For Shaw's real-life heroine, the trial centers on a larger-than-life personality and public deeds of strength, intelligence, and bravery that would have, if they had been accepted as valid expressions of a young girl's potential, demolished the system of gender opposition. Alma defines herself, though her songs and her life choices, as a woman devoted to and willing to sacrifice anything for love. Though accomplished in many ways, Alma faces trial and social judgment explicitly for murdering her husband, but implicitly for a host of sexual and gender-role transgressions acknowledged publicly, rather than kept in the dark realm of private shame. While Joan of Arc and Alma act vigorously and are tried for their actions, the fictitious character of Hermione is much more reserved, has done nothing, and is put on trial for something she has not done. She adopts an air of unwavering reticence as she literally disappears, albeit gracefully, with the help of Paulina, her most loyal confidant. All three women defend themselves primarily by enacting their self-constructed identities with solemn pride and often fierce modesty. In the end, all three women reflect on their lives and look to themselves for solutions about their futures or imminent deaths.

The actions and demeanor of the women on trial in these three plays undermine a simple division of males and females into active and strong *versus* passive and weak. Hermione and Alma are initially presented as dynamic and charming women, who are also strong and happy as mothers, whereas Joan of Arc begins as a peasant girl and develops into a defiant teenage rebel with a spiritual militant cause. In all three plays, the women's roles and identities are shaped and revealed by their trials, both inside and outside of the courtroom. Dramatic turning points in the plays bring out opposing qualities that contrast with their previous personalities or behavior. In Bryans' play, for example, the scene is literally covered in blood when Alma discovers her husband's lifeless body at the beginning of Act II, and it is at this very moment that Alma begins drinking and acting wildly. She daringly flirts with a police officer and tries to manipulate him, with the goal of implicating herself in the murder, while protecting her lover; later, however, she retracts her confession. Similarly, Shaw's Joan of Arc shows a wild and inexplicable side, which she attributes to her visions and voices, when she insistently rejects the authority of the politically biased judges who were determined to paint her as a heretic and ultimately discredit her (Spoto 16). When subjected to loss of her husband's affection, separation from her son, and childbirth in prison, Hermione becomes a haunting shadow of her former vivacious self. Alma's suicide, with its aggressive, stereotypically masculine, repeated self-stabbing, combined with the passive, stereotypically feminine, submission to the currents of a river, provides a richly symbolic moment of gender-role transcendence.

As judgment is not limited to the verdict of the judges, Shakespeare, Shaw and Bryans all integrate a degree of societal judgment in terms of the motivations behind the acts that lead to accusation. All three playwrights create and manipulate this dimension of judgment both inside and outside of the courtroom. *The Winter's Tale* ends happily: in spite of the fact that Leontes had firmly believed that his beloved wife and loyal friend had deceived him, the accusations are ultimately forgotten and harmony returns. Hermione's motivations are never explored. In the plays by Shaw and Bryans, the protagonists are explicitly questioned about their motivations during the trials. The motive in Alma's case is established quite early in the trial: they wanted the husband out of the way and the act of murder was linked to an uncontrollable impulse on the part of the jealous and deranged lover. As for Joan of Arc, the motivations of this pious protagonist are much more complicated, since she claimed that her actions were an extension of divine intervention. When theologians were brought in to determine her motivations, they subjected her to repeated questioning, as well as starvation, torture and sleep deprivation. The historical record indicates that her answer to each question eventually became a simple repetition of "I look only to my God" (Spoto 174). The play *Saint Joan* clearly represents mentality behind the Court and the clergy in the following statement from Bishop Cauchon in the epilogue: "the heretic is always better dead. And mortal eyes cannot distinguish the saint from the heretic."

In the cultural and social contexts of their times, the three protagonists pursued their goals with the crucial help of supporters. Hermione had the unfaltering support of Paulina, while Alma was backed by her "darling"[5] housekeeper Irene. Joan of Arc had extraordinarily won the support of her male troops. In all three of the plays, this support, which reflects the social status of the primary characters, affects the management and the outcomes or aftermath of their trials. In Shakespeare's play, the link between social status and identity intensifies both the pathos of Hermione's situation during and after her trial and the victorious resurgence of domestic harmony at the end. Hermione's staged death reveals a pseudo-suicidal attempt which is fully reversed with her romantic resurrection at the end of the play. Her Shakespearean renaissance is quite an idyllic contrast when compared to the tragic final scenes of Joan of Arc and Alma Rattenbury. Even though the roles and identities of the three women are very different in terms of social class—a queen, a peasant, and an upper-class citizen—each woman is stripped of her social class and character in the course of the trial. All three are considered merely women according to the law of the time. The theatre audience, however, places each woman in the context of her unique circumstances and often sides with the woman's supporters.

Analysis of the heroines in these three theatrical representations reveals the way in which each of these female protagonists comes to be viewed as a threat to masculine authority and put on trial. Though Hermione does not disobey or overtly challenge her husband, she falls victim to his need for absolute control—control so complete that he can see into her mind and understand her deepest desires and motivations. When her action of persuading Polixenes to extend his visit raises doubts in Leontes' mind, he will not rest until he satisfies himself that Hermione has been punished for what she might have been thinking. Both Joan of Arc, the girl military commander, and Alma Rattenbury, the sexual predator, actively challenge the gender norms for their time. Despite the overt nature of their challenges, both find their motivations and lives in general intensely questioned and closely scrutinized by male authorities (judicial or ecclesiastical). Their identities and roles are intimately probed since their actions do not reflect those of their contemporary counterparts as a typical mother or young, innocent adolescent. The presentation of all three characters as composed and courageous individuals both enhances the power of their responses to their accusers and normalizes their behavior. In the end, each character can be seen to represent a distinct challenge to patriarchy that continues to resonate with contemporary audiences.

Notes

1. Boas presents a fascinating comparison of the depictions of Joan of Arc in Shakespeare, Schiller and Shaw.
2. It was not until 1660 that women were allowed to appear on the stage of licensed theaters in England.
3. After Alma's death, George Stoner's sentence was commuted to life imprisonment; however, he was released early in order to serve in the army during World War II.
4. In Greek mythology Circe refers to a minor goddess of magic (a nymph, witch, enchantress or sorceress) who murdered her husband and was expelled by her subjects (see Grimal).
5. Alma shared a strong bond with Irene before taking her lover, and they would address one another as "darling" throughout the play.

Works Cited

"A Commentary." *The Criterion* 3.9 (October 1924) 1-5. Online.

Boas, F.S. "Joan of Arc in Shakespeare, Schiller and Shaw." *Shakespeare Quarterly* 2.1 (1951) 35-45. Print.

Beattie, J.M. "The Criminality of Women in Eighteenth-Century England." *Journal of Social History* 8 (1975) 80-116. Print.

Bryans, J. *By Some Divine Mistake.* Vancouver: 2006. Ms.

Castaneda, D. and Burns-Glover, A. "Gender, Sexuality and Intimate Relationships." *The Praeger Guide to The Psychology of Gender*, ed. Paludi, M. Westport, CT: Praeger Publishers, 2004: 69-91. Print.

Gilligan, C. *A Different Voice: Psychological Theory and Women's Development.* Cambridge, MA: Harvard University Press, 1982. Print.

Grimal, P. *The Dictionary of Classical Mythology.* Oxford: Blackwell Publishers, 1996. Print.

Holroyd, M. "A Tragedy Without Villains." *The Guardian.* July 14, 2007. Online.

Horner, M. "Toward an understanding of achievement – related conflicts in women." *Journal of Social Issues* 28 (1972): 157-173. Print.

Kent, Susan Kingsley. *Gender and Power in Britain, 1640-1990.* London: Routledge, 1999. Print.

Kermode, J. and G. Walker. *Women, Crime and the Courts in Early Modern England.* London: Routledge, 1994. Print.

King, P. *Crime and Law in England, 1750-1840.* Cambridge: Cambridge University Press, 2006: Print.

Martin, S. *George Bernard Shaw. The Order of Merit: One Hundred Years of Matchless Honour.* London: Taurus Press, 2007. Print.

McKay, L. "Why they stole: Women in the Old Bailey, 1779-1789." *Journal of Social History* 32 (1999): 623-639. Print.

Palk, D. *Gender, Crime and Judicial Discretion, 1780-1830.* Woodbridge: Suffolk, 2006. Print.

Pearson, J. and R. Davilla. "The Gender Construct. Understanding Why Men and Women Communicate Differently." *Women and Men Communicating: Challenges and Changes* (Second Edition), ed. Arliss, L. P. and D. J. Borisoff. Long Grove, IL: Waveland Press, 2001. Print.

Pernoud, R. *Jeanne d'Arc – La reconquête de la France.* Paris : Gallimard, 1995. Print.

Perry, Linda A. M., Lynn H. Turner, and Helen M. Sterk. *Constructing and Reconstructing Gender: The Links Among Communication, Language and Gender.* Albany, NY: State University of New York Press, 1992. Print.

Searle, W. *The Saint and the Skeptics.* Detroit: Wayne State University Press, 1976. Print.

Senzig, R. and M. Gay. *L'Affaire Jeanne d'Arc.* Paris: Editions Florent Masson, 2007. Print.

Shakespeare, W. *The Oxford Classics: Henry VI.* Oxford: Oxford University Press, 2003. Print.

Shakespeare, W. *The Oxford Shakespeare: The Winter's Tale.* Oxford: Oxford University Press, 2008. Print.

Shaw, G.B. *Saint Joan: A Chronicle Play in Six Scenes and an Epilogue.* New York: Penguin Books, 1946. Print.

Shoemaker, R. B. *Gender in English Society 1650-1850: The Emergence of Separate Spheres?* London: Harlow, 1998. Print.

Spoto, D. *Joan: The Mysterious Life of the Heretic Who Became a Saint.* New York: Harper Collins, 2007. Print.

Tannen, D. *You Just Don't Understand.* New York: Ballantine, 1990. Print.

Tannen, D. and R. Bly. *Men and Women: Talking Together.* New York: The New York Open Center: Cooper Union, 1993. Print.

Walker, G. *Crime, Gender and Social Order in Early Modern England.* Cambridge: Cambridge University Press, 2003. Print.

CHAPTER 6.

WHY DOES MARY QUEEN OF SCOTS ALWAYS GET HER HEAD CHOPPED OFF?

Verna A. Foster

In the four best-known plays featuring Mary Queen of Scots—Friedrich Schiller's *Mary Stuart* (1800), Maxwell Anderson's *Mary of Scotland* (1933), Robert Bolt's *Vivat! Vivat Regina!* (1970), and Liz Lochhead's *Mary Queen of Scots Got Her Head Chopped Off* (1989, revised 2009)—there is no trial scene, even though in the theatre trial scenes are almost always effective. This absence is true to the spirit of the historical judgment against Mary if not to the fact. Mary was, in fact, tried at Fotheringhay Castle in 1586 for her participation in the Babington plot to assassinate Elizabeth I and make Mary Queen of England. The trial lasted two days and was entirely pro forma. Mary had already been tried in the deliberations of Elizabeth's councillors, notably Cecil and Walsingham, and found guilty. At her actual trial, allowed "neither counsel nor witnesses in her defence" (Fraser 504) and in ill health, Mary behaved heroically. As the monarch of a foreign country, she rejected the legitimacy of her trial under English law; she admitted attempting to encompass her freedom but denied any complicity in a plot against her cousin Elizabeth's life. Despite her denial, Mary was likely guilty. As the center of repeated Catholic plots to make her Queen of England, Mary had long been dangerous to Elizabeth. While her participation in such conspiracies, culminating in the Babington plot, constituted the real and serious charges that led to her execution, in an important sense—even in history, but certainly in legend, popular culture, and literature--Mary's perceived crime, the source of both her condemnation and her later popular romantic image, was and is her love life. Her sexual attractiveness (compounded by her Catholicism), her impolitic marriages to Henry Stuart, Lord Darnley and then to his murderer, James Hepburn, Earl of Bothwell, her own implication in Darnley's death are stereotypically women's crimes, for all of which she is punished. In plays about Mary her whole life is on trial.[1]

In play after play and film after film, Mary of Scotland—Catholic, beautiful, willful, feminine, romantic, sexually fulfilled (at times), maternal, and ultimately tragic—is pitted against Elizabeth of England who, by contrast, is Protestant, clever, pragmatic, masculine (preferring to be known as a prince), "virgin" (despite her sexual involvement with Robert Dudley, Earl of Leicester), barren, and ultimately victorious, though not happy. In this essay I will focus on Lochhead's *Mary Queen of Scots Got Her Head Chopped Off*, but I will position this play within the context of the works by Schiller, Anderson, and Bolt. All four dramatists construct and explore the contrasts, but also the similarities between Mary and Elizabeth. Additionally, though historically Mary and Elizabeth did not meet, all four dramatists find a way to obviate this difficulty—Schiller and Anderson by introducing an unhistorical meeting between the two queens, Bolt and Lochhead in more theatrically inventive ways. All four dramatists, like numerous historians (Wormald 179, 15), judge Mary more in personal than political terms. Lochhead, however, writing from a Scottish and a feminist perspective, as obviously her predecessors did not, uniquely evaluates the life and death and afterlife of Mary Queen of Scots in light of what she perceives to be their historical consequences.[2]

The four plays provide varying perspectives on Mary's life through using different frameworks of time to tell her story. While Schiller sets his play during Mary's last days at Fotheringhay Castle after her trial, Bolt's *Vivat! Vivat Regina!* covers the most historical ground, beginning in France, where Mary, married as a teenager to the sickly Francis II, is queen, and ending with her execution and Cecil's prediction of Elizabeth's defeat of the Spanish Armada. Anderson and Lochhead focus on Mary's love life and her politico-religious difficulties in Scotland prior to her captivity in England. Anderson's *Mary of Scotland* concludes at the beginning of Mary's long years of captivity. Lochhead relegates the nineteen years of Mary's imprisonment in England to one scene out of fifteen (in the 1989 text) or seventeen (in the 2009 text). The penultimate scene in the 2009 version of *Mary Queen of Scots Got Her Head Chopped Off*, divided between Elizabeth and Mary, clarifies the historical events and the passage of time that has elapsed during Mary's years of captivity (somewhat confused in the 1989 text), but in neither version of the play is the Babington plot so much as mentioned. Rather, the play relegates the political conspiracies to a brief allusion: an English Adviser observes that Mary is the "focus of every Catholic hope, of every anti-Elizabeth faction in England." Elizabeth, exasperated, responds that even in a castle in the middle of an island Mary could "charm some man into helping her escape" (62, 69).[3] In Elizabeth's view of Mary the political is also personal, while Lochhead evaluates the seemingly personal as political.

Schiller, Anderson, and Bolt write in the long-established romantic biographical vein of historical drama (see Palmer, 3, 21-22, 27-28, 211-212). Schiller's *Mary Stuart*, while focusing as a tragedy on its titular heroine, is perhaps the most even-handed of the four plays in its presentation of the two queens, though Swales argues that Schiller sides with Mary and that his play is "not only about a trial, but turns itself into a trial which invites us as readers and spectators to sit in ultimate judgment" on Elizabeth and Mary (79). The play's scenic structure, alternating between Fotheringhay and Westminster, underscores the personal and political conflict between Mary and Elizabeth and the difficulties each faces. While Schiller makes his audience aware of the European political and religious issues at stake in this conflict (Swales 26, Sharpe 257), he also introduces, in the foreground action of the play, an old romantic relationship between Mary and Leicester, Elizabeth's favorite, that Leicester now betrays to save his own skin, as well as an invented character, Sir Edward Mortimer, as a final composite Catholic conspirator/lover who lusts almost indiscriminately for Mary and for a martyr's death.[4]

Thus even though Schiller's *Mary Stuart* seems to pay more attention to the political difficulties, especially in their moral dimensions (Sharpe 259), that divide Mary and Elizabeth than do the other three plays, it, like the later plays, couches the politics in romantic terms that require audiences to evaluate Elizabeth and especially Mary as women as much as rulers. Elizabeth says, "I had to strive to be a King while she/ Strove but to be a woman" (39). When the two meet in the central scene of the play, both lose their self control, and their debate descends into an altercation of sexual insults. At the end Mary goes heroically to her death, believing that her execution will atone for her long-ago participation in the murder of Darnley and her lust for Bothwell. The last scene, however, is devoted to Elizabeth, who, having lost her honor in deviously allowing Mary's execution to save her throne, is finally deserted even by her councillors. Though Mary seems to have triumphed in taking the moral high ground, there is an element of role-playing in her stance as Catholic martyr,[5] while Elizabeth's self-inflicted isolation is tragically real.

In *Mary of Scotland* Anderson turns the narrative of Mary's life into a love story focused on Mary and Bothwell and into a personal conflict between two kinds of woman, one of whom always, if unhappily, puts her rule (or, we might say, her career) first, while the other follows her heart. The play does not so much try Mary as serve as counsel for her defense. Mary and Bothwell love each other from the beginning, and Mary marries the drunkard Darnley (her cousin) only because she wants to preserve her Stuart bloodline and the future succession to the English throne of any child she may have, and also because the witchy Elizabeth sets her up to marry Darnley (as, contrary to historical fact, Elizabeth also does in Lochhead's play). Anderson protects Mary (and even to an extent Bothwell) from being implicated in Darnley's murder. The damaging slurs against her reputation, too, are arranged by Elizabeth, ably supported by Presbyterian minister John Knox, who confuses Mary's Catholicism with her sexuality, idolatry with adultery, as he sees it.

The short last act of *Mary of Scotland* takes place at Carlisle Castle in the early years of Mary's captivity. Here Anderson introduces a confrontation between Mary and Elizabeth, in which Elizabeth tries unsuccessfully to persuade Mary to abdicate in favor of the infant Prince James. Mary realizes finally that Elizabeth has always been her evil genius, and each queen asserts that she has "won" the struggle between them: Elizabeth because she controls "What will be said about us in after-years" (199), and Mary because she has loved "as a woman loves/ Lost as a woman loses" and has borne a son who will rule Scotland and England (201). The play ends with Mary alone looking ahead to years of captivity. The film based on Anderson's play, *Mary of Scotland* (1936), starring Katharine Hepburn, becomes even more of a love story between Mary and Bothwell and a love poem to the Scottish queen. Taking Mary's life to its end, John Ford's film does actually include a trial scene in which Mary answers the charge of conspiracy before meeting Elizabeth, but the film ends as tragic romance with Mary ascending her scaffold, bagpipes playing, and anticipating reunion with Bothwell in death.

Bolt's *Vivat! Vivat Regina!* updates the dialogue and some of the stage conventions of the romantic historical biographical drama, as Richard H. Palmer notes, but essentially continues in the same vein as Anderson's *Mary of Scotland* or Gordon Daviot's *Queen of Scots* (1934) (Palmer 137, 211-212). The "overtly theatrical" form of Bolt's staging in *Vivat! Vivat*

Regina! enables his play's wide geographical and historical range (Bolt xi). Nevertheless, despite the longer time span and more detailed attention to religio-political issues in Scotland and England, including the Catholic conspiracies, Bolt, like Schiller and Anderson and to a lesser extent Lochhead, unsurprisingly assesses Mary in personal rather than political terms, particularly by contrasting her with Elizabeth. To enforce the contrast, and even more the similarities, between Mary and Elizabeth, Bolt fuses together Scottish and English scenes. Throughout the play one queen enters the stage as the other leaves; they echo each other's words; and sometimes they appear simultaneously, for example, speaking aloud their letters to each other.

Bolt offers the most volatile and scandalous of the four Marys. While married to Darnley, she is sexually intimate with her Italian secretary, Rizzio, and later Bothwell (whom she loves), and she is clearly complicit in Darnley's death. Elizabeth, by contrast, allows Cecil to restrain her from marrying Leicester so that she may maintain her power. Nonetheless, or rather because of the behavior that costs her both her child and the Scottish throne, at the end, as in Anderson's play, the queen marked for death claims victory over the one who retains her throne and her life. Mary insists that she, rather than Elizabeth, has signed her own death warrant by putting her name to a conspiratorial letter to Babington even though she suspects that it will go first to Walsingham. At her execution, throwing off her black robe and "*revealing scarlet head to foot,*" she asserts, "There is more living in a death that is embraced than in a life that is avoided across three score years and ten" (95). In this play, however, the scarlet that Mary wears denotes the whore rather than the Catholic martyr. As Palmer observes, Bolt "reduces the political conflict between Mary Queen of Scots and Elizabeth I to a drama of repressed sexuality" (137).[6]

Certainly the ways in which the Scottish and English queens, traditionally or mythically, express or repress their sexuality, in their demeanor as well as their actions, allow Schiller, Anderson, Bolt, and Lochhead to make rather clear-cut distinctions between the personalities and the political acumen of the two queens. This is not surprising. What is more curious, perhaps, though it has its basis in historical fact, polemics, and literary convention, is the conflation in the later three plays of anti-Catholic and misogynistic sexual slurs against Mary, a conflation that constrains her ability to operate effectively in the political sphere. Anderson's Knox, speaking in prophetic vein, identifies Mary with the Catholic Church as "the whore of Babylon—the leprous and cankerous evangel of the Beast" (12), and later he refers to Mary in the same breath as "idolater" and "adulterer" (99). Bolt's Knox similarly connects Mary's Catholicism with her whoredom (specifically adultery with Rizzio): "The Great Whore in the Book of Revelations is no Queen—though Queens may be great whores—she is the Church of Rome" (19). The identification of Mary's sexuality with her religion is especially pointed here, since Mary is wearing a red dress as she listens to Knox preaching his sermon on the "Great Whore; dressed in scarlet; sitting on a throne" (18). Lochhead's Knox uses similar language.

The imagery, certainly, is old and familiar. Some of it derives from the historical John Knox's own notorious polemic, *The First Blast of the Trumpet Against the Monstrous Regiment of Women* (1558), directed at Catholic women rulers: Mary Tudor; Mary of Guise, who ruled Scotland on behalf of her infant daughter; and Catherine de' Medici. Lochhead actually has Knox preach "an extrapolated précis" (McDonald and Harvie 142) of this work as he declaims against "the vanity and iniquity of the papistical religion" and "all its pestilent manifestations in Sodom priesthooses and poxetten nunneries" (19, 16). One need only think, too, of Duessa, the devious temptress representing the Catholic Church in Spenser's *Fairie Queene*; in fact, in the historical allegory of Book Five of the poem Duessa represents Mary herself. Lochhead makes particularly interesting use of this familiar trope. Writing out of her own historical, Scottish, and feminist ideological context, Lochhead goes further than her dramatic predecessors in demonstrating the intertwining of the religious, the sexual/gendered, and the national in the story of Mary, in the conflict between Mary and Elizabeth, and most importantly in the present-day consequences of that historical fusion.

Mary Queen of Scots Got Her Head Chopped Off is historically the least inaccurate and dramatically the least realistic of the four plays about Mary.[7] A choric figure, La Corbie (the crow, appropriately clad in feathery black), presents and comments cynically, and sometimes sorrowfully, on the action. The play uses Brechtian scene titles, songs, episodic structure, and stylized action. In the 1989 version a Fiddler and a Dancer, subsequently dispensed with, create non-verbal symbolic actions that Lochhead combines with more realistic exchanges of dialogue.[8] There is a good deal of effective doubling. All of the subsidiary historical figures, given their proper names in the other three plays—such as Cecil, Walsingham, and Davison in England and Moray, Ruthven, and Morton in Scotland—are played by the ensemble as generic ambassadors, English advisers, or Scottish nobles. Lochhead finds even more ingenious ways than did Bolt to bring Elizabeth and Mary together without introducing an unhistorical meeting. On stage for almost the whole play, the two characters exist in "*separate and different*" worlds (2009: 11) while sharing parallel experiences. For example, early in the play various ambassadors, played by the same actors, offer unsuitable suitors to Elizabeth and Mary in turn and, as Scots and English commoners and Scots nobles, make acerbic remarks about their queens' options. In addition, the actress of Mary plays Elizabeth's maid, Marian, and the actress of Elizabeth plays Mary's maid, Bessie. Mary and Elizabeth are also Mairn and Leezie, two beggar girls, and in the play's final scene, they are Marie (1989)/ Maree (2009) and Wee Betty, two twentieth-century Scottish children. The transformations are made on stage gesturally (as when Mairn straightens to become "totally MARY" [33, 33]) or through slight changes in costumes that are already anachronistically contemporary, though eccentric.[9]

Through these doubling techniques, in particular, Lochhead constructs a dynamic connection between Mary and Elizabeth to draw out the contemporary implications of their historical roles: the vexed relationship between Scotland and England; the ways in which women negotiate between their femininity and power; and especially the legacy of the conflicts between Catholic and Protestant embodied in Mary and John Knox, whose diatribes against Mary's religion are interlaced with misogynistic sexual slurs. In the play's last scene, "Jock Tamson's Bairns," the historical characters become their contemporary equivalents among Scottish schoolchildren—pretty Catholic outsider Maree Stewart, spiteful Wee Betty, repressed Smelly Wee Knoxxy, tough James Hepburn, and others—who play out the sexual and religious conflicts of their ancestors, taunting Maree and ending with a vicious game of "Mary Queen of Scots got her head chopped off" (67, 78).[10] As the other children surround her, grabbing at her throat, so Maree/Mary does, again. La Corbie, "*compelled*" (explicitly in the 2009 text) to "*watch all over again*" (2009: 68) and to narrate a tragic story whose ending she knows but cannot change, registers awareness of the way history repeats itself: "*we've got to play this bloody game again*" (2009: 73). It is the sad and frustrating inevitability of this *again* that is Lochhead's final verdict on the life and death and afterlife of Mary Queen of Scots.

Lochhead wrote *Mary Queen of Scots Got Her Head Chopped Off* at the request of director Gerry Mulgrew for Communicado Theatre Company to produce at the Lyceum for the Edinburgh Festival Fringe in 1987, the 400th anniversary of Mary's execution. (The Official Festival put on Schiller's play.) In an interview given as she was writing her play, Lochhead noted, "It's really about Scotland, more about the present than the past, how those myths of the past have carried on into the present malaise of Scotland today" (Somerville-Arjat and Wilson 9). In her introduction to the 2009 revision, first performed by the National Theatre of Scotland, Lochhead underscores the contemporary concerns shadowed in the play's action: Scottish nationalism, women's relationship to power, and religious conflict. It is in light of these contemporary concerns that Lochhead's play evaluates Mary.

There was a need, Lochhead says, "for us to tell our own stories and find our own language to tell it in" (2009: x). Indeed, her Scottish characters speak Scots English (Mary with a French accent). La Corbie opens the play with a disquisition on the idea of Scotland—"Scotland. Whit like is it?" (11, 5)—and introduces the story she has to tell in the manner of a fairy tale: "Once upon a time there were twa queens on the wan green island, and the wan green island was split intae twa kingdoms" (12, 6). Lochhead feels that her play illuminated "the then current state of affairs between Scotland and England" (2009: x). As she was writing her play in 1987, much to her despair, Margaret Thatcher was voted into office for a third time. Scotland, which had voted overwhelmingly against the Tories, would be ruled by them again. Lochhead invokes similarities between Elizabeth I and Thatcher as illustrating "questions of women and power" (2009: x). Here the nationalist concern shades into a feminist one. After the devolution of the Scottish parliament in 1999, Anglo-Scottish relations may have seemed less pressing.[11] In any case, by 2009, Lochhead sees the play as being "fundamentally about Mary and Elizabeth, the passion of these women to have sex and love and marriage —or not—for can they, without losing power?" (2009: xi).

Important as this feminist theme is, it seems to me less interesting in establishing parameters by which to evaluate Mary's career than Lochhead's exploration of the intricate relations among gender, religion, and nationhood that are writ large in both versions of the play and are to a great extent embodied in Mary and Elizabeth.[12] In her introduction to the 2009 text, Lochhead explains the genesis of her particular articulation of the religious conflict. She notes that director Gerry Mulgrew, of Irish Catholic descent, and she herself, coming from a Scottish Presbyterian background, had grown up with different versions of the Mary Queen of Scots myth, indicating that the centuries-old conflict was still alive (Varty 161).[13] According to Lochhead, the Catholic Mary is "a martyr and almost a saint," while the Protestant version "veers between limp victim and politically inept nymphmaniac devil woman who almost scuppered Our Glorious Reformation" (2009: vii). Reacting against their own traditions,

Mulgrew saw Knox as a proto-democrat, while Lochhead strongly rejected Knox's misogyny. Lochhead believes that Knox's misogyny left an "enduring anti-feminist, anti-feminine legacy in Scottish society" (vii), as she depicts in her play's final scene of religious and sexual "school yard bullying" (McDonald and Harvie 145). The scene's title, "Jock Tamson's Bairns," an expression asserting that we are all children belonging to the same Scottish family, ironically underscores the destructive differences inculcated in the youthful inheritors of the 400-year-old sectarian conflict and the misogyny accompanying it that we have just witnessed.

In *Mary Queen of Scots Got Her Head Chopped Off* Lochhead represents both Scotland and Catholicism as gendered female and England and Protestantism as male.[14] Scotland is the smaller and poorer of the two kingdoms, while England has riches and military strength (12, 6-7). Mary feels the need for a husband so that she can "begin [her] reign at last," while Elizabeth, "the Lass-Wha-Was-Born-To-Be-King" (in La Corbie's words, ironically echoing the epithet of Bonnie Prince Charlie in the Skye Boat Song), believes that only by not marrying the man she loves can she continue to rule her kingdom (1987:17, 23; 2009: 13, 21). Most strikingly, Mary imagines her own position as feminine and Elizabeth's as masculine when she says that if Elizabeth were a man she would marry her (15, 11).[15]

Queen Mary and the Virgin Mary are set off against the masculinized Elizabeth and within Scotland against John Knox. La Corbie tells Mary that Knox "has torn the Mother of God from oot the sky o Scotland and has trampit her celestial blue goon amang the muck and mire," leaving in her place a "black hole, a jaggit gash, *naethin*" (23, 20). The image is of a nurturing feminine Marian Catholicism destroyed by Knox's rough, masculine Presbyterianism. Margery Palmer McCulloch notes Lochhead's linking of Knox's "dethroning" of the Virgin Mary and Queen Mary with "a suppression of the female principle in Scotland" (8). In the Protestant imagination the Virgin Mother was replaced by the Whore of Babylon, linking disreputable female sexuality with Catholicism (as in

Spenser's Duessa). In a similar vein, Lochhead's Knox, appearing in one scene anachronistically in the guise of a marching Orangeman "*in bowler hat and with umbrella*" (19, 15), refers to Mary as a "French hoor" and, conflating her with her manifestation as the beggar girl Mairn, he does indeed call her "ya wee hoor o Babylon," continuing, "Wi yir lang hair lik a flag in the wind, an advertisement o lust tae honest men" (32-33, 32-33). As Knox threatens to strike Mairn/Mary, Lochhead's 2009 stage direction notes that this is a "*moment of lust, madness and ambiguity*" (33). Knox's misogynist anti-Catholicism is then also a mark of his repressed and fearful sexuality, as is made explicit when his own later embodiment, Smelly Wee Knoxxy, recoils in terror at having his head thrust up Maree Stewart's skirt in the "Jock Tamson's Bairns" scene: "Ma faither says I'm no tae play wi lassies!" (65, 75).

Lochhead's depiction of Mary's husbands also furthers her play's gendering of religion. Described as a "*brute but magnetic character*" (1987: 25), Protestant Bothwell presents as markedly masculine, but unlike Knox, he aggressively flaunts his sexuality. In interactions replete with sexual innuendo, he seduces both Mary and her maid, Bessie. In the 1989 text he first appears before Mary, symbolically, as a huntsman pursuing a stag, played by Dancer. Bothwell clearly contrasts with both the feminized Catholic Darnley with his childish curls and his "cheek as saft as ony baby boy" (37, 38) and David Rizzio, Mary's Italian secretary and, in this play, platonic confidant (despite rumors to the contrary), who is "*small and slight but with a face both beautiful and gentle in his twisted body*" (2009: 40). Though sexually attracted to Bothwell, who supports her rule in order to preserve Scottish independence, Mary chooses romantically (and without even the political motives assigned to her by Anderson and Bolt) to follow her emotional yearnings and marry young Darnley for love (after feeding him broth while he is sick with the measles).

Sent to Scotland by Elizabeth to ruin her rival by marrying her, the weak, vain, and frequently drunk Darnley does just that. The Protestant Scottish lords who oppose Mary use Darnley to murder Rizzio in the

Queen's chamber during an entertainment, the Mummers' *Masque of Salome*, in which a further feminized Darnley plays a grotesque Salome. The disguised lords (who speak anachronistically like contemporary Glaswegian thugs—another nod to the contemporary implications of the violence the play depicts[16]—force Mary to play the masculine role of Herod and, in effect, order the murder of John the Baptist. The death of the unfortunate Rizzio, who is killed in play and in actuality, foreshadows the execution of Mary herself and the mock beheading of Maree at the end of the play. Disgusted with her husband, Mary acquiesces in Bothwell's plan to murder Darnley in the name of "*justice*" (60, 66) for Rizzio, and turns at last to Bothwell's embrace with a kind of "black joy" (62, 71), the sexual abandon of despair. To the cries of "Burn the hoor!" (60, 67), again emphasizing both her contemporaries' and popular history's view of her as sexual criminal, adulteress and murderess, Mary and Bothwell separate.[17] Mary flees to England, where she is imprisoned for nineteen years and finally executed after Elizabeth, who can no longer tolerate Mary's magnetic power, even in prison, as the center of plots against herself, finally tricks her advisers into "trick[ing]" her into signing Mary's death warrant (63, 69).

Lochhead's Mary is warm-hearted, independent, generous, forbearing to the point of foolishness towards both Knox and Darnley, but rash and impolitic in pursuing her goals. Trying to have it both ways, she tolerates Protestantism, including Knox's abusive insults, but continues to hear mass privately. She exercises independence in choosing her own husband, but the choice itself is disastrous. She is implicated in the murder of Darnley since, after one moment of hesitation, she does nothing to stop it and throws herself into the murderer Bothwell's arms. Elizabeth's advisers cite the political danger that Mary represents, but Lochhead's play is silent about Mary's role in the plots against Elizabeth, possibly because the conspiracies are an English rather than a Scottish political problem, and in any case Mary had already condemned herself to her ultimate trial and death when she fled Scotland for England. The last nineteen years of English captivity are a coda. At the end of the play

Mary goes bravely to her death. By contrast, Elizabeth subdues her sexual desire, at a cost, and schemes skillfully and successfully to keep both her throne and her reputation as a wise and virgin queen.

Less even-handed than Schiller, less sentimental than Anderson, and more politically astute than Anderson or Bolt, Lochhead guides the audience to respond sympathetically but not uncritically to Mary in a variety of ways: through the contrast with Elizabeth certainly, but also through the approving comments of Bothwell and especially through the acerbic choric voice of La Corbie, whose role as commentator the 2009 text reinforces. Bothwell praises Mary because she has "affordit oor New Truth toleration" (49, 52) and supports her because by remaining on the throne she assures Scottish independence from "the bliddy English" (50, 53), a sentiment likely to resonate with contemporary Scottish audiences. La Corbie is at times overtly, but often amusingly, critical of Mary, advising her, ineffectually, to get rid of Knox, despising her choice of the boy Darnley as a husband, and, though sympathizing with Mary's sexual desire ("Ach, here we go. . ." [2009: 36]), approving rather Elizabeth's refusal to subject herself to a husband: "Thon's a quine wi her heid screwed oan. An Mary . . . ?" (2009: 23). Despite these concerns, La Corbie "*is, always and quite openly, partial*" on Mary's side (2009: 7), supporting her as Scottish queen, Catholic, and woman. La Corbie is appalled by the story she has to tell and "*devastated*" by Mary's execution (2009: 72).

Lochhead's re-evaluation of the life and death of Mary Queen of Scots—woman, monarch, and myth—focuses, however, not as much on reinterpreting historical facts or prejudices for or against Mary, as Schiller, Anderson, and Bolt do, but on looking at the consequences of these factors, which we may see as literal or metaphorical, but in either case actual. Through the judicious use of anachronism, Lochhead imbricates contemporary sectarian prejudice and cultural sexism in the events of Mary's life and death.[18] The followers of John Knox singing their anti-Catholic "*Good and Godly Ballad*" (47, 50) are also contemporary marching Orangemen. Knox's misogynistic belittling of the Queen of Scotland as

Mary Queen of Scots 151

a "silly spilte wee French lassie" (34, 34) resonates with patronizing put-downs of powerful women centuries later. Equally familiar is Knox's justification of sexual violence with reference to the Bible. Speaking to Mairn/Mary, he says, "Nae wunder it is written in the Guid Book that your kind are the very gate and port o the devil – Ah'll leave the rid mark o ma haun on your white flesh afore Ah – " (33, 33). Here Knox articulates the intertwining of religious and sexual anxieties that, in Lochhead's reading of events, forced Mary to flee to England, and thus to her trial and death.

The contemporary Scottish children's merciless re-enactment of Mary's beheading in the theatrically powerful "Jock Tamson's Bairns" scene serves as Lochhead's final indictment of the historical events she has depicted. Inasmuch as little Maree Stewart *is* Mary Queen of Scots (played, of course, by the same actress), the audience, like La Corbie, has been compelled to watch "*this bloody game again*" (2009: 73) and to understand that Maree/Mary, with Johnny Knox up her skirt/in her face and Wee Betty directing her tormenters, is victimized because she is pretty, female, and Catholic. The scene depicts Scotland still troubled by religious tensions that are still played out in gendered forms of torment. This is why La Corbie despairs, and this is why Mary Queen of Scots *always* gets her head chopped off.

Notes

1. Both Mary and Elizabeth were sexually vilified by their political enemies (Eggert 135-136), but the charges of adultery and murder made against Mary in what was, in effect, her first trial in 1568—charges that were politically useful to Elizabeth in providing moral grounds for refusing to help restore a sister queen regnant to her throne—continued to be debated after Mary's death and indeed took over the historiography of her life and reign until the latter part of the twentieth century (Wormald 178-179, 15).
2. Liz Lochhead is (since 2011) the Scots Makar (national poet of Scotland).
3. When quoting lines that are, essentially, identical in both texts, I give the page number from the 1989 text first and the 2009 text second. Quotations from all four plays discussed in this essay are taken from the texts listed in the Works Cited. The quotation from Schiller's *Mary Stuart* is taken from Jeremy Sams's translation.
4. In the Preface to his own translation/ adaptation of *Mary Stuart* Stephen Spender suggests that Mortimer is a "composite ghost" from Mary's past.
5. See Swales 46, 66, 73; Sharpe 271. Mary's view of herself as a Catholic martyr is historical. At her execution she wore, beneath her black dress, a red petticoat and bodice. Red is the Catholic liturgical color for martyrdom (Fraser 538).
6. An almost contemporaneous film, *Mary, Queen of Scots* (1971), starring Vanessa Redgrave as Mary and Glenda Jackson as Elizabeth, attempts, somewhat unsuccessfully, to combine elements treated in all three of the preceding plays: Mary is romantic, sexual, implicated in murder, outwitted by crafty Elizabeth, and dies as a Catholic martyr, though the scarlet dress she reveals at her execution evokes whoredom at least as much as martyrdom.
7. A reading of Antonia Fraser's comprehensive biography, *Mary Queen of Scots*, which Lochhead may well have known, indicates how much in both event and dialogue Lochhead draws on historical sources for her play.
8. In dispensing with Fiddler and Dancer, the 2009 text loses some of the wild strangeness of the earlier version, but other changes create greater narrative and thematic clarity—for example in the role of La Corbie

as sympathetic, if acerbic, commentator, linking sixteenth-century and present-day Scotland.

9. See Varty 163.
10. The childhood game entails chanting "Mary Queen of Scots got her head chopped off" while flicking off the head of a dandelion (Lochhead 2009: vi). La Corbie in both the 1989 and 2009 texts substitutes a (symbolically named) marigold as she chants the words that the children enact.
11. See Scullion, "A Woman's Voice," for a discussion of the Scottish political and cultural context in which *Mary Queen of Scots Got Her Head Chopped Off* was written and received. I would suggest that the more recent debates over Scottish independence, culminating in the vote to remain part of the United Kingdom, reassert the importance of *Mary Queen of Scots Got Her Head Chopped Off* as a play about nation.
12. Several critics have commented on the links among nation, religion, and gender in *Mary Queen of Scots Got Her Head Chopped Off* and the way in which the final scene draws out the implications of those historical links for the present day. See Koren-Deutsch 429-430; Varty 161-162; McCulloch 7-8; Braun 204, 207, 209. These critics are responding to the 1989 text. While drawing on both texts, I focus especially on the 2009 revision. In her Foreword to *Liz Lochhead: Five Plays* (2012), which reproduces the 2009 text of *Mary Queen of Scots Got Her Head Chopped Off*, Lochhead asserts her willingness to "stand by *these* versions" of the collected plays (vii).
13. An early draft suggests that the "Jock Tamson's Bairns" scene, originally the first scene of the play, is set outside a Glasgow tenement in 1953 (Varty 161), the period of Lochhead's (born 1947) own childhood.
14. McCulloch notes that in the 1980s Lochhead began to bring gender and country together explicitly in her work, culminating in *Mary Queen of Scots Got Her Head Chopped Off* (7). Varty quotes Lochhead's comment "Scotland is like a woman" from an interview with John Cunningham in the *Guardian*, February 8, 1990 (164).
15. This wish is based on a joke historically made by Mary (Fraser 167).
16. See McCulloch 42-43. On violence connected to sectarianism and football in contemporary Glasgow, see Macmillan 17-18.
17. For the historical shouting of "burn the whore," see Fraser 331.
18. On continuing tensions between Protestants and Catholics in contemporary Scotland see McCulloch 7-8, 46-47; Devine. For gender inequality see www.Scotland.gov.uk/Topics/People/ Equality/18500/GenderBackground. Updated July 8, 2011. Viewed August 21, 2012. While anti-

Catholicism has significantly diminished in Scotland in the last forty years, "the catcalls of 'Fenian Bitch'" directed at Helen Liddell, the Catholic Labour candidate in a 1994 by-election (Macmillan 21), echo only too clearly the conflation of sexual and religious bias to which Mary Queen of Scots was subjected.

Works Cited

Anderson, Maxwell. *Mary of Scotland*. New York: Doubleday, Doran & Company, Inc., 1934. Print.

Bolt, Robert. *Vivat! Vivat Regina!* London: Heinemann, 1971. Print.

Braun, Anne-Kathrin. *Dramatic Laboratories: Figurations of Subjectivity in Liz Lochhead's Writings*. Leipzig Explorations in Literature and Culture 9. Glienicke, Berlin and Madison WI: Galda and Wilch Verlag, 2004. Print.

Devine, T.M., ed. *Scotland's Shame? Bigotry and Sectarianism in Modern Scotland*. Edinburgh and London: Mainstream Publishing, 2000. Print.

Eggert, Katherine. *Showing Like a Queen: Female Authority and Literary Experiment in Spenser, Shakespeare, and Milton*. Philadelphia: University of Pennsylvania Press, 2000. Print.

Fraser, Antonia. *Mary Queen of Scots*. New York: Delacorte Press, 1969. Print.

Koren-Deutsch, Ilona S. "Feminist Nationalism in Scotland: *Mary Queen of Scots Got Her Head Chopped Off*." *Modern Drama* 35 (Sept. 1992): 424-432. Print.

Lochhead, Liz. *Liz Lochhead: Five Plays*. London: Nick Hern Books, 2012. Print.

--------. *Mary Queen of Scots Got Her Head Chopped Off and Dracula*. Harmondsworth: Penguin Books, 1989. Print.

--------. *Mary Queen of Scots Got Her Head Chopped Off*. London: Nick Hern Books, 2009. Print.

MacMillan, James. "Scotland's Shame." *Scotland's Shame? Bigotry and Sectarianism in Modern Scotland*, ed. Devine, T. M. Edinburgh and London: Mainstream Publishing, 2000. Print.

McCulloch, Margery Palmer. *Liz Lochead's* Mary Queen of Scots Got Her Head Chopped Off. Glasgow: Association for Scottish Literary Studies 200, rpt. 2007. Print.

McDonald, Jan, and Jennifer Harvie. "Putting New Twists to Old Sories: Feminism and Lochhead's Drama." *Liz Lochhead's Voices*, ed. Crawford,

Robert and Anne Varty. Edinburgh: Edinburgh University Press, 1993: 124-147. Print.

Palmer, Richard H. *The Contemporary British History Play.* Westport, CT, 1998. Print.

Schiller, Friedrich. *Mary Stuart,* trans. Sams, Jeremy. London: Nick Hern Books, 1996. Print.

-----. *Mary Stuart,* trans. Spender, Stephen. New Haven and New York: Ticknor and Fields, 1980. Print.

Scullion, Adrienne. "A Woman's Voice." *The Edinburgh Companion to Liz Lochhead.*, ed. Varty, Anne. Edinburgh: University of Edinburgh Press, 2013: 116-125. Print.

Sharpe, Lesley. *Friedrich Schiller: Drama, Thought and Politics.* Cambridge: Cambridge Univerity Press, 1991. Print.

Somerville-Arjat, Gillean, and Rebecca E. Wilson. *Sleeping with Monsters: Conversations with Scottish and Irish Women Poets.* Edinburgh: Polygon, 1990. Print.

Swales, Erika. *Schiller: Maria Stuart.* London. Grant and Cutler Ltd., 1988. Print.

Varty, Anne. "Scripts and Performances." *Liz Lochhead's Voices,* ed. Crawford, Robert and Anne Varty. Edinburgh: Edinburgh University Press, 1993: 148-169. Print.

Wormald, Jenny. *Mary, Queen of Scots: Politics, Passion and a Kingdom Lost.* London and New York: Tauris Parke Paperbacks, rev.ed. 2001. Print.

Chapter 7.

Witchcraft Trials in Arthur Miller's *The Crucible* and Caryl Churchill's *Vinegar Tom*

Amelia Howe Kritzer

Witchcraft Trials in History

Belief in witchcraft was once ubiquitous, and for a span of two centuries was defined as a crime and judged in the courts of western countries. During this period, witchcraft was treated as an actual, if unusual, phenomenon in plays like Shakespeare's *Macbeth* (c. 1606) and the co-authored play *The Witch of Edmonton* (Thomas Dekker, John Ford, and William Rowley, 1621). In England and the English colonies in America, persecution of those perceived to be witches rose in the sixteenth century, peaked in the seventeenth century, and even as it peaked began to be questioned.¹ By the end of the seventeenth century, the belief had died out. The English Parliament repealed the legislation outlawing witchcraft in 1736, amid renegotiation of the relationship between church and state (Bostridge 180-181); but, as Bostridge notes, "by the time of the repeal... this belief had become a matter for ridicule, seriously entertained only by the marginalized, the eccentric, or the vulgar" (203).

In the modern period, rejection of the idea of witchcraft has become as common as the belief in witches was in earlier times. Thus, when modern and contemporary playwrights dramatize witchcraft trials, they write from the standpoint of outrage regarding the misuse of the courts and the miscarriage of justice represented by those trials. The drama that characterized many witchcraft persecutions provides rich material for constructing characters and situations through which audiences may identify with the accused and more fully understand the nature and extent of the injustices that were perpetrated in the witch hunts. Both plays considered in this essay—*The Crucible* (1953) by Arthur Miller and *Vinegar Tom* (1976) by Caryl Churchill—rely on the audience's understanding of the witchcraft trials as flagrant examples of prejudice and scapegoating.

The witchcraft persecutions provide a classic example of women subjected to accusation, trial, and punishment because of perceived failure to comply with gender expectations. David H. Hall notes that in seventeenth-century New England women were accused of witchcraft four times as often as were men, and that women over the ages of forty were disproportionately charged (6-7). Hall goes on to write:

> The prosecution of women as witches occurred in a society in which men exercised substantial authority—legal, political, ideological, and economic—over women. It is possible to interpret witch-hunting as a means of reaffirming this authority at a time when some women (like the charismatic spiritual leader Anne Hutchinson) were testing these constraints, and when others were

experiencing a degree of independence, as when women without husbands or male siblings inherited property (7).

In supporting this argument, Hall cites as an example the case of a Connecticut woman who, in 1669, complained of physical abuse at the hands of her husband, but saw the charges overturned when her husband claimed the bruises on her body were produced by witchcraft (*ibid.*). He emphasizes that "witch-hunting was... a process that began at the village level before moving to the courts" (10). Thus a woman whose appearance or behavior did not conform to local expectations, and especially any woman who quarreled with her neighbors, expressed anger towards anyone, or became a burden on the charitable apparatus of the community was vulnerable to accusations.

The two plays considered in this essay differ markedly in their treatment of the gender politics of the witch hunts. *Vinegar Tom*, which Caryl Churchill wrote in association with the feminist theatre company Monstrous Regiment, presents witchcraft as an ideology aimed at controlling women. It consciously and specifically prompts audiences to analyze the witchcraft trials of seventeenth-century England as an example of the gender policing that continues to exert powerful effects on contemporary women. *The Crucible*, uses and adapts historical material from the best-known witch hunt of the American colonial era, which took place in Salem, Massachusetts in 1692-93, to make a statement about the then-current persecution of those thought to be Communist and to highlight one man's struggle to remain true to himself when placed under the pressure of an unjust accusation. Miller's play sidelines the women, limits their dimensionality, and in doing so reveals the patriarchal structure of gender relations that prevailed in the 1950s and is replicated without question in the play.

The Crucible

In an essay published in *The Guardian* in 2000, Miller acknowledged the link between his portrayal of the Salem witch trials and his perception of the hearings spearheaded by Senator Joe McCarthy during the 1950s, aimed at discovering clandestine Communist sympathizers within the United States:

> It would probably never have occurred to me to write a play about the Salem witch trials of 1692 had I not seen some astonishing correspondences with that calamity in the America of the late 40s and early 50s. My basic need was to respond to a phenomenon which, with only small exaggeration, one could say paralysed a whole generation and in a short time dried up the habits of trust and toleration in public discourse ("Are You Now Or Were You Ever?").

At the basis of both persecutions Miller saw a kind of hysteria at work. He goes on to write, in the *Guardian* essay, of "anxiety, sometimes directed towards foreigners, Jews, Catholics, fluoridated water, aliens in space, masturbation, homosexuality, or the Internal Revenue Department" (*ibid*). He also identified, in both instances of ever-widening accusations and little or no actual evidence, the crucial role of the informer: "Should the accused confess, his honesty could only be proved by naming former confederates. The informer became the axle of the plot's existence and the investigation's necessity" (*ibid.*).

To dramatize the effect of pressure to inform, Miller chose, out of the twenty victims of execution, the dozen who died in jail, and the two hundred accused—many of whom had their lives permanently disrupted, even if the charge was dropped—one man: John Proctor. John is the character whose trial we witness in detail. This focus expressed the artistic-political vision Miller articulated in his 1949 essay "Tragedy and the Common Man," published in the *New York Times*, in which he argued for the continuing possibility and relevance of Aristotelian tragedy. He proposed that "the tragic feeling is evoked in us when we are in the presence of a character who is ready to lay down his life, if need be, to secure one thing—his sense of personal dignity." Miller shaped John Proctor as an Aristotelian tragic hero: a respected man in his community, he attracts admiration when subjected to the pressures of the dramatic situation, but falls from his respected position because of a tragic flaw. John's tragic flaw is a simple one: he had succumbed to his sexual attraction to Abigail Williams, a leader within the group of adolescent girls whose bizarre behavior and accusations set the witch hunt in motion.[2] Thus, while he has been known to express scorn at the very idea of witchcraft—an offense likely to bring him under suspicion—it is because Abigail wishes to take the place of his wife Elizabeth that first Elizabeth and then John are arrested.

Placed in the crucible of emotion-fueled accusations set in motion by adolescent girls but propelled by the fear, zealotry, and arrogance of other men, John encounters and accepts the truth of his life. Intent on saving Elizabeth, he reveals to the court examiners his infidelity to her in order to undermine Abigail's credibility; this confession, however, depends on Elizabeth's confirmation, and she refuses to acknowledge this shame publicly in court. Accustomed to feeling strong and independent, John finds himself helpless to stem the tide of mendacity that overwhelms his family and community. Finally, on the eve of being hanged, he considers offering a false confession for the sake of remaining alive; as he explains to Elizabeth, he cannot pretend to the virtuous life of others among the condemned, and therefore should not die a martyr's death among them. At the last, however, though he has offered a verbal confession, he refuses to sign it, because, as he says, "it is *my name*. . . . I may not live without my name" [emphasis original] (90).[3] John Proctor's name is the public emblem of his identity, and he cannot allow others to control it—in this case, to validate the proceedings and continue the prosecutions. As John goes to his death, Elizabeth says, "He have his goodness now" (Miller, *Crucible* 91).

Elizabeth's pronouncement, which ends the play, emphasizes her role in it as a witness to John's moral struggles and eventual decision to give his life in order to maintain his "sense of personal dignity" (Miller, "Tragedy and the Common Man"). Her speech recalls that of the long-suffering Linda Loman in *Death of a Salesman* (1949), who insists that "attention must be paid" to her husband Willy because "he's a human being, and a terrible thing is happening to him" (Miller, *Collected Plays*: 162). Neither Elizabeth nor Linda, despite the centuries separating their fictional lives, has access to personal dignity except through identification with her husband. In *The Crucible* Miller signals implicit acceptance of this differential between husbands and wives by referring to John Proctor as "Proctor" and Elizabeth Proctor as "Elizabeth" in the script's stage directions. Elizabeth, like Linda, is married to an unfaithful man, but cannot make this violation known to others; thus, her own claim to dignity depends on denial of truth. Elizabeth's own trial on charges of witchcraft is not presented in the play; instead, her trial occurs when she is called in to testify as John is being examined. He has told the court that she "cannot lie" (69). Nevertheless, when she is ordered to answer the direct question, "To your knowledge, has John Proctor ever committed the crime of lechery?" (70), she denies that he has, even though private conversations between Elizabeth and John previous to this scene indicate her certain knowledge of his infidelity. To be accorded respect as a wife, she must maintain the good name of her husband. To lose the respect of those around her would place her in the first category of women who were tried and convicted of witchcraft—those like Bridget Bishop, Goody Osburn, and Sarah Good, marked by poverty, unfeminine behavior such as "smokin' a pipe," and, worst offense of all, having "*no husband*" [emphasis original] (33).

The lack of a position from which to express the individual truth of her own thoughts and experience and make a claim to individual "goodness" or "attention" forms a central aspect of gender construction in patriarchal systems. Catherine Belsey writes of this gender mechanism as "an uncertain place" (149) in her study of Renaissance-era tragic drama.

Her description of women characters and readers in Renaissance drama clearly applies to *The Crucible*:

> Permitted to break their silence in order to acquiesce in the utterances of others, women were denied any single place from which to speak for themselves. A discursive instability in the texts about women has the effect of withholding from women readers any single position which they can identify as theirs. And at the same time a corresponding instability is evident in the utterances attributed to women: they speak with equal conviction from incompatible subject-positions, displaying a discontinuity of being, an 'inconstancy' which is seen as characteristically feminine (149).

The virtuous women, like Rebecca Nurse and Martha Corey, who go heroically to their deaths are almost silent in the play's scenes. Both Rebecca Nurse and Elizabeth Proctor speak with authority at times, but only in private contexts, and only in relation to matters such as childbearing, child-rearing, and the protection of children. When they are arrested, their husbands speak for them. In her trial, Martha Corey begins giving simple, spare answers to the questions of the judge, but the proceedings are almost immediately interrupted by the clamorous speech of Giles Corey and Francis Nurse, demanding that the judge take into account evidence they have brought into court. The only last words reported from the executions are the two of Giles Corey: "more weight" (85), as he is pressed to death by stones.

The women who do speak out, attract attention, and ultimately gain power and freedom within the context of the play, are the young accusers, led by Abigail Williams, the teenage girl labeled a whore by John Proctor. The label "whore" sets Abigail apart from the other women and serves as a paradoxical emblem of her power. She exerts a magnetic pull on John Proctor, of which she is aware and which gives her confidence that he will return to her and eventually marry her, in spite of his repeatedly stated intention to end the relationship. Furthermore, her knowledge and enjoyment of the sexual act has evidently given her the power to judge the people of the Salem community as "hypocrites in their hearts" (49). The theatrical and highly sexual act of dancing naked in the woods attributed to Abigail in the play (a Miller invention rather than a historical report) serves to initiate the witch hunt. The dramatic and sexually charged demonstrations of being bewitched given by Abigail and the other girls in court hold the entire community in thrall; though the veracity of these demonstrations is questioned by the accused, those with the power to judge never think to put the accusers on trial. That this hypnotic effect on the all-male legal officials owes something to sex appeal is suggested in Abigail's admission to John Proctor, during their secret meeting, that she has been at the local tavern every night to "play shovelboard with the Deputy Governor" (48), who has been brought in to preside over the court. When Mary Warren joins the others in court testimony, her newfound authority prompts her to announce to the Proctors that she will "not stand *whipping any more*" (33) and will "not be ordered to bed *no more*" [emphases original] (34). Finally, the chaos engendered by their accusations allows Abigail, along with the "sly, merciless" (10) Mercy Lewis, to escape from Salem with money stolen from Reverend Parris. Miller shows these young women as the source of potent evil in the community and strongly suggests that their evil originates in their sexual magnetism and potential for sexual pleasure.

As Iska Alter notes, Miller places the play's most visible women, Elizabeth Proctor and Abigail Williams, at opposite poles of feminine power. Elizabeth, the wife, concerns herself primarily with defending those she cares about, and does so by means of her place in the community: as she is taken away by the authorities, she gives instructions regarding the children, and when John is also arrested she arranges for their care. Elizabeth, whose execution is postponed because of pregnancy, evidently does not lack fertility, but she does not embody the kind of sexual promise that is the source of Abigail's power. John often refers to Elizabeth as sickly, and she describes herself as "a cold wife. . . so plain, so poorly made" (86), blaming his adultery on her own lack of warmth and beauty. These competing forms of feminine power highlight John

Proctor, suspended between them and ultimately unable to negotiate them in a way that preserves his life and the community's fabric. This feminine duality effectively emasculates John Proctor: rendered impotent, he is hanged with the convicted women.[4]

The play engages the audience at the emotional level, as it takes them through a succession of efforts that seem to have the potential to save the accused, only to show the ultimate failure of each one. John Proctor dominates this protracted emotional contest between the accusers and the accused, while the play downplays the violence against women that characterized the witch hunts.[5] This arousal of emotional identification accords with Millers' structuring of the play as an Aristotelian tragedy. As a political play, however, it presents two characters whose lack of involvement in the emotional contest between the accused and the accusers suggests the possibility of a different outcome. The two are Tituba and Reverend Hale. Tituba, a black slave woman brought from Barbados to Massachusetts by the Parris family, stands out as the quintessential outsider. Her expressed attitudes contest those of the Puritans: she does not fear the devil, whom she views as a "pleasure man" (76), and calls upon to "take [her] home" (77) to Barbados.[6] The implication that a pervasive guilt in relation to sexual and other pleasures may lie at the basis of the witch hunts and subsequent persecutions is not developed, but merely offered as a hint in a historical period known for sexual inhibition as well as for scapegoating those suspected to have some Communist connection. The second person is the learned Reverend Hale, also an outsider, who arrives with a load of books and hovers around the proceedings observing everything. By the end of the play, Hale has seen enough to consider the imminent hanging of John Proctor to be murder, but at this point it is too late to do anything to save him or the others. Thus, Hale the intellectual, like Tituba, the adherent to an alternate belief system, ultimately serve merely to heighten the emotion of the tragedy through their powerlessness. The audience, as its emotion is purged, may be left with an uncomfortable impression created by the sexual politics beneath the surface of the main story—the impression that women, whether the good ones who follow the rules for their gender or the bad ones who violate them, inevitably prove to be a source of trouble for men.

Vinegar Tom

Caryl Churchill's 1976 play *Vinegar Tom* confronts the idea of women as trouble by presenting a community, though not a historically specific one, in which everyday failures and conflicts between individuals coalesce into a general sense of dread. This feeling culminates in an urgent desire to identify witches, rid the community of them, and thus purge the uncomfortable and inexplicable fear that has come to dominate their lives. Working with the feminist theatre collective Monstrous Regiment, Churchill attempts not only to view the well-known story of the witch hunts through a contemporary feminist perspective, but also to resist conventional paradigms for drama, such as Aristotelian tragedy, and communicate through new dramatic forms and unconventional combinations of character, narrative, and theme. Therefore, while dealing with a historical phenomenon, *Vinegar Tom* simultaneously comments on the persistence and significance of the attitudes underlying the witch hunts through a series of songs, written in contemporary language and performed by actors in contemporary dress, that point to continuing misogyny. This play, in contrast to *The Crucible*, has no protagonist and does not heighten emotion through the use of oppositions. Instead, it questions oppositions through doubling (in which actors play more than one role), and emphasizes what Churchill has referred to as the "petty and everyday" (130)[7] nature of the offenses with which the accused women were charged, rather than exploiting the melodramatic aspects of the witch hunts. Its twenty brief scenes reveal a collage of village life in the seventeenth century, suggesting the period with costumes and a few props.

Vinegar Tom shows the accused as women marginalized in their community, who are then accused, persecuted, and condemned when they do not accept the subordination inherent in their gender and class

Witchcraft Trials 167

position. Alice, an unmarried mother, copulates with an unidentified gentleman in a roadside ditch. "Am I the devil?" 135), he asks her, initiating a one-sided conversation about beliefs in which he simultaneously yearns for and bitterly attacks religion. Despite the hints he gives of sadism, she asks eagerly to go away with him, but he spurns her, calling her "a whore" (137).[8] Joan, Alice's mother, a widow living in poverty, asks her neighbor for a bit of yeast, but the neighbor refuses coldly, and Joan responds with anger. Ellen, an herbal healer, operates outside the regular economy of the village and employs knowledge not understood by her neighbors. Susan, a young mother exhausted by continual pregnancies, goes to Ellen for help to abort the fetus conceived while still nursing her baby. Each of these women exemplifies some type of gender nonconformity, and each finds herself accused of witchcraft in the course of the play. Churchill created this group of women on the basis of her observation, following her historical research, that "women accused of witchcraft were often those on the edges of society, old, poor, single, sexually unconventional. . . ." (129-130). The lack of value accorded these women becomes clear in a gestic moment late in the play, when Joan, desperate to postpone her hanging, claims to be pregnant; her statement, dismissed with scorn, emphasizes the fact that she is no longer fertile or productive.

Fertility and productivity appear as preoccupations among the villagers, and thus form the basis of anxieties. Fertility, potency, prosperity, and success are central to the lives of these people, but always uncertain. When good fortune turns sour, do its victims blame themselves, remain baffled by the change, or seek to blame someone? Accusations among the villagers arise out of the kind of everyday misfortunes and grievances compiled in historical studies of witch hunts.[9] Margery and Jack, prosperous tenant farmers, have plans for expanding their holdings, but encounter difficulties. Margery cannot get butter to "come" (142), despite her endless churning and chanting; she associates this failure with the presence of Joan's cat, Vinegar Tom, sneaking around her dairy. Jack, who has become impotent with his wife, accuses her of laziness. Jack pursues

Alice for sex, but she refuses him. He persists in harassing her until Joan intervenes, and when he threatens to "break [Joan's] neck," she retorts with a curse: "You lift your hand to me, may it drop off" (148). The uneasiness expressed by Margery and Jack escalates sharply when first a cow, then several calves die of an unrecognized ailment. Margery feels herself struck by an invisible blow, and Jack complains that his penis has been stolen and that his hand has become paralyzed. Measuring their escalating misfortunes against their sins, they decide they must be victims of witchcraft, and their suspicion immediately targets Joan. Packer, the witch finder, is summoned, and his inquiries soon result in not only Joan, but also Alice, Susan, and Ellen, being charged.

The trials of the suspected witches take a physical form. The women's words are disregarded, and their speech is rendered meaningless, as the witch finders seek evidence on the women's bodies. Goody, Packer's assistant, who considers herself privileged to "work with a great professional" (168), conducts physical examinations in which she pricks each accused woman repeatedly with needles to find the spot "made insensitive to pain by the devil" (165). Goody views this work, for which she is well paid, as normal and beneficial to society. Proceeding in a methodical manner, despite the screaming and cursing of the women being pricked, Goody also shaves the women's genital areas to search for "devil's marks" (173) that are considered proof of guilt, though Packer observes that the absence of such a mark does not establish the woman's innocence. Alluding to other practices for identifying witches, Ellen considers that she might "ask to be swum" (169) when she learns that she is suspected:

They think the water won't keep a witch in. . . so if a woman floats she's a witch. And if she sinks they have to let her go. I could sink. Any fool could sink. It's how to sink without drowning (*ibid.*). Thus in various ways, the play shows that the trials offer no possibility for the accused woman to establish that she is not a witch, or even to establish an identity through speech. To be accused is to be placed in a double-bind situation with no way out, to have one's identity erased, to be judged guilty, and to be hanged.

The only speech act on the part of the accused woman considered to have meaning by the witch finders is the confession. Goody and Packer take turns in beating a drum to keep the women awake, using sleep deprivation as a form of torture to force confessions. Goody laments the fact that England is "too soft with its witches" (168), forbidding the methods practiced elsewhere:

> [I]n other countries they have the thumbscrews and racks and the bootikens which is said to be the worst pain in the world, for it fits tight over the leg from ankle to knee and is driven tighter and tighter till the legs are crushed. . . And very few continue their lies and denials then. (*ibid.*)

The accused women, denied any route to exoneration, are subjected to the worst forms of torture their society permits in order to further deny them an authentic voice. The four accused women react to this pressure in different ways. Joan makes a voluble confession in which she names those toward whom she has harbored resentment and hatred. Susan, agonized by guilt over the abortion and the subsequent death of the baby she was nursing, confesses to sins she is sure she has committed, naming others in her grief. Ellen, who had thought, or hoped that rationality would prevail when she explained that "healing, not harm" (170) was the intent of her work, is given no final speech; instead, she is shown with Joan at the end, hanging from the gallows—an anonymous body. Only Alice retains her defiant voice: as she watches the hanging of Joan and Ellen, while awaiting her own, she expresses anger at the women's complete powerlessness:

> If I could meet with the devil now I'd give him anything if he'd give me power. There's no way for us except by the devil (175).

The play shows a parallel course for the young woman Betty, who is the daughter of the local landowner. Despite her privileged circumstances,

Betty lacks power and freedom. She has been promised in marriage to someone of her own class (perhaps the cruel, shadowy man with whom Alice has sex in the opening scene), but she is refusing to marry the man and even wishes that he would die. Betty continually seeks personal freedom: like the undeveloped character Betty Parris in *The Crucible*, she wants to fly. Her powerlessness leads to hysterical fits of screaming, like those of the adolescent girls in *The Crucible*. Betty is captured, locked up, tied, and subjected to repeated bleeding to force her compliance. Her situation thus shows elements of coercion and torture that are similar to those of the accused witches, but with this difference: while they are condemned for their inability to appear and behave in accordance with gender expectations, Betty is coerced into conforming to those expectations.

Vinegar Tom consciously presents the gender politics of the witchcraft trials. While indicating rational explanations for some of the events recorded as the basis of witchcraft accusations, it also highlights the social attitudes about gender that create double-binds for women in the past and today. The final scene of the play features an appearance by the historical Kramer (who used the Lain form of his name, Institoris, as a pen name) and Sprenger, co-authors of *Malleus Maleficarum*, the fifteenth-century handbook of witchcraft theory. The actors who have just been shown hanging, as Joan and Ellen, play the parts of Kramer and Sprenger, quoting from the text that linked witchcraft with female sexuality, asserting that woman "is more credulous. . . more impressionable," and "a liar by nature"—"an imperfect animal" that "cannot keep faith" (177) and is characterized by "insatiable malice" and "carnal lust. . . which is in woman. . . insatiable" (178). This recitation of the explicit ideology underlying not only the witch hunts but also more contemporary oppressions of women, exposes it to questioning, if not outright ridicule. However, the fact that female actors deliver these gems of misogyny suggests the extent to which women have been complicit in the oppression of all women through self-policing in order to achieve and maintain a relatively privileged position, and through the exclusionary attitudes and accusatory acts toward other women that often constitute the bitterest factor in gender politics.

Vinegar Tom attempts to move audiences beyond mere recognition of patriarchal gender ideology toward a more active involvement in contesting it. It counteracts the passivity inherent in viewing scenes of historical injustice with the Brechtian technique of songs that break up and refocus the action. The songs focus on aspects of contemporary gender oppression, with references to age discrimination, cosmetic surgery, psychiatric control, nationalism, and prejudice toward minority groups. The most important single issue highlighted in the songs is the externality of definitions of women. Just as the *Malleus Maleficarum* defined women in a way that was entirely outside their control and likely very separate from their lived experience, the gender norms of contemporary society are created by advertising and by visible celebrities. The final two songs address women and men separately, suggesting that women "ask how they're stopping you now" (176) and questioning men as to whether "evil women" play an important part in their system of erotic desire. The play thus exhibits the witchcraft trials as a phenomenon that is clearly part of past history, but also contextualizes it as one of many continually evolving forms of demonizing women.

Both *The Crucible* and *Vinegar Tom* are political plays. Both try to channel the outrage generated by the trials and convictions of innocent persons to propel the audience toward resistance to contemporary oppression and injustice. Both express concerns typical of the particular playwrights, with Miller presenting sexual tension in political terms and Churchill analyzing the politics of gender relations. *The Crucible*, which premiered during the time when Joseph McCarthy, the U.S. senator who led the anti-communist crusade, was active and influential, inspires audience members with a heroic male who stood up to the oppressors in spite of his character flaws. The women on trial in Miller's play serve primarily to call attention to this central, heroic male. Thus, an alternate story separate from the attempt to expose the injustices of McCarthyism plays out, in which Miller compounds the injustices toward women exemplified in the witch hunts by not giving the women a significant voice on their own behalf and by implicitly blaming the difficulties of the hero on conflicts arising from the sexuality of women. *Vinegar Tom*, which was conceived and produced in the context of a women's theatre company intent on articulating the feminist activism of the late 1970s, moves the focus to a group of female characters that collectively represent all women—young and old, learned and simple, weak and strong. It uses fear to warn audiences of the double binds inherent in patriarchal gender construction, and Brechtian-style analysis to summon energy to resist patriarchal norms that control women today. *The Crucible*, some sixty years after its premiere, has itself become a marker of history, while *Vinegar Tom*'s haunting suggestion to "ask how they're stopping you now" (*ibid.*) remains current.

Notes

1. In the Salem witchcraft trails in 1692-1693, for example, unease with the convictions mounted with the execution of well-respected citizens who refused to confess and died courageously, uttering prayers. The trials were halted, and when they were resumed under the newly instituted rule that "spectral" evidence would not be admitted, most of the accused were exonerated. During the subsequent two decades, as Peter Charles Hoffer records, the General Court dealt with the aftermath of these trials by "reversing the convictions, repudiating the trials, and paying off claims to kinsfolk of those who were executed" (136).
2. A number of critics have noted that Miller aged the historical Abigail Williams six years (from eleven to seventeen) to make the character's relationship with John Proctor plausible. See, for example, Alter, 1989.
3. All page numbers refer to the acting edition of *The Crucible*, originally published in 1954.
4. The fear of being emasculated by witchcraft is detailed in the account of witches stealing and collecting penises in the classic manual of witchcraft, *Malleus Maleficarum* (1486)—doubtless one of the "heavy books" (19) brought to the scene by Reverend Hale.
5. The accused in Salem were not subjected to torture, but did have to endure winter in unheated jails, supervision by male jailors, and forced intimate examinations of their bodies.
6. The play downplays the role of the historic Tituba in naming those who would be indicted for witchcraft. It also does not reveal her eventual fate: she was taken to Boston for trial, but freed when "the grand jury simply refused to believe her" (Hoffer 84). As Hoffer relates, her lengthy incarceration resulted in considerable costs, which her owner was required to play; lacking the money to do so, he sold her.
7. All page numbers refer to *Churchill Plays: One*.
8. Paola Botham, in an essay on *Vinegar Tom* that contrasts it with *The Crucible*, emphasizes the difference between Miller's character Abigail and Churchill's character Alice: unlike Abigail, who "tries to save her own skin by confessing (and encouraging others to confess). . . Alice in *Vinegar Tom* refuses to take part in the man's fantasy and reverses the terms of the proposition" (110).
9. See, for examples, Rosen and Gibson.

Works Cited

Alter, Iska. "Betrayal and Blessedness: Explorations of Feminine Power in *The Crucible, A View from the Bridge,* and *After the Fall,* in *Feminist Rereadings of Modern American Drama,* ed. June Schlueter. Cranbury, NJ: Associated University Presses, 1989. Print.

Belsey, Catherine. *The Subject of Tragedy: Identity and Difference in Renaissance Drama.* London and New York: Methuen, 1985. Print.

Bostridge, Ian. *Witchcraft and Its Transformations c. 1650-c. 1750.* Oxford: Clarendon Press, 1997. Print.

Botham, Paola. "Playwrights and Plays: Caryl Churchill," in *Modern British Playwriting: The 1970s,* ed. Megson, Chris. London: Methuen Drama, 2012. Print.

Churchill, Caryl. *Churchill Plays: One.* London: Methuen, 1985. Print.

Gibson, Marion, ed. *Witchcraft and Society in England and America, 1550-1750.* Ithaca: Cornell University Press, 2003. Print.

Hall, David D., ed. *Witch-Hunting in Seventeenth-Century New England: A Documentary History 1658-1695.* Second edition. Boston: Northeastern University Press, 1999.

Hoffer, Peter Charles. *The Salem Witchcraft Trials: A Legal History.* Lawrence: University Press of Kansas, 1997.

Miller, Arthur, "Are You Now Or Were You Ever," *The Guardian* June 17, 2000. Online.

--------. *Collected Plays.* New York: Viking Press, 1957. Print

--------. *The Crucible.* New York: Dramatists Play Service, 1954. Acting edition. Print.

--------."Tragedy and the Common Man." *New York Times* February 27, 1949. Online.

Rosen, Barbara, ed. *Witchcraft in England, 1558-1618.* Amherst: The University of Massachusetts Press, 1991. Originally published as *Witchcraft,* 1969. Print.

MODERN DRAMA

CHAPTER 8.

THE FLAPPER ON TRIAL IN *MACHINAL*

Miriam López-Rodríguez

WOMEN AND MURDER

A quick overview of those American plays where a woman is put on trial highlights an interesting feature: the most often repeated charge against the accused female seems to be that of murdering her abusive husband or partner. This characteristic is no accident, as evidence shows that in real life this is also the most common reason for an American woman to be accused of murder. As contemporary playwright Lynn Nottage states in an author's note in her short play *Poof!*, "nearly half the women on death row in the United States were convicted of killing abusive husbands" (i). This statement was Nottage's way of making clear to her readers or audience that the drama she had written was not simply a product of her imagination but was closely linked to real life. In spite of its employment of magic, Nottage's play, as many other plays on the subject written by American female playwrights, is closely linked to reality not only because statistics show that most American women convicted of murder had killed their abusive partners but also because the plots of most American plays where a woman is on trial for murder are based on real events. Such is the case, for example, of Sophie Treadwell's expressionist landmark *Machinal* (1928).

Social Context: Flappers and Sob Sisters

This essay analyzes Treadwell's often-dissected play, but not for the purpose of exploring its expressionist elements or its portrayal of structural violence; instead, it will focus on how Treadwell used the device of a trial to frame and highlight the construction of gender in 1920s America. At the center of *Machinal* is a trial where a female defendant faces a male judge, male lawyers, and male jurors—and is thus denied her constitutional right to be tried by a jury of her peers. To fully understand attitudes toward the female culprit both on the part of other characters in the play and of American audiences in the period when it was first produced, we must bear in mind historical aspects such as the economic and social consequences of the First World War, the struggle for woman's right to vote, the emergence of the flapper and the sob sister as media types, and, finally, the influence on Sophie Treadwell of real life trials she had covered as a journalist during the decade before writing *Machinal*.

The beginning of the twentieth century was marked both in Europe and the United States by an atmosphere of optimism and widespread hopes for a new period of new experiences and improved opportunities. The growing industrialization of the western world promised a better standard of living and more leisure time, among other things. This initial optimism, however, soon subsided as the political tensions in Europe made it clear that an international conflict was imminent. Once the First World War was declared, American politicians proclaimed the neutrality of the United States while their industries continued supplying the Allied forces. When the country became officially involved in April, 1917, the authorities launched a campaign to raise awareness among American women of their important role in the so-called home front by practicing economy in household expenses and applying to those jobs left vacant by the young men fighting in Europe. As Michael E. Parrish states, "with over one million men called to military duty by the first draft in 1917, employers [...] had little choice but to recruit women for these traditional male tasks" (140).

Whether women accepted the challenge in order to help the nation or to obtain economic independence, the fact is that the number of women working outside their homes rose significantly. However, as the war ended and soldiers returned, most of those women lost their jobs. Furthermore, the financial crisis of 1920 created a situation in which there were not enough jobs, even for men. Something good came out of this: President Woodrow Wilson urged Congress to reward women for their war effort by giving them the right to vote. The achievement of this historical landmark, however, proved disappointing, as most women were not interested in politics and either did not bother voting or "when they did vote, they cast their ballots much as their husbands, fathers, and male relatives did" (Parrish 142).

Women's suffrage was not the only consequence of the First World War: for many Americans, the war's end did not eliminate the effects of the shock they had endured in armed conflict on a scale never seen before. The war's thirty-seven million casualties led to collective trauma both in North America and Europe.[1] Compounding the trauma was a feeling that the sacrifices made during the conflict had been pointless. Both British and American societies feared the threat of a second Great War, and as time went by the political situation in countries such as Germany and Italy made it clear that another international conflict was more than just a mere possibility.

Those who fought in the war and never recovered from the experience became known as "the lost generation." Having witnessed the death and mutilation of so many young men, these survivors reacted by living as if there were no tomorrow. Life had to be enjoyed to the full, it was there and then. "*Carpe diem*" seemed to be the motto of a whole generation. With a clear disregard for what this generation felt and wanted, American authorities reacted to this pleasure-seeking attitude with the zeal of Puritans. In January, 1919, the government passed legislation making illegal the distillation, distribution and sale of alcoholic beverages. However, this initiative did not result in abstinence from alcoholic drinks or an attitude of temperance. Contrary to expectations, the implementation in January, 1920, of this legislation did not solve social problems connected with alcoholism or social violence, but led to the proliferation of speakeasies, the flourishing of gangsters and mafia organizations, and a general contempt for Prohibition.[2]

The sense of wasted youth, the disappointment with politics, and the general disdain for authority led to a questioning of social and moral values. The decade following the end of the conflict then referred to as the Great War saw the emergence of the flapper, the Jazz Age, and an intense thirst for the immediate pleasures of life difficult to understand by many. This change in ways of thinking strongly influenced new attitudes regarding the role of women in society. Given that a culture's construction of feminine gender is usually reflected in the attire considered appropriate for her, it is only logical that the new woman who emerged after the First World War did not dress like her pre-war counterpart.

During the nineteenth century American females were characterized by their "long hair, high brow, thirty-six-inch bust, narrow, anatomically precise waist, broad hips and well-concealed legs" (Yellis 44). This model woman preserved the nineteenth-century's prevailing value system with its concept of true womanhood and the defense of what were considered the four cardinal virtues of any female wanting to be considered a lady (or at least, a respectable woman): piety, purity, submission and domesticity. The quest for these four virtues was a life-long endeavor for many women, who had to fight back their longings for an existence outside the constraining limits of the domestic sphere; but the fear of becoming a social outcast if labeled a heathen, a tomboy, or a slut, kept most women compliant.

A small number of women resisted the cult of domesticity, in spite of the power it exerted in American culture, and fought for sexual equality. Woman suffragist activists such as Elizabeth Cady Stanton or Susan B. Anthony, and writers such as Louisa May Alcott and Kate Chopin advocated in their speeches and writings a different type of woman, a woman who questioned the rightness of some patriarchal values and looked for alternatives. In contrast to the "true woman," this politically and socially committed woman was labeled the "new woman." The new woman dressed as conservatively as her sisters, but without a corset, in an attempt to emphasize her rejection of patriarchal constraints and her wish to adapt female clothing to the new realities of women attending college or working in factories. Coexisting with the "true women" and the "new women," a third group of nineteenth century American women went one step further and refused to wear traditional long skirts. The so-called Bloomer girls wore, below a short skirt, long baggy trousers inspired by those traditionally worn by Turkish women. This loose fitting garment was intended to preserve a Victorian sense of modesty in public attire while at the same time providing women with less restraint on their movement and even permitting them to ride bicycles.

The abrupt end to life as it had been known that occurred with the First World War, along with the social developments that occurred in its wake, brought about further modifications of female attire. Young women from both Europe and Northern America altered their appearance, rejecting long hair put up in a bun in favor of a short hairstyle dubbed the bob, substituting short skirts that left the lower parts of their legs uncovered for the old-fashioned long ones, and eschewing form-fitting corsets for straight dresses that hid their waists and flattened their breasts. The finishing touch to this new look was the use of make up, a lot of it. Critics of these new fashions argued that the short hair and the curveless figure defeminized women, and indeed it can be seen that the women who adopted the new styles were interested in rejecting an entire construct of femininity that curbed their freedom in many ways.

The eradication of traditionally female features was not limited to appearance, as it also affected the behavior of young women: they smoked, drank alcohol, drove cars, danced provocatively, dated freely, and treated sex in a casual manner. All this, together with their increasing economic independence, made these young women freer than ever before. It was as if these girls were sowing their wild oats before settling down to a more traditional life as wives and mothers, but the changes of the Jazz Age affected not only young single women. Many middle-aged housewives also adopted a milder version of the new fashion, bobbing their hair and dancing the Charleston, the fox-trot and other popular dances considered provocative. Although most housewives remained at home taking care of the domestic chores and depending economically on their husbands, they also enjoyed a certain amount of emancipation and a better standard of living. As Kenneth A. Yellis indicates,

> Smaller, centrally heated houses were easier to clean, and many other families lived in apartments. Canned and frozen foods began to dominate the American diet, along with store-bought baked goods. Out-of-home housekeeping services and the availability of inexpensive mechanical and electrical devices in the home also tended to ease the housewife's burden. (55)

The most conservative members of society considered the increasing independence of females a threat, as they thought new women—both single and married—jeopardized social stability, marriage and the traditional family. Unsurprisingly, they questioned the morality of the women who adopted the new fashion. Going beyond criticism, they resorted to sneering at the young, fashionable women using the derogative term "flapper." The word had originated in England at the end of the nineteenth century to designate a young prostitute, and it made clear their opinion about the moral standards of the women to whom it was applied.

The Flapper on Trial in *Machinal*

In the first decades of the twentieth century, at about the same time of the appearance of the flapper, and for very similar reasons, another female prototype came into existence in the United States: the so-called "sob sister." This second type of woman is also essential to understand Sophie Treadwell's creation of *Machinal*, its protagonist and her trial. As previously mentioned, the developments that occurred early in the twentieth century meant that "women on all social levels were facing changes in life-styles, expectations, and responsibilities. This led to a great deal of confusion about women's role in the house and at the workplace" (Abramson 3). Alterations in the concept of womanhood brought, of course, a transformation of society and the workforce. One of the fields of work women entered was that of journalism. Women began writing for newspapers and magazines, initially in what were considered female fields such as cooking, and fashion. Soon, however, women journalists asked for more. At the same time, as Abramson indicates, "the press, too, was undergoing profound changes. There was a shift in emphasis from editorial comment and preoccupation with affairs of the government to wider fields of news and human interest" (3). It was in this field of "human interest" that women journalists found a new niche of opportunity: taking advantage of patriarchal prejudices, they contended that, if women were morally superior and intrinsically more sensitive, it was only logical that they covered this type of news.

Along with the increasing number of women in journalism, another fact of great significance for the change of assignments given to women journalists was the transformation of the average newspaper readers. Little by little, largely motivated by the increase of leisure time among middle-class women, a growing number of females became regular readers of newspapers, journals, and magazines. For them the press became a way to escape the boredom of their lives, while at the same time staying at home; thus, preserving their reputation as wives and mothers. Avid businessmen were quick to respond: "Publishers and editors, recognizing this trend, began to cater specifically for them with news, features, and pictures" (Abramson 23). Men of questionable ethics but undoubted success, such as William Randolph Hearst, owner of the *San Francisco Examiner* and the *New York Journal*, or Joseph Pulitzer, of the *New York World*, found a gold mine in sensational journalism. Putting aside their sexism, they hired more and more women to write for these new female readers who were eager for the vicarious thrill of sensational human-interest coverage. Scandals were welcome; the more gruesome the details, the better. The exposés, crusading stories, and undercover serials of journalists such as Djuna Barnes, Winifred Black, Willa Cather, Dorothy Dix, Edna Ferber, Zona Gale, Martha Gellhorn, Susan Glaspell, Nixola Greely-Smith, Josephine Lawrence, Ada Patterson, Katherine Anne Porter, Tess Slesinger, Rose Wilder Lane, and of course Sophie Treadwell, revolutionized the history of American journalism and the role of women in it.

It was in 1907, with one of these scandals, that the term "sob sister" was coined. A wealthy man named Harry Thaw and his beautiful wife Evelyn were having dinner at the Madison Square Garden restaurant one night when Standford White arrived with some friends. Mr. White had known Mrs. Thaw when she was Evelyn Nesbitt, a dancer on Broadway, and they had been lovers until she met Thaw. Thaw had revealed a violent streak, regularly beating Evelyn, and that night at the restaurant he suddenly stood up, crossed the room to White's table and shot him dead. Many newspapers decided to offer extensive coverage of Thaw's trial, knowing that the details of Evelyn's sordid relationships with both men that would certainly come out would help their papers sell like hot cakes. Four female journalists were assigned to the trial, as editors assumed that women would find it easier to sympathize with the young widow and would tell the story from a more appealing perspective for the prospective readers.

It was so unusual to have women covering a murder trial that they were granted privileged seats from which to follow the case. As Abramson explains, it was the journalist Irwin Cobb, "reporting the trial for the *New York Evening World*, [... who] dubbed them the 'sob sisters,' a name chosen to describe their sentimental reportage" (60-61). With shameless sentimentality, the four women journalists provided their readers with moving accounts of the way White had treated Evelyn, of how she escaped him by becoming Thaw's lover only to find herself in the hands of another brutal man, of how once married she told her husband about White's sexual abuses and how Thaw—in one of his outbursts of violence —killed White in a room full of witnesses. They also gave very detailed descriptions of Evelyn Thaw's appearance and demeanor. Her figure, her clothes, her reactions, and her deep sadness were carefully discussed in the hope of helping readers empathize with her. When in January, 1908, Harry Thaw was sent to the Asylum for the Criminal Insane, the concept of "sob sister journalism" had been born and a new trend in court reporting began. Just as with "flapper", the term "sob sister" expressed contempt. It was society's way to voice disdain towards those wanting to challenge the *status quo*—in this case, the women who did not content themselves with typing the news covered by men or with writing about recipes and fashion, but instead wanted to enter the male realm of court reporting. The roots of this disdain lay deeper than the worry that men might lose their jobs.[3] Permitting the presence of ladies in a courtroom dealing with all types of criminals went against the concept of true womanhood—first because it meant sanctioning women's entrance into the public sphere, and second because making women witness all the details of murder trials undermined the traditional construction of woman as someone of such delicacy that she required protection from anything gruesome or disgusting.

Disrespect for women journalists was further evident in the tendency to refer to them as girls, regardless of their age. This designation inferred they lacked experience and professionalism, although the truth was that they were not expected to rise to the level of expertness required from men. The terms of their employment made stereotypical assumptions about both writers and readers. Sob sisters were assigned criminal cases "to provide the so-called woman's angle by reporting on their own sympathetic reactions to news events. Their reports were expected to express the conventionally emotional responses of women, documenting not just the news but the femininity of its tellers" (Lutes 3). In other words, as women they were "assumed, by virtue of their gender, to be incapable of deliberating rationally, transcending their personal interests, or making neutral judgments" (Lutes 7), and the presumption regarding their female readers was that they would not be interested in this type of reportage. Sob sisters used some features of the sentimental narrative of the Victorian age, a genre traditionally connected with women writers and women readers, and just as women novelists of the nineteenth century had been scorned for their emphasis on feelings, so were the women journalists of the first decades of the twentieth century. Though an analysis of some of the trials covered by men shows the existence of very similar sentimental features, women were criticized for their style as a means of denying them legitimacy in a profession that had been the exclusive domain of men.

Therefore, if we analyze the role of women journalists in the first decades of the twentieth century we detect a curious ambivalence towards them. On the one hand, we find newspaper editors trying to cash in on the fact they were hiring more and more women reporters by emphasizing that the articles they published were written "as seen by a woman" or "as seen by woman's eyes" (Lutes 70). Notably, "while editors also published photographs and promoted name recognition of male columnists, they made women's pictures bigger and promoted their names more aggressively" (Lutes 70). On the other hand, many fellow journalists and members of society with a sexist attitude did not bother hiding their disdain of the sob sisters. Journalism historian Howard Good indicates that "most women reporters resented this label because it reinforced the stereotype of women as big-hearted but soft-minded, emotionally generous but intellectually sloppy" (50).

The Snyder-Gray Case

It was within this background of social change and coldness that sometimes verged on animosity towards modern women that a sensational murder hit the headlines. The infamous Snyder-Gray case filled newspapers and tabloids for weeks describing the murder of Albert Snyder, the art editor for *Motor Boating Magazine*, at the hands of his wife, Ruth May Snyder (neé Brown) and her lover, Judd Gray. Day after day the public waited anxiously for whatever information the media could provide. In this way they learned that in 1914, nineteen-year-old Ruth Brown had met Albert Snyder, a thirty-something executive with a reputation as a womanizer, and that she managed to marry him in 1919, subsequently giving up her job as a telephonist and becoming a middle-class housewife. In spite of achieving her initial goal, Ruth Snyder was not satisfied, as hers was an unhappy marriage. Tired of her loveless life, Ruth began an affair with Judd Gray, a corset salesman. After 18 months as lovers, Ruth convinced Gray that her husband had threatened to kill her and that murdering him was their only option.

On March 1927 Queens police was called to the Snyder home. They found Albert Snyder dead in bed. He had his hands tied with picture wire, a rope around his neck and a broken skull. Mrs. Snyder said two men broke in and knocked her unconscious, when she finally woke up she found herself tied up and her husband dead. The police realized immediately there was something wrong: the coroner could see no injury to Ruth's head; there was no evidence of a forced entry; and investigators found in the basement a blood-stained pillow cover and a sash weight. Furthermore, at the foot of Albert Snyder's bed they found a pin with the initials J.G.; coincidentally enough, in Mrs. Snyder's address book there was one Judd Gray. To make things worse, the police found out Mrs. Snyder had forged her husband's signature in a double indemnity insurance policy.

Ruth Snyder was immediately arrested and questioned. The police fooled her into believing that Judd Gray had been arrested too, and that he had already confessed to being her accomplice. She fell into the trap and confessed that on Saturday evening March 27, 1927, the Snyders were attending a party and Ruth's mother, who lived with them, was away for the evening. Ruth left the back door unlocked. When Ruth and Gray thought Snyder was asleep, they entered his room. Gray struck him twice but did not hit him with enough force to cause immediate death. Snyder woke up and struggled with Gray. Then Ruth hit her husband for a third time, this being the fatal blow. Ruth and Gray tied Snyder's hands, placed a rope around his neck and disarranged the house to make it look burglarized. Then they had sex and a few drinks to relax while they waited for Snyder to die. Afterwards Gray gagged Ruth and left.

Six weeks after the murder, Snyder and Gray were tried and, as they accused each other of being the one who planned the killing, both were convicted of murder and sentenced to die in the electric chair. The culprits' alibis were so ridiculous that one reporter called the case "The Dumbbell Case," thus making a pun with Snyder and Gray's dumbness and the weight used to strike Snyder's skull. The trial, which lasted eighteen days (April-May 1927), made public many details of Ruth Snyder's relationships with her husband and with Judd Gray. The journalists covering the case publicized every single detail, regardless of how intimate or sordid.

As the lovers waited in jail for an appeal, they granted several interviews to newspapers and magazines. No longer a team, both wanted to tell the world their version of the story and gain the public sympathy, as newspaper readers were all potential jurors. Facing an "every man for himself" situation, Snyder and Gray were quite aware that how they were portrayed by the press could be literally a question of life or death. Ruth Snyder, for example, tried to win the readers' liking (as she had strived to do with the jurors) by talking about her disastrous wedding night and her husband's philandering. Her complaints about Snyder's attempts to control her whereabouts backfired on her. She explained how, after her father's death in 1924, Albert Snyder bought a bigger house in Queens and invited Mrs. Brown to move in with them, thereby reducing Ruth's freedom, and causing her to resent her mother's presence. Unfortunately for Ruth, she did not gauge the reaction this information could trigger in her readers. As jurors had done before, readers questioned why Ruth's husband felt the need to control her and why her attitude towards her mother differed so much from the image of dutiful daughter that Snyder's lawyer had tried to portray during the first trial. Readers noted with disapproval that Ruth left her husband, daughter, and mother at home while she went out partying as some sort of middle-aged flapper.

Things got worse for Ruth Snyder when Judd Gray's lawyer decided that the only way to save his client from the death penalty was to destroy her reputation. Taking advantage of the double standard that chastises women's adultery while ignoring men's, Gray's lawyer presented him as a mere puppet manipulated by a heartless seducer. Snyder herself unintentionally reinforced this idea, as she had declared to the press that she enjoyed Gray's adoration, because it was the first time in her life she controlled someone else's life, and she liked that type of power. The photographs of Snyder entering the court did not help either: her appearance wearing make up, a fashionable fur coat and a cloche (a felt bell-shaped hat common among flappers) was far from the image of conventional housewife and mother that her lawyer was trying to sell to the jurors. With all this in mind, it came as no surprise when in the appeal (November, 1927) the death sentence was confirmed. Snyder and Gray were executed in Sing Sing prison on January 12, 1928.

Treadwell's Observation

From the moment of the arrest on March, 1927, until the execution ten months later, playwright and journalist Sophie Treadwell was highly interested in the Snyder-Gray case. As a sob sister, she had covered other murder cases and had become very interested in the idea of what drove ordinary women such as Ruth Snyder to kill their partners. Although Treadwell was not hired to cover this case, she decided to attend the trial sessions all the same, hoping she could find an answer to this question.

With the freedom of not having to worry about deadlines or having to adapt her articles to make them more appealing to readers, Treadwell could focus on the female defendant and her reasons for murdering her husband. Listening to the way lawyers, judge, and other court officials treated Snyder and reading what her fellow journalists wrote about the defendant, Treadwell became convinced that Ruth Snyder did not stand a chance. It was not only that the all-male jury denied her the constitutional right to be tried by a jury of her peers; it was also the sexism Snyder had to endure from everyone involved in the case. Unlike Gray, who was judged only for murdering Albert Snyder, Ruth had to face the legal charge of murder but also the accusations of being a bad daughter, a bad wife and a bad mother. At a time when many in American society feared that the new women threatened the survival of the traditional family and the preservation of the *status quo*, these last three accusations were even more serious than that of murder.

Treadwell rebelled against this double standard, and the discrimination suffered by women in their encounters with the American legal system. However, there is another element to bear in mind when analyzing Sophie Treadwell's state of mind at the time of the Snyder-Gray trial: with the objectivity gained by not covering the trial for any newspaper, Treadwell could analyze the work and attitude of the journalists who covered the case. She felt disgusted by the sensationalism they used to sell more newspapers, regardless of the consequences it could have on the accused. Connected with this disgust towards her fellow reporters, Treadwell began to feel angry with herself because she had been part of that destructive machinery. Her eagerness in the early 1900s to be a journalist had made her accept a certain level of mendacity, but now, at the end of the 1920s—having decided to leave aside her journalistic career to focus on her playwriting—her feelings of guilt were strong.[4]

As a sob sister Treadwell had covered at least two sensational murder cases that made a deep impact on her: in 1914 the case against the milliner Leah Alexander for murdering her lover, the wealthy J. D. Van Baalen;

and in 1916 the case against housewife Elizabeth Mohr for murdering her husband, Dr. Charles Franklin Mohr, and injuring his lover, Emily Burger. These cases filled the pages of tabloids for many weeks, and the press found them highly lucrative. In spite of all the evidence of abuse endured for years at the hands of their partners, both accused women, Leah Alexander and Elizabeth Mohr, were declared guilty of murder. During those two trials Treadwell had fulfilled to perfection her role as sob sister, emphasizing in her coverage of the court sessions those morbid elements she knew would attract her readers' attention. Following her editors' indications, Treadwell had focused her articles on detailed descriptions of the two female defendants, what they wore, what they looked like, their tone of voice, their deep suffering—in short, anything to move the readers' sympathy and make them go on buying the newspaper morning after morning to see what became of the protagonists of these two tragedies. Had Treadwell sacrificed the truth in order to keep her editors happy? Had she sold her soul for the sake of her journalistic career? These questions must have crossed her mind in 1927 as she witnessed the way her fellow journalists behaved in court, and how they portrayed Ruth Snyder.

As soon as the Snyder-Gray trial finished, Treadwell fell into a writing vortex as she began working on her next play. What she had seen and heard in court during the trial sessions and what she had read in the newspapers during those weeks had such a deep impact on her that she felt compelled to devote her time and energy, not to mention her writing skills, to creating a play that would expose the hurdles encountered by American women when they were accused of murdering their partners. *Machinal* would offer a dissection of the structural violence that patriarchal society resorts to in order to maintain the *status quo*, especially with regard to gender issues. This expressionist tragedy would also provide spectators with the unique opportunity of watching a real trial, because Treadwell was adamant that this play would provide a faithful portrayal of what had happened in court during Ruth Snyder's questioning and cross-examination.

The Play

If we compare the court proceedings and newspaper coverage of the trial with the play we can see how the description of the protagonist's clothing is a detailed account of what Ruth Snyder wore in court. This accuracy also encompasses Helen Jones's way of talking: Sophie Treadwell did not make Helen Jones express herself in a *staccato* telegraphese just to follow the expressionistic style; that was the exact way in which Ruth Snyder had expressed herself during the trial. Some scholars have stated that Helen Jones's testimony during the trial offers a perfect example of expressionism, but the truth is that Snyder's statements when questioned by her lawyer and by the district attorney were most of the time hesitant, clipped, and lacking fluency.[5] At some points, towards the beginning of the proceedings, Snyder had presented herself as friendly and talkative; but then, as she became aware of what would happen to her, she was often paralyzed with terror. Most of the time she seemed confused and unbalanced; she often contradicted herself. This gave jurors and journalists the idea that she was lying and was undoubtedly guilty.

When it came to portraying Snyder in court and how the other characters in the courtroom reacted to her, Treadwell wanted to be painstaking meticulous. However, when Treadwell formulated the outline of *Machinal*, she introduced many changes regarding Judd Gray, Ruth Snyder's mother, and Snyder's behavior. These changes highlight the playwright's intentions in writing. The first significant change we find in the play is that the description of the Young Woman's mother has nothing to do with that of Ruth Snyder's mother, Josephine Brown. While in *Machinal* the character of "Mother" is presented as a manipulative parasite living off her daughter and always using emotional blackmail to keep her under control, the actual Mrs. Brown was a hard-working woman, devoted to her family, who had accepted living with Ruth and Albert Snyder to help with the housework and with the upbringing of her granddaughter, Lorraine. Although Albert Snyder could have easily provided for his mother in law, she insisted on working some evenings as a companion to the sick. While in *Machinal* it is Young Woman who endures her mother's moods, in real life it was Mrs. Brown who suffered because of her daughter's whims and her refusal to accept her responsibilities as wife and mother. Obviously, the character of Mother was not based on Ruth Snyder's mother but on Sophie Treadwell's.

Another interesting change made by Treadwell in the play was the character of the Young woman's lover. While Judd Gray was a married corset salesman, who devoted his spare time to singing in his parish choir, Man/Richard Roe was an adventurer, living between New York and Mexico. While Gray lacked a masculine appearance and liked to call Ruth Snyder "Mommie," Man/Richard Roe is presented as an independent man with no wish to tie himself to anybody. While Gray was thin and myopic, with thick glasses that gave him a permanent look of surprise, Man/Richard Roe is presented by Treadwell as masculine and attractive. Why did Treadwell change this character in such a way? Perhaps she found Gray such an insignificant fellow she could not understand Snyder's attraction to him, or perhaps, as it had happened with the character of Mother, Treadwell moved away from the Snyder-Gray case to focus on her own life: Man/Richard Roe has nothing in common with Ruth Snyder's lover but he certainly resembles Treadwell's. While married to William McGeehan she had had an affair with the also married Maynard Dixon. As a painter highly interested in Native Americans and the West, Dixon had spend time travelling around the Southwest and he undoubtedly had adventures to tell, just like Man.

In connection with Young Woman's decision to have a lover, in *Machinal* Treadwell presents her protagonist as someone with little sexual experience and hardly any social life. During the Snyder-Gray trial, however, it became clear that Ruth Snyder had a very active social life and that Judd Gray had not been her first extramarital relationship. At the time of her arrest, Snyder had a little black book with the telephone numbers of 28 men. Although she declared these men were only friends she went out with, the jury and the newspaper readers condemned her for what they saw as inappropriate behavior for a married woman. The idea of Snyder going out night after night, drinking and dancing with other men, while her husband, daughter, and mother remained at home was very damaging for Snyder's reputation. Perhaps by hiding this information about Ruth Snyder, Treadwell hoped to make Young Woman/Helen Jones more acceptable to her readers. If she was presented less like a selfish flapper and more like a victim of her circumstances, readers would find it easier to sympathize with her.

A final change made by Treadwell when writing *Machinal* concerned Snyder's relationship with her daughter. During the trial Snyder confessed not only to leaving her daughter at home while she went out partying, but also to using the child as an excuse for going to town and meeting Gray. Saying she was taking Lorraine downtown, Snyder would go to the Waldorf Astoria Hotel for her sexual encounters with Gray. Snyder would leave the child waiting in the lobby while she went upstairs. Jurors and readers were rightly scandalized by this total lack of moral responsibility; thus it is understandable that Treadwell decided to overlook this aspect of Snyder's character revealed in the court proceedings. However, there is another element of Snyder's connection with her daughter that is not so easily explained: In the play Young Woman has no wish whatsoever of becoming a mother and, when her baby is born, she is very disappointed she has given birth to a girl. The actual Ruth Snyder insisted she wanted to be a mother, as she considered that was the main purpose of marriage. It was Albert Snyder who refused having children, and he was furious when he found out Ruth had lied to him about contraceptives to get pregnant. He finally accepted the idea of having a child, hoping the baby would be a boy with whom he could share his outdoor activities. When Lorraine was born he was deeply disappointed and wanted no interaction with the child. That Ruth Snyder was very conventional about the idea of motherhood as a compulsory requirement for married women helped her with the jury, as it complies with the patriarchal notion of maternal instinct as a desirable feature for all women. Then, we can wonder, why did Treadwell change this in the play. The decision goes against Treadwell's attempts to make Young Woman more likeable. Again we find the explanation not by looking at the Snyder-Gray case, but instead at Treadwell's own life. Her mother was too selfish to want the responsibility of having a child, but on the other hand she hoped it would help her keep her husband by her side. When Sophie was born, blonde blue-eyed Nettie Treadwell was very disappointed to see that her baby was not only a girl but also one who had inherited Alfred Treadwell's dark eyes and hair—indicators of his Mexican origin.

Thus, while Treadwell wanted to write a play expressing her displeasure over distortions that appeared in newspapers and to offer readers a true account of the injustices suffered by females in the justice system, the truth is that her own experiences as daughter, wife, lover, and journalist played a big role in her playwriting. At the end, rather than remaining strictly faithful to the Snyder-Gray case, she ended up interposing information from her own life into Ruth Snyder's story. As a result, Young Woman/Helen Jones is not an *alter ego* of Ruth Snyder but a mixture of Snyder and Treadwell herself. Nevertheless, Treadwell did fulfill her original idea of using the device of a trial to frame and highlight the construction of gender in the 1920s America.

Works Consulted

Abramson, Phyllis Leslie. *Sob Sister Journalism*. New York: Greenwood Press, 1990. Print.

Critoph, Gerald E. "The Flapper and Her Critics." *Remember the Ladies: New Perspectives on Women in American History*, ed. George, Carol V. R.. Syracuse, NY: Syracuse University Press, 1975: 145-160. Print.

Dickey, Jerry and Miriam López-Rodríguez, eds. *Broadway's Bravest Woman: Selected Writings of Sophie Treadwell*. Carbondale, Illinois: Southern Illinois University Press, 2006. Print.

Dumenil, Lynn. *The Modern Temper: American Culture and Society in the 1920s*. New York: Hill & Wang, 1995. Print.

Good, Howard. *Girl Reporter: Gender, Journalism, and the Movies*. Lanham, MD: Scarecrow Press, 1998. Print.

Gourley, Catherine. *Flappers and the New American Woman*. Minneapolis: Twenty-First Century Books, 2008. Print.

Kennedy, David M. *Over Here: The First World War and American Society*. New York: Oxford University Press, 1980. Print.

López-Rodríguez, Miriam. "New Critical Approaches to *Machinal*: Sophie Treadwell's Response to Structural Violence." *Violence in American Drama: Essays on Its Staging, Meanings, and Effects*, ed. Ceballos, Alfonso and Ramón Espejo. Jefferson, NC: McFarland Books, 2011: 72-84. Print.

------. "Sophie Treadwell." *Otros scenarios*, ed. Ozieblo, Barbara. Barcelona: Icaria, 2005: 187-200. Print.

--------. "Sophie Treadwell. A Profile." *The Literary Encyclopedia*, ed. Clark, Robert, Emory Elliott and Janet Todd. London: The Literary Dictionary Company. Online.

--------. "*Machinal*. A Profile." *The Literary Encyclopedia*, ed. Clark, Robert, Emory Elliott and Janet Todd. London: The Literary Dictionary Company. Online.

Lutes, Jean Marie. *Front-Page Girls: Women Journalists in American Culture and Fiction, 1880-1930*. Ithaca: Cornell University Press, 2006. Print.

Parrish, Michael E. *Anxious Decades. America in Prosperity and Depression, 1920-1941.* New York: Norton, 1992. Print.

Rosenberg, Jennifer. "Flappers in the Roaring Twenties." *About.com 20th Century History.* Online.

Sagert, Kelly Boyer. *Flappers: A Guide to an American Subculture.* Santa Barbara: Greenwood Publishing Group, 2010. Print.

Saltzman, Joe. "Sob Sisters: The Image of the Female Journalist in Popular Culture." *Image of the Journalist in Popular Culture (IJPC).* University of Southern California. 2003. Online.

Yellis, Kenneth A. "Prosperity's Child: Some Thoughts on the Flapper." *American Quarterly* 21. 1 (Spring 1969): 44-64. Print.

Zeist, Joshua. *Flapper: A Madcap Story of Sex, Style, Celebrity, and the Women who Made American Modern.* New York: Crown Publishers, 2006. Print.

Notes

1. We must also bear in mind the additional trauma caused by the 1918-19 influenza epidemic. Statistics indicate that between twenty and forty million people died of this flu.
2. A speakeasy was an establishment illegally selling alcoholic beverages during the Prohibition era. Unlike "blind pigs" (a.k.a. "blind tigers"), speakeasies were usually higher-class establishments with elegantly dressed customers.
3. As Jean Marie Lutes indicates, between 1920 and 1930 women had gone from making up sixteen per cent of all working journalists to twenty-three per cent (9).
4. Sophie Treadwell began writing for the *San Francisco Bulletin* in 1908. A decade later, after covering the Alexander and Mohr cases, she left the United States to serve as a foreign correspondent in France during World War I.
5. In *Machinal* the protagonist is called "Young Woman" for most of the play, to become "Helen Jones" towards the end.

Chapter 9.

Defining Gender and Sexuality in *The Children's Hour*

Araceli González Crespán

The Original Source

When Lillian Hellman (1905-1984) started writing for the theatre, she used as a resource a book on legal cases suggested by her friend Dashiell Hammett, a recognised and respected detective fiction writer. The origin of her first play *The Children's Hour*, was thus a forensic one. In fact, the section she chose, "Closed Doors, or The Great Drumsheugh Case" was part of *Bad Companions*, a compilation of real court proceedings by William Roughead. It was a suitable inspirational text for the former detective turned novel writer; for Hellman, it proved to be a good start for a playwriting career that would span almost three decades.

The scandalous nature of a case which had taken place in Edinburgh, Scotland at the beginning of the 19th century hinged on the accusation of lesbianism and revolved around the trials to which two women were subjected when a girl in their all-female boarding school charged them with "inordinate affection" (Dick 32) for one another. Hellman realized that this case presented the elements of drama. The setting would be a school for well-to-do girls. The characters would include a resentful, illegitimate, exotic, and maladapted pupil; her rich, righteous grandmother who is also her guardian and an important patron for the institution; two young, independent women in charge of the school; one of the headmistresses' aunts, a troublesome former actress. The plot would entail an accusation, an exodus from the school, a lawsuit and the ensuing appeals.

After drafting the play, Hellman kept rewriting it, heeding Hammett's advice and often sharp criticism, adding and eliminating characters and scenes, reworking dialogue until she thought it was ready for its debut. Producer and director Herman Shumlin presented the play on Broadway in 1934 for a successful run of 691 performances. From the beginning, the scandal of suggesting lesbianism on the commercial stage functioned both as an incentive and a discouragement for audiences and critics alike. The play was actually banned in Boston and Chicago, but became a colossal success in New York, and Hellman's financial take amounted to $ 125,000 (Lederer 3). It was shortlisted for the Pulitzer Prize in drama, but the thorny subject eventually made the jury choose Zoe Akins' *The Old Maid*. This decision provoked the protest of New York theatre critics and the establishment of the Drama Critics' Circle awards (Griffin and Thornsten 27). Despite its controversy, or perhaps as a result of it, the play certainly helped to inscribe Lillian Hellman in the Broadway roll of accomplished playwrights.

From Text to Play

Hellman's adaptation of the source involves changes in time, setting, characters, and elements of the plot. Most significant is the disappearance in her play of any representation of the trial itself whose records, as previously mentioned, formed the basis of the story by William Roughhead. The playwright made a substantial decision to bring the story into her own time and place so that she could control the dramatic action on her own terms and base it on her own experience. The chronological and geographical jump from Scotland at the beginning of the 19th century to a small New England town in the 1930s, would allow Hellman some leeway to comment on her own society and time. It is not irrelevant that she placed the action in New England, noted for the persistent influence of the Puritans who settled the original Massachusetts Bay colony and based its culture on a radical conviction of their covenant with God, of being a chosen people, and of founding a society that combined democracy with religious zeal.

The 1930s, of course, was a critical time period for the United States, as it brought the Great Depression following the financial crash of 1929. The economic situation was at an all-time low; poverty was a reality for millions of people; and unemployment was at its peak. These conditions, in which many were driven by the pressures of anxiety, created a breeding ground for ideologies that identified enemies. Thus, after an upsurge of feminism and the emergence of liberating mores for women in the roaring twenties (the image of the flapper being its epitome), this decade saw independent women as a threat. On the one hand, women who had jobs would be considered to be taking them away from men and thus emasculating them by robbing them of their primary function as breadwinners. On the other, women who did not need a man for their survival and chose work instead of family entailed a particular danger for the continuity of a society based on separate but complementary functions for males and females in heterosexual relationships, where women were assigned the role of wife and mother, responsible for homemaking and looking after the family (Loeffelholz 1-15). Any alternative to this model posed questions that society was not ready to address at a moment when there were more pressing problems to solve.

The Children's Hour is conservative in style, using the conventions of realism, following the Aristotelian model of unity of action, and dividing the drama into the usual three acts. Everything takes place in two distinct settings: a room in the Wright-Dobie school for girls, "a converted farm-house eighteen miles from the town of Lancet" (1. 5)[1] and Mrs Amelia Tilford's living-room. The time period for the play spans April to November of the same year. The first and second acts take place within the same day, from afternoon to evening; and the third act, with its climax, shows the audience the effect of the trial, which has occurred between the second and third act, but which Hellman chose not to represent on stage. Fundamental to the absence of the trial is the predominance of women characters in the main roles of the drama. This emphasis on women locates the play firmly in female spaces and excludes the locus of a public, masculine sphere. Though this play in some respects exemplifies feminism in its presentation of women as active subjects, the fact that the main characters in the drama—both the accusers and the victim—are all female complicates the reading from a feminist perspective. Hellman would later justify her decision by explaining: "I can write about men, but I can't write a play that centers on a man, I've got to tear it up, make it about the women around him, his sisters, his bride, her mother and—" (*Pentimento* 508).

FEMALE DISCOURSE AND THE APPROPRIATION OF PUBLIC SPEECH

In a documented essay about the origin of the female subject, Miguel Cereceda analyzes tension that arose during the late Middle Ages between the irruption of women into the literary domain and the misogynistic texts resisting their presence. He argues that to gain access to the public use of language, women had to fight not only against specific social conditions but also against a tradition which insisted on denying them their voice (308). The patriarchal order assigns a specific area of language to the feminine and defines as masculine the languages of ownership, propriety, logic, science, and economics. It offers women their own space within literary language, and simultaneously devalues that sphere as superfluous and useless (Cereceda 311). It follows, then, that the problem is not women's linguistic ability, but that women are denied the public use of language. Teresa Moure also points to the value of language and the difference between men and women:

> Therefore, language is not a banal power, it is simply the power. That might be the reason why our age is characterised by an almost morbid interest in language, in its signs, in its meanings. The *homo sapiens* could adequately be called *homo loquens*, since knowledge is also shared by other species but language however is not (Moure 54).[2]

As Cereceda stated, Moure also explains that masculine discourse is accorded prestige, while feminine discourse is devalued (Moure 57). The most important concepts offered in these two essays are the recognition of language as a battleground and the distinction among discourses with different values, some acceptable for public use and restricted to men and others considered appropriate to the domains of women.

The first act of *The Children's Hour* presents the main characters, their relationships and the origin of conflict. It also sets a mood which will serve as a contrast to the following scenes, and particularly to the last act. Hellman introduces several intertextual references to trigger the audience's response and build on their knowledge by connotation. The play opens with a student, Peggy, reading aloud part of Portia's speech in Shakespeare's *The Merchant of Venice.* For most of the audience, familiar with Shakespeare's plays, it would be easy to remember that when delivering this speech, Portia is dressed as a doctor of law. A woman who is not entitled to participate in a public act such as a trial uses disguise and deception to defend her friend Antonio against Shylock's demand. Therefore, in the Elizabethan comedy, Portia manipulates a patriarchal institution which denies her the power and the right to be a citizen because of her sex, by resorting to costume and manipulating a language that is forbidden to women. Her speech pivots on the comparison between mercy and justice. Describing mercy as a godly attribute in contrast to blind, human justice, Portia eloquently demands from Shylock the greatness of the former, asking him to forgive Antonio. When her articulate address does not achieve the desired outcome, she takes a further step by reminding him that the debt should be paid by "a pound of flesh" (4. 1. 116), literally insisting on the substance, only flesh and not a single drop of blood, and on the amount, not one inch more or less than that. In specifying the forfeit in this way, Portia makes it physically impossible for Shylock to receive his payment. The quality of mercy as superior to justice has a double benefit: "It is twice blest; it blesseth him that gives and him that takes" (1. 5) and it stands in sharp contrast to temporal, human law and justice.

A further reference in the text appears when another student, Catherine, practices for a Latin test. The section she is reciting comprises Cicero's famous opening lines of the Catiline Orations. It is a prime example of oratory, a speech delivered in front of the senate in order to convince its members of the manipulations of Catiline who was planning a coup d'état against the Roman Republic. Again, this second speech points to the oral ability in public forums which was restricted to male citizens, the locus of institutionalized power thus banning women from their presence and their right to speak publicly.

THE ELEMENTS OF THE TRIAL IN *THE CHILDREN'S HOUR*

Karen Wright and Martha Dobie, the two women who stand accused as a result of the slanderous statements of a pupil, are educated young women who chose to set up a school for girls after graduating from college, where they had become friends. They have gone through difficulties in becoming established, but at this point the institution is working reasonably well, and its financial position looks promising. Karen is engaged to Joe Cardin, the village doctor and a relative of Amelia Tilford. She has kept postponing her marriage but is now ready for it. Martha's anxiety has to do with the feeling that Karen's new status will be incompatible with the job, as it was common at the time to view working outside the house as acceptable for single women but not for those who were married. Unexpectedly, they find their livelihood abruptly cut off when the girls, one after another, leave the school on the same night, without any explanation. Martha and Karen decide to confront Mrs Tilford when they finally find out what the problem is. Their indignant reaction and decision to go to court in order to free themselves from the calumny unleashes the drama. The two women's naive belief in the mercy of the jury will lead to the demise of their reputation. Their expectations of the trial prove their lack of knowledge about the functioning of language and ideology.

The duplicitous accusers, Lily Mortar and Mary Tilford, show some commonalities. Both are uneasy at the school, feeling that they are not being treated fairly. They are constantly creating uncomfortable situations, and they share an attitude of superiority. Lily Mortar is Martha Dobie's aunt, a retired actress with delusions of grandeur. She is in charge of the students' elocution classes, and she spends most of the time talking about her supposedly grandiose past. Her conceit is clearly identified by the girls who keep asking her about her experiences on the stage just to avoid studying. She prides herself in never being wrong, claiming that "[i]n my entire career I've never missed a line" (1. 8); but, significantly, Mrs. Mortar skips the lines directly addressed to Shylock: "therefore Jew, / Though justice be thy plea, consider this, / That in the course of justice, none of us should see salvation" (4. 1. 112). When one of the students points out the slip, instead of accepting her mistake, she changes the topic, demonstrating her pride and mean spirit. Out of the blue, she utters Alexander Pope's line from *Essays on Man*: "one master passion in the breast, like Aaron's serpent, destroys all the rest" (1. 9). Mortar's unexpected comment foregrounds Martha's feelings, but also Mary Tilford's malevolence and the speaker's own disputable moral position. As an actress, she is used to performing other people's discourses, but ironically, in the play her words are used by Mary Tilford to charge the headmistresses. Out of spite, Mortar refuses to declare when asked to testify. She chooses silence, and her lack of speech has dramatic consequences for the verdict.

Mary Tilford has a "sullenly dissatisfied expression on her face" (1. 8) and is constantly causing trouble. She is conscious of her power over her grandmother and manipulates her classmates by bullying, so that they second her attempts to avoid punishment and leave the school. She can get away with lying to vain Mrs. Mortar, but neither Karen nor Joe will buy into her faked fainting and heart trouble. Mary's precocious interest in sexuality is shown by the French book she is secretly reading: *Mademoiselle de Maupin.* In Roughead's account, she felt "odd and unwanted" (qtd. in Joseph). She shares with Mortar a flair for acting, as a sign of duplicity and equivocation. Both lie and perceive themselves as undervalued, deserving a higher status, more respect, and better treatment. Both are egotistical and seem unable to empathize with the people around them. They manipulate language, appropriating the discourses of others and using them for their own benefit and interest.

The accusation from Mary Tilford is represented on stage when she shows up suddenly at the home of her grandmother, Mrs. Amelia Tilford. An aged widow and Mary's guardian, Mrs. Tilford has helped Karen and Martha set up the school, both with financial help and by using her influence to attract the daughters of other families in the area. According to her nephew Joe Cardin's humorous description, she is a prominent member of this society: "You can look at Aunt Amelia and tell: old New England stock; never married out of Boston; still thinks honor is honor and dinner's at eight thirty. Yes ma'am, we're a proud old breed" (1. 21). The calculating girl prepares her act very carefully, rehearsing in front of the mirror as if she were an actress about to step on stage. She employs several different strategies to convince her grandmother, who says she is a "coaxer" (2. 1. 35). She ranges from endearing and lovable attitudes to playing the victim, telling Mrs. Tilford she does not love her. Her ability to manipulate is shown by her perfect modulation of the language used to talk about lesbianism. She is very vague at the beginning, using generic, unspecific terms: "things... secrets... funny... unnatural" (2. 1. 37). Then she qualifies what she has not named yet: "Bad things" (2. 1. 38), "funny noises... funny things" (2. 1. 39). When she finally shifts to greater explicitness, she highlights the inappropriateness of this discourse to be spoken aloud: "I can't say it loud" (2. 1. 38), "I'd tell you, but I got to whisper it" (2. 1. 39). Mary has adapted and appropriated a comment from Martha's aunt, Mrs. Lily Mortar, overheard by two other students, eavesdropping, in the course of an argument with her niece:

> MRS. MORTAR: I know what I know. Every time that man comes into this house, you have a fit. It seems like you just can't stand the idea of them being together. God knows what you'll do when they get married. You're jealous of him, that's what it is.
>
> MARTHA: (*her voice is tense and the previous attitude of good-natured irritation is gone*) I'm very fond of Joe, and you know it.
>
> MRS. MORTAR: You're fonder of Karen, and I know that. And it's unnatural, just as unnatural as it can be. You don't like their being together. You were always like that even as a child. If you had a little girl friend, you always got mad when she liked anybody else. Well, you'd better get a beau of your own now – a woman of your age (1. 19-20).

When Mary confronts Karen and Martha in the presence of her grandmother, she says she saw them kissing through the keyhole. Karen explains that there is no keyhole through which she could have seen them. With this evidence disproving her allegation, Mary resorts to a false witness: Rosalie Wells, another student who has stolen a bracelet and has been previously forced to pledge obedience to her. The process of disclosing the charge exhibits Mary's ability with discourse and her control of what her elders can accept as reasonable knowledge from a girl. Her anger at feeling mistreated and determination to get away from punishment and not to return to the school spur her harmful use of a piece of information she never heard but received second-hand from her roommate. The rhythm in unveiling the accusation presents a supreme example of controlling language and discourse.

IMPLICATIONS FOR GENDER AND SEXUALITY

For a long time *The Children's Hour* has been the only play in the American canon dealing with lesbianism (Hart 275). With the advent of the second wave of feminism, it has received quite a lot of critical attention from this perspective. Since its presentation of lesbianism is indirect and it allows the lesbian no way out but suicide, the play has often been critiqued as a profoundly homophobic text (Titus; Fleche). However, in the last decade or so, there have also been new analyses which consider the play as an indictment of a homophobic, conservative, repressive society (Spencer; Cuenca and Seguro). It is the axis created by the normative function of institutions and the use of language that provides the key to my interpretation this play and understanding of its comment on gender and sexuality.

The school and the court both represent what Althusser has named ideological state apparatus. Both are central social institutions that propagate received ideas using suitable methods of punishment—expulsion, selection, etc.—to enact discipline. Both function as keepers of morality, tradition, justice, and are associated with specific uses of language in the form of distinct discourses considered appropriate for public and private situations. They guarantee the transmission and enforcement of an ideology by educating future citizens and by protecting or punishing those who evade the norms. Schools function primarily by ideology and only secondarily by repression. The fact that Karen and Martha run a school for girls, responsible for their education and for providing role models of appropriate behaviour in accordance with the prevailing social values, turns the possibility of lesbianism into a terrible crime which forces the well-meaning Mrs. Tilford to warn every family and cause a stampede of withdrawals. As she tells Joe Cardin: "What they are may possibly be their own business. It becomes a great deal more than that when children are involved" (2. 2. 49). This remark refers very explicitly to two separate and clear-cut spheres: the personal and the social, the private and the public, the individual and the collective. Sexuality in general, and non-normative sexual practices in particular are not issues to be dealt with in public and must definitely be banned from a school setting. The school complements the function of the family and reinforces the work of the whole community to teach the individual to internalize its dominant ideology.

The court functions primarily by violence and secondarily by ideology. Martha Dobie decides to go to court to defend her honour, because she believes public exposure and open discourse will cancel out a privately whispered lie:

> All right. That's fine. But don't get the idea we'll let you whisper this lie: you make it and you'll come out with it. Shriek it to your town of Lancet. We'll *make* you shriek it— and we'll make you do it in a court room. (*Quietly*).Tomorrow, Mrs. Tilford, you will have a libel suit on your hands" (2. 2. 50).

However, Martha's attempt to secure protection through a libel suit backfires, as the court dismisses the complaint of libel and thus implicitly validates the accusation. As Bersani notes, institutions apply disciplinary mechanisms to prevent deviation from the norm:

> In schools, prisons, courtrooms, and mental hospitals, the seriousness of the offence and the gravity of the illness are measured in terms of their distance from a normative ideal and punishment is inseparable from a corrective, curative process designed to close the gap between the normal and the anomalous (Bersani 2).

The legal proceeding affirms the reality of a lesbian relationship which the characters have never experienced. Martha and Karen are charged with "sinful sexual knowledge of one another" (3. 63).

Access to the social is necessary in order to become full individuals, and the tenets of that given society are learned and internalized in such a way that they become one's own basic, unquestioned principles. However, the familiar, protective function of the social does also contain in itself an opposite effect. The process of socialization can only be realized by limiting the possibilities of the child's personality, by taming the instincts, by repressing the desire; it is only by doing so that we can integrate and live with others. This contradiction, the conflict between individual desire and the need to adapt to social norms, has very frequently been shown in dramatic literature. When analyzing that contradiction, we may understand how the social institutions work to mold our personalities, to give us positive and negative images of normal behavior, and how the conformity with or rebellion towards those norms shape our identities. Language, a social construct, shows through usage what is considered real. Societies try to exercise control over language either by creating new words or by erasing others which refer to realities no longer acceptable. In this process, the non-existence of certain models, the silence regarding some attitudes, the lack of an appropriate vocabulary to describe alternatives to the mainstream is a clear sign of violence and repression. When emptiness replaces an image, it illustrates the denial of the human capability to describe; when silence substitutes for a word, it highlights the violation of the creative power of language. The ability to represent, and therefore to admit as real, is eliminated by the social institution which imposes that void.

Martha Dobie undergoes a process that redefines her identity. She internalizes the charge of lesbianism and commits suicide, unable to contest the definition imposed on her by society. The sexual and social repression of a traditional, conservative, Victorian-like society uses external condemnation to produce internal guilt, and thus victimizes a character whose real sexual tendency is never fully disclosed. In this case, the reading of society, a reading out of silence, lies and malevolence, exerts a powerful effect on the psyche of an individual who is unable to find her real feelings and explore her sexuality in freedom, provoking a tragic end and leaving the reader/spectator pondering on the pressure of ideological, economic, institutional and social forces which have real, direct and maiming consequences on individual lives. The verdict is for Martha Dobie a mirror that gives back a new, unsuspected, and fraught image of the individual. This image which talks back is so powerful that it creates a new reality from what is not named.

It is for the Audience to Judge

As spectators, we see the consequences of the trial. The once lively, bright, warm school becomes a gloomy, silent and dark place where Karen and Martha feel isolated and secluded, away from the society which has judged them so harshly. They cannot muster the strength to face the town, renouncing their normal activities and daily chores:

> KAREN: (*suddenly*) Let's go out.
>
> MARTHA: (*turns over, stares at her*) Where to?
>
> KAREN: We'll take a walk
>
> MARTHA: Where'll we walk?
>
> KAREN: Why shouldn't we take a walk? We won't see anybody, and suppose we do, what of it? We'll jus-
>
> MARTHA: (*slowly gets up*) Come on. We'll go through the park.
>
> KAREN: They might see us. (*They stand looking at each other*) Let's not go (MARTHA *goes back, lies down again*) We'll go tomorrow.
>
> MARTHA: (*laughs*) Stop kidding yourself.
>
> KAREN: But Joe says we've got to go out. He says that all the people who don't think it's true will begin to wonder if we keep hiding this way.

> MARTHA: If it makes you feel better to think there *are* such people, go ahead.
>
> KAREN: He says we ought to go into town and go shopping and act as though-
>
> MARTHA: Shopping? That's a sound idea. There aren't three stores in Lancet that would sell us anything. Hasn't he heard about the ladies' clubs and their meetings and their circulars and their visits and their- (3. 59- 60).

Contact with the outside world only offers confirmation of the new opinion the town now holds of the two teachers. As an emblem of this outside world, the grocery boy stares at them, fascinated by the monstrous, the grotesque, the abnormal. He stands, giggles, walks towards them, examines them, and keeps giggling when he goes, without looking away (3. 60). Martha, pressed by isolation and anguish, after learning Karen has just broken up with Joe, confesses her love for her. In speech resembling the modulating rhythm of the accusation by Mary, Martha reproduces a movement from ignorance to disclosure which is shown through her statements. At first, she keeps the official version, her own truth: "I've loved you like a friend, the way thousands of women feel about other women. . . It's perfectly natural that I should be fond of you"; but then, for the first time, hesitates: "I love you that way—maybe the way they said I loved you. I don't know"(3.71). As a reaction to Karen's denial, she insists "*I have loved you the way they said*," and she even delves into her own memories, in her identity as a subject, to confirm the verdict and redefine her feelings: "There's always been something wrong. . . But I never knew it until all this happened" (3. 71). Significantly, she again uses indirect and negative words. It is impossible to use the right, exact language, because it is not part of the socially accepted repertoire.

Martha's love "without a name" (3. 71) demands "a new language" (3. 72). She reformulates her identity and defines her new sexuality only under the pressure of punishment and by internalizing the opinion of society as officially delivered by the court: "Suddenly a child gets bored and lies—and there you are, seeing it for the first time. (*Closes her eyes*) I don't know. It all seems to come back to *me*. In some way I've ruined your life. I've ruined my own. I didn't even *know*" (3. 72). However, she is unable to accept this new being which defies the model of romantic love and attraction toward the opposite sex. Although she has never had any sexual contact with Karen, the burden of a new reality, a different self is unbearable for her. She cannot resolve the conflict and shoots herself. How can lesbianism, a possibility unknown and unexplored, be the source of conflict? In the process, it becomes an unveiled reality, with no previous record or reference. The lack of a language to describe it had eliminated the possibility of that experience prior to the conflict, and as spectators we witness the process in which that reality is created, from the moment of alluding to it indirectly, through the reaffirmation by the court's verdict, to the final incorporation of that reality in the definition of the individual subject. This is a common pattern in lesbian literature and criticism:

> This problem of definition is exacerbated by the problem of silence. One of the most pervasive themes in lesbian criticism is that woman-identified writers, silenced by a homophobic and misogynistic society, have been forced to adopt coded and obscure language and internal censorship. Emily Dickinson counseled us to "tell all the truth/ but tell it slant," and critics are now calculating what price we have paid for slanted truth. The silence of heterosexual women writers may become lies for lesbian writers, as Rich warns: "'a life 'in the closet' [may] spread into private life, so that lying (described as *discretion*) becomes an easy way to avoid conflict of complication" (Zimmerman 207).

The referential power of language is here highlighted. When Martha accepts the term, she refuses, however, to live with it. There is a substantial creative power in the ability to name, because it is clear that speaking may be a form of knowledge:

> And not an insignificant one. Among the human searches, searching the word is fundamental (...) I want a new discourse and producing it becomes a most succulent way of learning about the world, a most tasty way of experimenting with pleasure. That is why there is no possibility but revolt: the construction of a new world—a world of renewed words (Moure 30-31).

The intimate connection between reality and language is further explored by Deats and Lenker:

> The way in which individuals perceive the world is largely determined by the language they use to describe the phenomenon they experience as reality. Thus language constructs as well as encodes the conventional perceptions of individuals in a given society; it intervenes in history even as it reflects history. It follows, therefore, that literature, the only art form composed entirely from words, not only mirrors society's conventions but also creates them (7).

The representation by absence reflects a mode of sexuality which does not exist because it has not been uttered. Only when the legal system, the institution of the court, names it, even if indirectly, does it become real, and that reality is then projected in Martha's psyche. She appropriates alien words to incorporate them into her own definition. The idea of the lesbian defies social values to such an extent that language has to be violated to erase the possibility of that reality.

Lying is the equivocal veil which discovers some inner truth Martha was not prepared to confront unless society screamed it at her. For all its melodramatic qualities and the tragic end of a character for whom facing reality meant no way out, the play served (and continues to do so) to stage the ideological functioning of a society which cannot and will not admit the possibility of an "unnatural" feeling which overturns the social order based on the secondary role of women and a notion of the heterosexual, traditional family. By representing on stage the limitations, injustice, and drawbacks of an inflexible social organization that maims individuals by restricting freedom and failing to recognize alternatives, the play gives audiences the opportunity to read it as a critique of that same conservative society stifling any individual's efforts to challenge the status quo.

The Children's Hour is a journey that starts with a lie, provokes disclosure for the protagonist and culminates in her death. As readers and spectators we do know Mary was lying, but the construction of the lie is always based on indirect verbalizations. If the focus is indeed a lie, it is a very negative one whose representation we may not trust. The word lesbian is never uttered, and Martha's inability to cope with it accounts for a tragic ending; however, the value and the importance of such a text should not be underestimated. Lesbianism cannot take center stage dressed as such, and Lillian Hellman has chosen to show it in an unstable way, mirroring social censorship. We could interpret the play as a critique of a society which has forced language to eliminate a direct reference to lesbianism, in the hope that by doing so, that reality disappears. The slant representation of the lesbian, by never overtly naming her, to some extent equates lesbianism with a lie, but it also points to a society (and an audience) which has violently repressed the possibility of a more open, direct representation. As homosexuality deviates from normative behavior, the lie may not only be the accusation by the child, but also society's effort to eliminate lesbianism by erasing the language which can appropriately name it.

What we have to judge is not Martha or her lesbianism but the society that is responsible for crushing her feelings, eliminating her options, and forcing her to die. Unlike Portia, who adroitly manipulates public, legal speech and disguises herself in order to be heard in a forum in which she is not entitled to speak, Martha goes openly, candidly to the legal institution seeking protection from slander. Unlike Portia, Martha's plea is not heeded even in the absence of definitive evidence. Unlike Cicero, she will not be able to stop the conspiracy and publicly denounce it. By eliminating the trial from the stage, the play forces us, as readers and spectators, to become part of the jury and give a verdict. Should we remember Portia and question justice, claiming more than limited human law to assess and judge Martha's feelings and possibilities, and pronounce a negative verdict on a society which does not allow her to continue living?

Notes

1. All quotations from the play include the act followed by the scene (when there is one) and the page. Page numbers refer to *Six Plays by Lillian Hellman* (1979).
2. All quotes from texts in Spanish are translated by the author.

Works Cited

Althusser, Louis. "Ideology and Ideological State Apparatuses," *The Louis Althusser Internet Archive.* Online.

Bersani, Leo. "The Subject of Power." *Diacritics* September 1977: 2-21. Print.

Cereceda, Miguel. *El origen de la mujer sujeto.* Madrid: Tecnos, 1996. Print.

Cuenca, Mercè and María Isabel Seguro. "'Making Something Out of Nothing': Lesbianism as Liberating Fantasy in *The Children's Hour*." *Atlantis. Journal of the Association of Anglo-American Studies* 30.1 (2008): 115-127. Print.

Dick, Bernard F. *Hellman in Hollywood.* East Brunswick: Associated University Presses, 1982. Print.

Fleche, Anne. "The Lesbian Rule: Lillian Hellman and the Measures of Realism." *Modern Drama* 39 (1996): 16-30. Print.

Griffin, Alice and Geraldine Thorsten. *Understanding Lillian Hellman.* Columbia: University of South Carolina Press, 1999. Print.

Hart, Lynda. "Canonizing Lesbians?" *Modern American Drama: The Female Canon.* ed. Schlueter, June. Cranbury NJ: Associated University Presses, 1990: 275-292. Print.

Hellman, Lillian. *The Children's Hour, Six Plays by Lillian Hellman.* New York: Vintage Books, 1979 (1934). 1-78. Print.

--------. *Three: Unfinished Woman, Pentimento, Scoundrel Time.* Boston: Little, Brown and Company, 1979. Print.

Joseph, Craig. "Study Guide," *The Children's Hour.* Chicago: Timeline Theatre Company. Online.

Lederer, Katherine. *Lillian Hellman.* Boston: Twayne, 1979. Print.

Loeffelholz, Mary. *Experimental Lives. Women and Literature 1900-1945.* New York: Twayne, 1992. Print.

Moure, Teresa. *A palabra das fillas de Eva.* Vigo: Galaxia, 2004. Print.

Roughead, William. *Bad Companions.* New York: Duffield and Green, 1931. Print.

Shakespeare, William. *The Merchant of Venice*. Ed. John Russell Brown. London: Routledge, 1955. Print.

Spencer, Jenny. "Sex, Lies and Revisions: Historicizing Hellman's *The Children's Hour.*" *Modern Drama* 47.1 (2004): 44-65. Print.

Titus, Mary. "Murdering the Lesbian: Lillian Hellman's *The Children's Hour.*" *Tulsa Studies in Women's Literature* 10.2 (1991): 215-232. Print.

Zimmerman, Bonnie. "What Has Never Been. An Overview Of Lesbian Feminist Literary Criticism." *The New Feminist Criticism: Essays On Women, Literature And Theory*, ed. Showalter Elaine. London: Virago Press, 1986. 200-224. Print.

CONTEMPORARY DRAMA

Chapter 10.

Stoning Maries

The Ethics of Justice Vs. Ethics of Care

Valentina Mikluc

Gender and Tragedy

In *A Room of One's Own* Virginia Woolf asks women if they are aware that they are "perhaps, the most discussed animal in the universe" (24). Tragedies often put women central stage as the focus of judgments, insights, and attitudes, but despite the focus on women and the range of action exhibited by women in the course of the play, tragedies usually restore the hierarchy of gender relations. The presence and even centrality of women in tragedy, however, has its basis in the family, and the presence and centrality of women in the family cannot be denied. Tragic drama derives its power from the tragic limitations of kinship (Simon 14), which become apparent as families are divided and destroyed by internal violence.

Modern tragedy is mediated by the insights available in psychology. Woolf wrote: "I thought of [...] the shut doors of the library; and I thought how unpleasant it is to be locked out; and I thought how it is worse perhaps to be locked in" (*Room of One's Own* 22). Since they were "locked in," just as women were "locked out" and invisible at the time, the creators of orthodox psychoanalysis did not take women into account when theorizing human development and patterns of thought and feeling. Femininity thus remained something unknown and ignored. In its neglected corner, it came to be seen as internally and externally divided along the lines of a whole set of binary terms. Femininity ranked low in the notorious Lawrence Kohlberg's scale of moral development, but some years later, the feminist ethicist and psychologist Carol Gilligan analyzed feminine qualities that are usually neglected and often underestimated. Gilligan introduced an ideal of ethics based in common female experience, which she called the ethics of care, comparing the significance and validity of this ideal with the ethics of justice, based in and related to common male experience. The ethics of justice respects universal principles and rules, and claims to be fair and objective. The ethics of care, on the other hand, functions through taking care of the specific needs of an individual in a specific situation. The ethics of justice and the ethics of care can initially seem to represent extremes, but their integration best functions to close the circle of making an informed ethical decision.

The social value of an ethical orientation depends on the cultural background or cultural stereotyping of gender. If an ethics of care, as Carol Gilligan suggests, specifically promotes interpersonal communication and development, it seems that it is not inferior to the universalist ethics of justice. The assumption of feminine inferiority in the work of Lawrence Kohlberg focuses on the supposed female inability to overcome pre-social basic instincts and self-centered desires, including the desire to please others, and move on to abstract principles of social sensitivity to the common good. These ideas have implications for both genders, as social organization fosters the control and subordination of most men, as well as women. Thus, the ethics of justice may neglect care and responsibility to others if attempts at objectivity exclude emotions, as the best interest of the human being at the center of an ethical dilemma is not then taken into consideration. According to Gilligan, moral development occurs in the following three stages: (1) a person cares only about and for himself or herself; (2) he or she recognizes a responsibility to care for others; (3) he or she accepts the principle of care as a universal ethical criterion. What is most interesting about Gilligan's categorization is its simplicity.

Both *Stoning Mary* (2005) by Debbie Tucker Green and *Five Kinds of Silence* (2000) by Shelagh Stephenson are tragedies with women at their center. In both plays, women have murdered aggressive, socially unadjusted male characters. As a result of their actions, the women are viewed as maladjusted. In common with classical tragedies focused on women, both plays are purposely uncomfortable and unpleasant. The irritation they cause is linked to their tragic quality: as Bennett Simon observes, "If Aristotle had known only plays by Euripides, I think he could have made the notion of irritation as much a part of his definition of tragedy as catharsis" (97 - 98). Aroused through mysterious action that hints at but does not clearly define the disintegration of families through violence, the irritation is then calmed through explanation. The female characters, however, cannot be explained completely. They are accused, and they make no denials, and yet the audience does not know how to judge them.

This essay argues that the women in these two plays, which are both written by British playwrights but suggest quite different social worlds, react out of care for their loved ones and their community. They did not kill their victims in self-defense; rather, they did what they thought was necessary to defend their community. Theirs are not crimes of passion, but acts aimed at protecting the social order, despite the fact that they have been victimized by it. Does the ethics of care demonstrated by these female characters stem from a universal maternal role that women are conditioned to accept? Is it, as a product of limited circumstances, limited itself? Or is it more insightful, more realistic and more informed, because it comes from a subordinate, actively passive observing position, from a dim dusty corner of the kitchen or living room? The plays present women who are confined to the private sphere, where they imagine their true connection to the world is the television set; they dust inside the rooms whose walls are constantly narrowing to smother them.

Five Kinds of Silence

Though the play is based on an actual event, the originality of *Five Kinds of Silence* is visible from the opening moments. It begins with a crime scene, and the perpetrators are known and undenying. The investigators are poking about for the motive. The play is evidently about the conspiracy of silence that surrounds a terrorized family. It deals with the causes and consequences of psychological, physical, and sexual abuse of not only women and children, but also of the abuser—in other words, it deals with the way society shapes people into being abusive or forces victims into putting up with the abuse. Billy, the patriarch of the family, whose two favorite scents are fear and blood, has been killed. The ties that bind their family have fed on these scents and emotions which hold the abused and their abuser together. Most of the play is structured in the form of monologues showing the effects on the abused and the motivation of the abuser. When he returns to haunt the house, the murdered abuser becomes a modern combination of the Greek chorus and a Shakespearian ghost trying to restore his system of values. Despite his abuse of his wife and two daughters, he does evoke empathy after a monologue about his childhood memories reveals that he possesses feelings, if perverted ones, and loves his victims in his deviant way.

The ugliness of the deviance and abuse within this family never comes to the surface through language. The characters do not offer graphic details of their physical and sexual abuse, but make it clear through their emotional reactions that they have been living in extreme conditions. Dreams and reality intertwine. Billy shares a dream of himself as a dog who sees and smells everything without being seen, which indicates his self-division, both in his self-concept and in the way he is perceived by others. His wife and daughters explain to the authorities that they killed him while he was unconscious, because he was a sick and sad dog who needed to be put down. At the same time, Billy's daughter Susan has nightmares about enjoying sex with her father, and she is embarrassed to share them. The murdered abuser expresses disgust at his killer's weakness: "Water streaming down her leg. Her eyes streaming. The dam is breached, the walls have collapsed" (Stephenson 27). The dam has been put back into working order, however, as the women allow shame to stifle expression of their real feelings.

The play exemplifies the fact that "...the silences and narrative interruptions in tragedy are the implementations in *form* of the problem in the *content* of the play. That problem can be stated in two complementary ways: how do we speak of unspeakable deeds done by one family member to another? And will there be a terrible interruption in the chain of generation?" (Simon 16). The institutional guardians are eager to file the case away, but they cannot reason with these women. When the policeman asks why they killed Billy, they all together answer that they do not want to talk about it, followed by Mary's "If you don't mind" (Stephenson 8). In the wake of the crime, Billy's wife Mary is calm not because she is cold-blooded, but because she feels that the problem that had to be dealt with is over; she asks, "Can I get you a cup of tea, Officer?" (Stephenson 7). Once in the past she had tried to run away from Billy, but bumped into the wall of stern patriarchy: "...father said: you made your bed. Now lie in it. Marriage is a sacrament. Marriage is for life" (Stephenson 17). As Janet explains, they have felt they had to "...smile, or people might catch on –" (Stephenson 14); they have kept "smiling smiling smiling for our lives..." (Stephenson 19).

In their isolation, the women have clung to television for a sense of connectedness. In Five Kinds of Silence, background noise comes from a television cartoon, a ubiquitous household sound. Billy's wife and two daughters have claimed for themselves the power of invisibility and soundlessness, as they go through their version of life hoping nobody notices their deviance. The only sounds they hear from the outside world are mechanical in nature: television is supplanted by the inquries and comments of police, psychiatrists, and lawyers, but no words that acknowledge them as distinct individuals. The fifth kind of silence of the title is that of the outside community. Because their severely limited life has not allowed them to imagine anything else, all the three women want is a safe and cozy room they can call their own. When taken into custody, Janet inquires, "Is this a cell?" and when the police officer affirms that it is, her sister Susan remarks, "It is beautiful" (Stephenson 9). In prison, Susan and Janet are on vacation for the first time in their lives. The letter they write to their mother is carefree and happy, as if from a summer camp. Mary, at home, must deal with Billy's ghost; she feels alone and guilty again. She fears being non-existent to others, remembering when she was six years old and her mother died just before Christmas, yet the neighbors were singing and celebrating while she was silently crying. Similarly, Susan and Janet understand that if they had not killed Billy, not only would they and their mother have been killed, but the silence surrounding their family would have made it seem as though they had never existed.

A woman remains a 'partially closed gestalt' (Simon 262), an ambiguous figure to which anyone can give their own kind of closure. Inside their private space, women are viewed as men's sexual property, and victimization is their occupational hazard. They are supposed to be afraid of strangers and therefore of crossing the threshold, of going out into the dangerous world they are supposed to be too weak to handle. They face no pressure of having to be in charge, which makes them more passive and prone to further levels of victimization. When he saw Mary for the first time, a shy girl sitting on her own, Billy's first excited thoughts were: "I'm a pioneer. I'm in enemy territory, I'm going to knock it into shape, impose a bit of order" (Stephenson 18). Billy chose Mary as an unprotected woman over whom he could exert control and through doing so finally take the reins of his own life back into his own hands. Mary repeated a pattern by choosing a depressed alcoholic, which her father had become after her mother's death. She tries repeatedly to justify men's behavior—first her father's, when she declares "It's not his fault. It's not his fault, I won't have that, he loves me, and I love him so hard that my chest hurts, but there's drink and a great sadness and I'm so small I can't help" (Stephenson 19), and then her husband's, when she says, "I looked into your eyes and my heart welled up. Oh, I will save you, I will, I will save you" (Stephenson 20). Mary plans to save Billy by providing him with a family, which contrasts with Freud's idea of a woman being saved by a man giving her a baby. A woman has an unacknowledged role and a disturbing significance in a man's life.

The ethics of justice is the convention established by masculine competition and dominance. As Virginia Woolf described in Three Guineas, aggressive patriarchal patterns enable the ethics of justice to persist and rule over family relations which are at the heart of the ethics of care. Though a family is a microsociety, the law must be respected if a member wishes to enjoy the rights and privileges of the society; but the play demonstrates the limits of conventional justice for the abused women. For Billy, his military discipline and perverted control over his family created an orgasmic transcendence. However, his abusive behavior led him to develop health problems that turned him into an outsider to society: "Sometimes he'd lie on the floor and shout. / BILLY: I don't want to live, I want out, I want out"; and as his daughters who killed him explain: "So really we did him a favour. Either he went, or we all did" (Stephenson 27).

Stoning Mary

In Debbie Tucker Green's *Stoning Mary*, Mary's crime resembles that of earlier revenge dramas: she kills the boy soldier who has slain her parents. In a series of scenes that include a married couple fighting over the one prescription for an AIDS drug they both need, a mother mourning her missing son, and Mary awaiting execution by stoning for killing the boy soldier, this play theatrically fuses elements of different cultures into the universal language of human archetypes that can readily be recognized and understood. Referencing a globalized world of contrasting cultures, the playwright evokes conflicts stemming from the AIDS epidemic, savage regional wars that impress young boys as fighters, and the ancient punishment of stoning to death—all typically associated with Africa—but demands that actors are white, and specifies that the setting must be the country in which the play is performed. Its tone is expressed in the words the wife, dying of AIDS, says to her dying husband: "Didn't think it would get to this [...] y'didn't think dyin would draw out so dramatic, didja?" (Tucker Green 5-6)

The pairs of characters who take the stage in the sequence of scenes do not display the emotions that could be expected of people in their situation. Fighting over the single supply of AIDS drugs, husband and wife both demonstrate stereotypically masculine toughness, avoiding crying or any demonstration of emotions, and thus shunning the formation of powerful memories that such emotions could produce. Self-division is apparent in their representation by two roles: Husband and Husband Ego battle Wife and Wife Ego. Despite these similarities, their status difference is revealed in the following exchange:

> HUSBAND: I liked you lookin after me.
>
> WIFE: You had to be looked after.
>
> [...]
>
> WIFE: When have you (ever) – you wouldn't know / how
>
> HUSBAND: You're never sick. (Tucker Green 14)

Their daughters exemplify a similar toughness. They hurt each other with words, avoid touch, and in many ways repeat the patterns of their parents' conflicts, as can be seen in the following passage:

> YOUNGER SISTER: What if your – 'you me' – never had no one else to call?

OLDER SISTER: I'd ask my 'me you' self why. If I was still *you*. Which I wouldn't be... (Tucker Green 55)

Similarly, the parents of the boy soldier do not express emotion. After their terrifying child has been killed, Mum is trying to cry, but cannot 'stream' as Susan, in *Five Kinds of Silence* was able to:

DAD: *I* know how dry your eyes were when was with us – and I can see how dry your eyes are. Even now. (Tucker Green 66)

The sisters of *Stoning Mary* are stunned by their helplessness, embarrassed and ashamed, not unlike the sisters of *Five Kinds of Silence*; but instead of being gentle, as Susan and Janet are, these two express their sadness through anger at each other, as if that could help make the situation less ominous. The older sister even continues the pattern of the parents' dialogue, as she has AIDS in a later scene and fights with her boyfriend over what remains of the last medicine they could afford. The parents of the murdered child soldier also run out of ways to change their habitual pattern:

DAD: Nothing?

MUM: ... Nothing.

... I can't think of nothing good... (Tucker Green 2005: 10)

Then they turn to rage and self-deprecating disgust before sinking back into numbness:

DAD: genetically modified [...]

contaminating naturally organic me / and he –

[...]

never naked of someone else's

bottled version...

[...]

just lose the real you for good.... (Tucker Green 2005: 23-24)

[...]

MUM: Outshone by our son. (Tucker Green 33)

African culture strongly resonates in *Stoning Mary*, but is theatrically linked to white European dominance. In African culture the mother is respected; her individual decisions lead family life. Placing such values and patterns within the framework of western civilization shows loss of the necessary feeling of protection within any kind of group. Seemingly, the play is written in prose, but the dialogues sound deliriously poetic, which is in accordance with the situations they present. *Stoning Mary* is African in the nature of its language. Words and melody are a unity, and in many African languages the intonation influences meaning. The form of the play resembles African poems, with a refrain, a preparation for a divine trance ending in a finalizing message in the last line, and then a new rhythmic cycle. Words of actors playing alter egos give rhyme, and conscious and subconscious give different gradations to words such as *sick, sicker, sad, sadder*. Polished reality is on the outside; a rough truth is under the surface. Content corresponds to the Brechtian form. European theatre deals with relations between people, and African theatre is interested in relations between people and everything that is not human. It transcends the factual in its representations of false forms of kinship. In its fusion of forms, the play exposes serious issues relevant to the survival of humankind.

Mary, the woman who has been tried and convicted in *Stoning Mary*, has an intentionally limited stage presence. Brought on stage very late in the play, she is in a prison cell, awaiting her execution. Although the title of the play points to her as the main character, she has had no introduction. The accusation and trial are not represented. Mary has but one scene just before being stoned to death, when she talks with her sister about her prospective photograph in the newspapers. Her sister thinks that Mary should take her ugly glasses off before the show; her sister also scorns her for accepting free medical help from the state. Mary speaks haltingly and cannot finish her sentences; only when she is angry do her words splash out whole and clear. Everything else is stammering, insecure, bewildered. She justifies her crime as an action acknowledging her parents: "Least I done somethin. [...] Mum and Dad'd be ... They'd been prouda / me" (Tucker Green 63-64). Her concern, however, goes beyond her own parents: "ourn weren't his first, he'd killed other people" (64). Mary delivers the longest speech in the play when she expresses her anger and frustration that the "feminist bitches... the professional bitches... the black bitches... the rootsical bitches... the white the brown bitches..." and on and on, describing women who are educated, rebellious, political, and powerful, have refused to sign petitions, march for her, or engage in any effort to save her from being stoned to death. In the end, she dies alone and without trust in human solidarity, deserted by her sister, who gives away her ticket and does not attend the stoning, and hated by the soldier's mother, who picks up the first stone.

Conclusion

Both plays exemplify the falsity of commercialized notions of equality between men and women and equality among women. The representatives of the youngest generation in both plays are "sterile hybrids" (Simon 100) of the wild and the civilized, human and robotic. Bennett Simon's thesis that "tragedy is centrally concerned with the problem of procreation within the family at war with itself" (Simon 49) is borne out in families that lack the harmony and strength to rear children and preserve the household. Feelings are split between prescribed empathy and inevitable aggression. Action is split between the ethics of care and the ethics of justice, but no common meeting ground for the two enables meaning.

One such reaction to the loss of meaning is what Nietzsche calls 'passive nihilism', 'will to nothingness,' when life turns away from itself, as there is nothing of value to be found in the world. Mary's desperate words of prayer in *Five Kinds of Silence*—"Let it end here. Let it end with us. I don't want grandchildren. Let the blight end here" (Stephenson 29)— thus sound like a sobering prophecy by an omniscient chorus. The dying husband in *Stoning Mary* comes to a similar conclusion: "God got bored before we did" (Tucker Green 17). *Five Kinds of Silence*, however, seems to contain the seeds, though blighted, of some form of continuation, of 'going on'" (Simon 259) beyond the end point of the play, because the women have bought shelving for the spare room in their new house (Stephenson 30).

Both plays highlight the incapability of official social instruments in dealing with victimized members of society. These institutions mostly make the problem even greater by putting the victim under the spotlight, into a laboratory-like setting where the weird thing may be examined from all angles while isolated from the real world. They are pressured into feeling what does not come naturally to them. Embarrassment and anger at the unprotective mother, which brings to mind the psychoanalytical *'mother, why did you have me a girl?'* is expressed before silent acquiescence to the patriarchal norm. The fictional, abstract ideal of the patriarchal ethics of justice, is the point of origin for the formation and differentiation of the given psychological resources into preparatory attitudes, susceptibilities, and character traits. The individual then wears the character traits demanded by this fictional goal, just as the character mask (persona) of the ancient actor had to fit the finale of the tragedy (Adler 94). Humiliation is the strongest opponent to progress as both genders waste their energy to react to it, either through aggression or passive sadness. Billy even suggests his own defense mechanism when giving a piece of advice to his female family members: "Gather your thoughts, say nothing, take your time, there's still time. [...] Laugh at him, go on. Laugh" (Stephenson 11). A woman can get support only if she can be pitied, i.e. if her crime was self-defense after a long time of putting up with abuse.

From a feminist aspect, it is important to point out that Maries are not good carers, as they have not recognised their own identities were worth caring for. Female ethics of care is able to bring results only when it is freed from the patriarchal demand for female self-sacrifice. Social regression is at the core of helplessness and acceptance of the status quo, such as the mother's in *Stoning Mary,* when she picks up the first stone while being unable to cry after the death of her son, the boy soldier. Possessive masculine ethics took her son away: "I never lost him," she insists, defending herself against her husband's accusations, "I didn't I didn't I didn't... They took him. They took him. They *took* him," (Tucker Green 35) she tries to convince herself. Her son's true colours have been forgotten or have even faded into an image of a hero since his murderer is waiting for a death sentence. Within the same ethics, the mother is expected to be a proud mourner; however, she is unable to cry and worries that everybody will notice her dry eyes. From this standpoint, she sees fitting in with the male pattern as the only solution and discards the very essence of the ethics of care she had only started to grasp. On the other hand, Mary's older sister is not weak when she adapts her ethics to protect her life or when she refuses to come to Mary's stoning after realizing how futile Mary's purely emotional and impulsive actions are. Harsh circumstances and the understanding that her life will soon end brings the realization that convention is a mere artificiality that will not alter the situation: "Like someone up there's gonna save you," (Tucker Green 11) wife ego says, and "...like some higher bein would bother bein here," (Tucker Green 17) even husband ego later agrees.

By provoking some sort of institutional attention, by refusing to slip "through it all like ghosts" (Stephenson 27), and by surprising everyone with their active reaction to violence, the women of these plays do, in some sense, advance their cause. They have managed to mobilize public efforts towards at least some kind of inclusion of ethics of care into general education through the new ideology of tolerance, general awareness that the desire to be cared for is an innate human characteristic every healthy human will positively respond to, and is thus a legitimate part of a combined ethics functional and applicable today.

WORKS CITED

Adler, A. The individual psychology of Alfred Adler: A systematic presentation in selections from his writings. Eds. Ansbacher, H. and R. Ansbacher). New York: Basic Books, 1956. Print.

Gilligan, C. In a Different Voice: Psychological Theory and Women's Development. Cambridge, MA: Harvard University Press, 1993. Print.

Saul, J. Feminism: Issues and Arguments. Oxford: Oxford University Press, 2003. Print.

Simon, B. Tragic Drama and the Family: Psychoanalytic Studies from Aeschylus to Beckett. New Haven: Yale University Press, 1988. Print.

Stephenson, S. Five Kinds of Silence. New York: Dramatists Play Service, 2000. Print.

Tucker Green, D. Stoning Mary. London: Nick Hern Books, 2005. Print.

Woolf, V. A Room of One's Own. Harmondsworth: Penguin Books, 1945. Print.

Woolf, V. Three Guineas. San Diego: Harcourt Brace & Company, 1966. Print.

Chapter 11.

Aileen Wuornos or, the Heroine of Last Resort

An Essay in Seven Parts[1]

Jules Odendahl-James

Part 1: Just because you're paranoid, doesn't mean they aren't out to get you.

On an early fall evening in October of 2011, at the first rehearsal with the cast of Carson Kreitzer's *Self Defense or, The Death of Some Salesmen* at the University of North Carolina, Greensboro, I read the following sentences from my copy of Caesar Lombroso's *The Female Offender*:

> The female born criminal surpasses her male counterpart in the refined, diabolical cruelty with which she commits her crimes. Merely killing her enemy does not satisfy her; she needs to watch him suffer and experience the full taste of death. [...] sexuality can be exaggerated in female born criminals; this is one of the traits that makes them similar to men. Due to it, all women born criminals are prostitutes. While prostitution may be their least significant offense, it is never absent. Eroticism is the nucleus

around which their other characteristics revolve. (Lombroso and Ferrero 182, 184)

Then I read from notes I'd made during my dissertation research (2000-2003), specifically an excerpt from State's Attorney John Tanner's opening statements during the trial of Aileen Wuornos, the Florida woman on whose case *Self Defense* is based, for the murder of pawn store owner (and convicted sex offender) Richard Mallory:

> Ultimately, the bottom line is, the evidence in totality will show that Aileen Carol Wuornos likes control. She had been exercising control for years over men. Tremendous power that she had through prostitution. She had a devised a plan now and carried it out to have the ultimate control. All that Richard Mallory had she took, including his life. Under the law, under the law, she must pay with her life. (qtd. in Kennedy 142-43).

Finally, I asked the cast to turn in their scripts to a moment late in Act 5, titled "Jesus told me to write to you," when an unnamed male prosecutor makes his opening statements regarding the evidence against *Self Defense*'s protagonist Jolene Palmer.

> PROSECUTOR: The evidence is clear. This man-hating lesbian became a prostitute for the control over men. And when that thrill was no longer enough, she moved on to the ultimate control— murder. She lured Tom Waldren into the woods in order to kill him and steal everything he had—his car, his personal possessions, even up to and including his life. (Kreitzer 63).

A hush fell over the room. While most of the cast knew that Kreitzer's play was inspired by Wuornos' life, the direct line of argument regarding inherent female criminality and sexual deviancy from a largely repudiated nineteenth-century criminologist to a Florida's state's attorney courtroom declarations in 1992 to his doppelgänger's arguments in this 2002 play was irrefutable. In that chain of associations, we found our way to a central dramaturgical question: How does this play and its production move an audience to want to understand someone whose entire forward progression as a character shatters every possibility of empathetic identification?

There is no doubt, I remember saying, *that Aileen Wuornos killed at least six men between 1989 and 1990 in central Florida. There is no doubt that during this time she was earning whatever money she could through sex work with mostly anonymous clients found hitchhiking along Florida's interstate highway system. There is no doubt that upon her arrest, an array of what seemed like stock characters from Hollywood central casting— a betraying female lover; a born-again Christian woman; a pot-smoking ambulance-chasing attorney; a feminist criminologist; an overworked female public defender; an evangelical, anti-pornography crusading prosecutor— influenced the tone and path of her criminal defense, or lack thereof. There is no doubt she was paranoid, violent, foul-mouthed, and seemingly devoid of conventional expressions of femininity. By the time of her October 9, 2000 execution she had publicly repudiated portions of her initial statements claiming self-defense. With such irrefutable evidence about the real-life inspiration for Jolene Palmer, how does Kreitzer offer the audience a way to identify with a violent offender without excusing or admiring her violence? Why should we care about someone like Jolene Palmer?* That, I said as I concluded my dramaturgical presentation, is what we are going to spend the next four weeks trying to figure out.

Part 2: Deathwatch

I have traveled to Florida only once to what might be called the unhappiest place on earth: the city of Starke. When I hit the "welcome to" sign midday on October 8, 2002, I realize the deep resonance of the name. A municipality of less than six thousand, it sits on a rather sprawling expanse of land for such a small population. Its largest "job creator" is the prison system, which includes four facilities in the space of twenty miles: Union Correctional Institution, New River East Correctional Institution, Lawtey Correctional Institution, and Florida State Prison, home of Florida's death chamber. I am struck by the way prisons gobble land, as if the gulf between "us" and "them" of non-criminals and criminals require physical acreage in order to keep the mental divide wide and clear. I was in Starke as part of my dissertation research on the Aileen Wuornos case. Her execution, delayed for a decade, was finally scheduled. The night before, I sat in a Day's Inn watching local newscasts hum with modulated excitement at the conclusion of a case that had made headlines since 1990. Much of the same themes and language about female criminality, the twists and turns of death penalty cases, and the prisoner's culpability and competency were on display as had been throughout the past ten years. At this moment, however, a particular sore spot—the popularity of Wuornos' story to non-journalists—emerged in almost every news report. My notes reflect my flipping through the channels:

> The Wournos case already has spawned two movies, an opera and several books.
>
> She's been the subject of films, a TV movie, a BBC special, a San Francisco opera, books, and scholarly essays.
>
> [...] countless newspaper stories, several books, a few movies and even an opera [...]
>
> Her life of crime has been told in two movies, three books, an opera [...]. (Odendahl 88)

The idea that such a criminal's life would rise to the level of an opera[2] seems particularly galling to newscasters. Television programmers, on the other hand, see a ripe opportunity. In the month prior to Wuornos's execution, "killer women" true crime and fiction shows appear throughout cable and network schedules. This includes the season four premiere of *Law & Order: Special Victim's Unit*, an episode titled "Chameleon," which starred Sharon Lawrence as a prostitute who robs and murderers her clients and claims self-defense.

It is during my weekly searches for Wuornos news updates that I find Carson Kreitzer's *Self Defense* in the summer of 2002. At that time, Wuornos's execution date sat in limbo and in an effort to speed up the process she retracted all earlier claims of self-defense and dropped both her death-sentence appeals and her abuse lawsuit against the Florida Department of Corrections. This turn of events was not lost on reviewers of the New York premiere of *Self Defense* in June of 2002. Writing for *The Village Voice* about the play's production at HERE Arts Center, Charles McNulty admires Kreitzer's refusal to "sentimentalize or condone" her killer protagonist but questions the "disproportionate amount of care in conveying Jolene's side of the story" (69). In a *nytheatre.com* interview along with Randy White, the director of the HERE production, Kreitzer addresses the interviewer's concern regarding what possible interest the public should have in "these women who have killed and admit it." The play, she argues, unapologetically foregrounds the extreme conditions under which Wuornos and sex workers like her exist without glorifying violence:

> I think we definitely have things to learn from their extreme lives. [...] Prostitutes have long been considered "disposable." This is one prostitute who stood up, who decided her life was worth more than someone else's. I may not agree with what she did, but I certainly have to admire the fact that she managed to survive a life that would certainly have killed me. (May 21, 2002)

Because of this willingness to take seriously the core social critique at the heart of Wuornos's claims, *Self Defense* stands alone in the myriad popular culture renderings of the case because it dares the audience to imagine what we might do in situations of clear and present danger and to consider our own complicity in a legal system which preemptively denies claims of self defense for "selves" that exist on the social margin.

Part 3: A Heroine of Last Resort

The Last Resort is the name of the Port Orange, Florida biker bar where Wuornos was arrested in January, 1991, on warrants dating from the mid-1980s related to charges against her registered under her Lori Grody alias.[3] After weeks in custody, suffering alcohol withdrawal and being plied with investigator-orchestrated calls from her lover Tyria Moore, Wuornos eventually confessed to and was charged with murdering multiple "middle-aged men."[4] In a life of events and characters "straight out of Jerry Springer" (McNulty 68)—encompassing an abusive, pedophile father; absent mother; proud but poor grandparents/guardians; fully active sex-life by age 12; unplanned pregnancy at 14 resulting in a son's adoption; an annulled marriage in her twenties to a man forty years her senior; a life lived out mostly on the streets—The Last Resort provides the *coup de grace* and an apt metaphor for Wuornos' biography. It also exposes the vast underbelly of the "Sunshine State," where theme parks, family resorts, lavish ocean homes, and celebrity nightlife are marketed to tourists and millionaires, while the state's median household income has languished in the mid-$40,000s since 1990.[5] Florida's high incidence of rape yield the statistic that one in six women will suffer rape,[6] and the stories of its violent serial murderers (e.g., Danny Rolling, Ted Bundy, and Gerald Stano) are staples subjects of true-crime programming.

Most of the Floridians we meet in Kreitzer's play live in this Last Resort world. Their marginal existence makes them ripe targets for victimization, and the playwright employs two theatrical devices to keep the audience's critical eye trained on the systemic erasure of certain kinds of victims. First, she creates "a Thanatos/Eros Greek Chorus of sorts" (Kreitzer 8). Three female actors are cast as characters based on real people (e.g., Wuornos's born-again Christian adoptive mother, Arlene Pralle; feminist legal advocate and scholar, Phyllis Chesler; public defender, Tricia Jenkins). Each also takes a turn as a relative of one of Palmer's victims or a member of the media reporting on the story. The most significant role each actor plays, however, is as one of three sex workers (Daytona,

Pandora, and Chastity) and as one of three corresponding, unnamed coroners. Through such double- and triple-casting, Kreitzer encourages the audience to see women's position as always a potential victim of sexual assault and murder and as a potential family or community member whose life will be touched by extreme violence. Women's relationship to victimhood is not simply a theoretical assertion. Kreitzer's second key dramaturgical choice reinforces the layers of ensemble characters' experiences by demanding a fluid approach to time and place. In her "Production Notes," Kreitzer insists that action "should flow more or less seamlessly from start to finish, a stream of quick cuts" (6). In her notes on setting, Kreitzer describes a "two-level set with three playing areas" that "suggest" distinct locations (5). Much like the actors, these places are double- and triple-cast to assist speedy transitions. For example, in the UNC-Greensboro production the place where interrogation scenes were played transformed into the courtroom by shifting a chair and changing the focus of the actors from upstage to downstage. The stripper poles were only activated when dancers used them. At other times, they became structural elements of the police precinct wall or a highway motel room.

Both Kreitzer's staging recommendations reinforce the pace and frequency of the text's change in time and place. It also supports the layering of perspectives she embeds in her casting model. For example, in the Prologue, we see three female coroners dissecting a male body—a body we come to learn is one of Palmer's victims. While their demeanor and appearance is clinical and medically authoritative, they wear stereotypical sex-worker gear underneath. In the UNC-Greensboro production, the height and shine of the heels and boots and the slightly heavy make-up were the only signs that there might be "more" to these professionals. This more is revealed in a sound cue, "Suicide Blonde" by INXS, which breaks the somber mood and ends the Prologue. At this music, coroners let down their hair and removed their glasses and outerwear in homage to thousands of pornographic film scenarios. They then proceeded to dance across the stage stopping at the metal poles on either side of the playing space. The stage transformed into a seedy men's club, complete with strobe and red lighting, as the title for Act 1, "Paranoid and Pussy Crazy," appeared on two large screens. Then as quickly as the location appeared, the music faded, the lights shifted from disco to fluorescent, the strippers made their way off-stage and were replaced by the police investigators and their captain, reviewing the details of the murder cases at the center of the plot.

The Prologue's melded identification of crime solver and potential crime victim is also a staple of contemporary crime stories. Female medical examiners appear on countless television police procedurals and in a multitude of forensic novels.[7] While either brusque and interpersonally awkward or warm and friendly when dealing with the living, these characters' devotion to the dead is unquestioned. They humanize the victims, by serving as a "medium" between their ravaged bodies and the legal system, forcing investigators to pay attention to the dead no matter the individual's history. They also humanize the legal system by interjecting maternal-like care into the rather brutal processes of autopsy and forensic pathology. In *Self Defense*, however, the link between sex worker and coroner illuminates another tension when the victims are female but lack standing as "women" or at least as the kind of women who have a right to justice. The shifts in character, time and place are so quick that over the course of the seven acts it is almost impossible to separate the sex worker from the coroner or from the other multiple female characters they portray. The aggregate effect is that an audience is able to see a kinship with women across strata of existence and potentially see a heroine, even if of last resort, in Jolene Palmer.

PART 4: NO HUMANS INVOLVED

In 1993, two years after Aileen Wuornos' conviction and receipt of six death sentences, a San Diego public art project made waves by calling attention to the abbreviation "NHI." Billboards sprang up across the city with the acronym emblazoned next to photographs of Donna Gentile, a victim of an as yet unidentified murderer of 45 women, most of whom, like Gentile, were sex workers and some of whom, also like Gentile, were police informants. Gentile herself was found strangled to death with gravel stuffed in her mouth a month after she testified against two officers accused of misconduct. "NHI" stood for "No Humans Involved" an abbreviation reportedly adopted by detectives in the San Diego police department in reference to this string of rapes and murders of sex workers between 1985 and 1992. The billboards were part of a corresponding art exhibit titled MWI: Many Women Involved, organized by artist Carla Kirkwood. The piece drew local and state attention to both the casual and institutionalized misogyny and discrimination cultivated by work in law enforcement.

NHI enters *Self Defense* as a charge leveled by Jolene Palmer to the story's one redeemable cop, Bucket. In Act 5, when Palmer and Bucket cross paths for the first time, in her initial interrogation, she demands to know if he has noticed the lack of "unsolved prostitute murders" in his "NHI files" since her crimes. He seems to recognize but is reluctant to admit the designation. She challenges him to "go through those files, there. Look for yourself" (55). Daytona then appears to fill in details for the audience:

> NHI.
>
> Is a police term.
>
> Prostitutes. Biker girls. If no family comes forward to put the heat on. Or if the family is powerless. Poor. Non English speaker.
>
> Goes in a file marked NHI.
>
> No Humans Involved. (56)

Towards the end of that same act, after consulting with one of the coroners about whether Palmer meets the definition of a serial killer, Bucket brings his findings to the attention of his captain. There have been fewer murders of prostitutes, a reduction of the same number as the number of men Palmer is charged with killing. The captain is a man whose credibility is already tainted by a moment in Act One when he demands a blowjob from one of the strippers he is questioning about the death of Tom Waldren. He dismisses Bucket's concerns in language that reminds the audience which citizens they have been sworn to protect and serve:

> Are you worried about Prostitute Quality of Life, here? Are you concerned that not enough fucking Hookers will choose the Sunshine State to ply their trade? [...] We're never gonna run out of hookers. [...] Now, if white middle-aged businessmen pick someplace else to live and work and spend their hard earned vacation dollars, THEN we're in TROUBLE. (65-66)

It would be easy to critique this speech as hyperbole born out of Kreitzer's emulation of hard-boiled, true crime language and (male) character construction in *Self Defense*. In the months leading up to the UNC-Greensboro production, however, North Carolina was the site of multiple NHI cases. Between 2005 and 2009, nine African-American women in Rocky Mount went missing, all with a history of addiction and/or prostitution, and all of whom lacked a permanent or consistent living situation. At this same time, a homeless man stabbed a prominent white female civic leader to death. A massive manhunt ensued with full-scale participation of state and local law enforcement. Her killer was apprehended in one day. As to the "Murdered or Missing Sisters," a name given by one of the victim's family members, it was only after their families banded together for a public vigil and a billboard campaign in early 2009 that the story was picked up nationally. As a result, law enforcement in the area focused efforts and resources in a way that eventually produced a suspect and an arrest. Just three weeks prior to the Greensboro premiere of *Self Defense* in November 2011, Antwan Pittman was found guilty of the murder of Taraha Shenice Nicholson and sentenced to life without parole. Whether he will be tried for the deaths of the other eight women is yet to be seen.

In an article that appeared in the June 2010 issue of *GQ Magazine* titled "The Lost Girls of Rocky Mount," Rocky Mount police chief Gerald Manley is quoted giving this advice to the families of the missing women, "You have to stay on us. Let us know that you're not going away until you know we've done everything we possibly could do. Because if you don't care, I don't know why we should" (Draper). All of us working on *Self Defense* found this an unsettling verification that the world of the play was alive and well over a decade after Wuornos' conviction and execution.

PART 5: DIFFICULT VICTIMS

Act one of *Self Defense* finds investigators frustrated with their first victim, a man who is "paranoid and pussy-crazy" (15). There are too many suspects but no motive, unless they take seriously the sex workers' claims about the victim's sexual proclivities. As Daytona tells the audience: "The kinda stuff he was into, the kinda *impulses* he was useta getting' satisfied, I'm not surprised the man is dead" (70). A difficult victim is difficult to rally around. Fortunately for the police, better victims turn up. "He's my great hope," Bucket declares about a "sausage delivery guy" whose sister we watch give an impassioned news interview: "She must have been posing as a stranded motorist because my brother would never have stopped to pick up a prostitute, but a woman in trouble? He would definitely have picked up a woman having car trouble." Not only does this victim have family to vouch for him, his general profile seems to satisfy even Bucket that he is not a potential john: "No priors, no beat-up ex-wives. A sister who loves him. Speaks pretty well for the guy" (74).

As the male murder victims in *Self Defense* become more legible, more legitimate, easier to cast as unsuspecting innocents, the more illegitimate and illegible the female killer becomes. Palmer is a prostitute, and therefore rape is deemed to be impossible. Perhaps she played a woman in distress, someone who tried to offer sex and, when rebuffed, resorted to robbery and murder. She's a foul-mouthed, loud, alcoholic who carries a gun. Her entire M.O. is masculine. As her lover Lu tells the captain, "Everybody said she was five-eight or ten. That's just how she acts. She's five-five. [...] She just acts bigger" (34-35). That detail further undermines her claims of physical abuse; what man could overpower *her*? She talks about her "wife" (56) so lesbianism taints her claim of prostitution. Her violence is both evidence of her lack of standing as a "normal" woman and proof of the inherent criminality of the female sex. All of these elements condemned Wuornos in real life and do the same for Jolene Palmer in the world of *Self-Defense*. She is doubly monstrous: too bad to be a woman and bad because she is a woman.[8]

In Starke, during the days before Wuornos' execution, journalists reminded the public that Wuronos was a dangerous animal, one who has claimed she "would kill again" if ever released. Feminist, LGBT, and sex-worker advocacy groups had long abandoned Wuornos's case. Those that remained were the usual forces that work against capital punishment itself; they were not specifically concerned with this woman's case. The refrain of local coverage was clear:

> One look at Aileen Wuornos, and you can almost feel the venom. Then, she opens her mouth.
>
> Unrelentingly grim and angry, she has screamed at judges and once called the jurors who convicted her "the scumbags of America."
>
> Aileen Wuornos, the venom spitting, teeth gnashing female resident of Starke Prison's "X" block. (Odendahl 88)

Up to the moment of her death, Wuornos remained outside any realm of public understanding where the particulars of her case and behavior could be considered. Kreitzer offers her this space through the theatrical creation of Jolene Palmer in *Self Defense*.

PART 6: SHOW THROUGH TELLING

In her *AisleSay* review of the 2004 Rivendell Theatre Ensemble production *Self Defense* at the Steppenwolf Theater Garage, Kelly Kleiman noted how director Ed Sobel's staging choices offer the audience "no escape." Seated "around the action in isolated little pockets of a few seats each" with no intermission to break the tension, Kleiman found herself forced to examine events and people from almost cell-like confinement. In the UNC-Greensboro production of *Self Defense*, the size of the Brown Theater (140 seats maximum) and the choice of stadium seating enhanced the audience's juror point-of-view. We were cognizant of watching each other deliberate as the characters moved and appealed to us directly even outside the play's courtroom scenes. Such public intimacy is critical for the most graphic moment of the play, which comes late in the action as part of Act 6. Palmer testifies in her own defense[9], recounting a brutal rape at the hands of the "paranoid and pussy-crazy" Tom Waldren whose death begins the play.

The monologue is devastating not simply because of the excruciating detail with which Palmer describes what happened to her but because of the way she continually asks pardon from the judge and jury for the language she uses and the emotion she feels:

> I'm sorry. This is very difficult for me. I don't – this is very embarrassing. I'm sorry.
>
> He got undressed and threw his clothes on the floor...he lifted my legs all the way up to where my feet were near the window. Then he started having anal sex. He's doing this in a very violent manner...And then I don't know if he came...or climaxed or whatever...I don't know what the proper word is, I'm sorry, I talk street talk...But he took himself very violently out and put himself very violently in my vagina. I was crying my brains out...he said he loved to hear my pain. That my crying turned him on. (67)

For all the sensational elements from the real-life case, this monologue is the closest the play comes to staging an act of sexual violence. Kreitzer deliberately distances the audience from the rape by bringing us closer to its only living witness through her courtroom testimony.

Bertolt Brecht argued that actors performing as eyewitnesses would offer an audience the means by which to "form an opinion" about an event. When he advocates an epic theater acting training in line with a testimonial style of performance, Brecht recognizes the double-edged sword of emotion. His acting advice sounds almost like the coaching a defendant might receive from legal counsel:

> There is no question that the street-corner demonstrator has been through an 'experience', but he is not out to make his demonstration serve as an 'experience' for the audience. [...]. The theater's demonstrator, the actor, must apply a technique which will let him reproduce the tone of the subject demonstrated with a certain reserve, with detachment [...] He must not go so far as to be wholly transformed into the person demonstrated." (Brecht 122, 125)

By refusing the true-crime impulse to stage Palmer's encounter with Waldren, Kreitzer leaves the question of credibility and empathy solely in an accused killer's hands. Such a choice comes with risk. Much of what we have heard from Palmer up to this point in the play is inflected with paranoia, conspiracy theories, and rage. The chorus of sex workers, however, counters our suspicions by corroborating Palmer's experiences. Barbara Ozieblo argues these dramaturgical choices create "an audience that becomes witness to the violence being denounced, and is therefore obliged to react" (166). Whatever nods to true-crime storytelling that Kreitzer makes, in tone and character construction, she insists that a *Self Defense* audience experience a complex web of causes and effects of violence (against the NHI victims, against the male victims, and against Palmer herself). As a result, as Ozieblo observes, Kreitzer "manipulates her spectator" but in socially conscious way, "by means of a fragmented story presented on multiple level that places her as witness, into a position from which she has to try and understand" (168).

PART 7: CALLED HIM SON

On the morning of October 9, 2002, I stand outside Florida State Prison in a field designated for members of the media and the public who have come to witness, at a distance, Wuornos's execution. While I wait in between religious advocates praying for the death penalty's elimination and those praying for its swift hand of justice, a local reporter approaches me. He seems amazed at the lack of turnout. "I was here for Bundy," he says, "there were thousands of people. This is ...." He trails off. I wonder if he was going to say, "this is sad." He looks at his watch. It is 9:15am. 15 minutes before it happens. "Well, maybe it's starting up. Maybe there's going to be lots more people in a little bit" (Odendahl 93-94).

Bundy remains the king of Florida serial killers. *Self Defense* references Danny Rollings's gruesome murder of seven University of Florida co-eds (Kreitzer 30-31, 70), but even in the play Bundy is the more significant cultural figure. There are many reasons for his standing. Bundy was, to all outside appearances, a handsome, accomplished, intelligent man who used these features to mask his sadism. True-crime novelist Ann Rule cemented his image and that of the modern serial killer as the "stranger beside me" with her book of the same name. There is, however, another, lesser-known reason why Bundy is relevant to Wuornos's case. John Tanner, the prosecutor for Wuronos's one and only murder trial, was a significant figure in Bundy's death penalty appeals. Tanner was part of a team of evangelical Christian anti-pornography crusaders rallying behind Bundy in the mid-1980s because Bundy, in what other observers saw as a rather blatant attempt to stay his execution, claimed an obsession with pornography led him to acts of sexual violence.[10] They were unsuccessful in their bid to save his life, but Tanner (and his wife) went the extra mile to assure that Bundy's soul would be saved, praying with the killer on the eve of his execution (Morris).

In *Self Defense* Palmer's only death row visitors are two inept spirits: Goodness and Mercy. They descend into Palmer's cell near the end of Act 7 in the same stripper outfits worn by Chastity and Daytona and tell her of their intention to "guide you at the end" (81). When Palmer recites the twenty-third Psalm and the two specters seem unfamiliar with its meaning or significance, the condemned woman responds a line that always got a laugh at each UNC-Greensboro performance: "I can't even hallucinate no shit that makes sense?" (82). With great effort, Mercy holds Palmer in her lap even though each time she touches the prisoner the phantasm is physically racked by the "fear" and "ANGER" coursing through Palmer's body (81). This tender, if comic, scene critiques the supposed salve of religion and leaves the heroine's afterlife uncertain. Even Bundy was offered the peace of redemption. Palmer/Wuornos has no such savior.

The final word of *Self Defense* rests with the coroner/Pandora. She does not mention Tanner by name, but refers directly to the efforts made to understand and empathize with Bundy as a flawed human being despite the depravity of his crimes. This story, spoken directly to the audience, is the play's second most damning piece of testimony, after Palmer's rape account:

> CORONER: When the judge sentenced Bundy, [...] to two death sentences for the murder of over thirty women he acted like—He—He said, "You're a bright young man. I would have liked to see you practice law in my courtroom. But you went the other way, son."
>
> Called him Son.
>
> Like it was some awkward misunderstanding that led them both to that position. (86)

In this moment, Kreitzer offers a gut-wrenching detail similar to those that often mark the epilogues of true-crime narratives. Just when we think we can settle comfortably into notions of justice served and justice deserved, there is a turn that unsettles the story's conclusion. Typically, this element focuses on our insecurity about how and when crime will touch our lives. In *Self Defense*, however, the worry is one that has been gnawing at our consciousness since the early acts of the play: what kind of self is worth defending, let alone worth saving? With what the play has shown us, to place Palmer in the same category as Bundy seems not only undeserved but downright perverse. By directing us back to Bundy's case, Kreitzer reveals a hierarchy of value even among killers. Psychologists, religious figures, and journalists solicited Bundy's attentions but, without this play, Palmer/Wuornos seems destined for the NHI file of popular culture. While Kreitzer does not redeem her protagonist's crimes, she demands that we take a closer look at the file before it is closed. Once offered a more complex understanding and context for Palmer's actions, perhaps we might come to an understanding that is neither empathic, so often lacking critical reflection, as we see in John Tanner's recounting of his relationship with Ted Bundy, nor empty titillation, the type had from true-crime recounting of these murders—a nuanced perspective on human beings and the inhuman acts they commit.

Notes

1. This organizational structure is in homage to Kreitzer's play, which is subtitled, "A play in seven acts."
2. *Wuornos* an opera by Carla Lucero premiered in 2001 at the Yerba Buena Center for the Arts in San Francisco, California. The project's website www.wuornos.org gives a synopsis and production history.
3. Lori Grody was the name of Wuornos' maternal aunt. A much younger sibling to Diane Wuornos, Aileen's mother, Lori and her brother Barry were raised as siblings with Aileen by Diane's parents, Lauri and Britta Wuornos.
4. While the title of Kreitzer's play inserts the designation "salesmen" as a deliberate play on Arthur Miller's *Death of a Salesman* and the notion of the everyman tragic hero, the phrase most often used to refer to Wuornos's victims was "middle-aged men" or "middle-aged male motorists." The distinction is small but significant because Wuornos's status as a sex worker of Florida's interstate system is critical to contextualize both her actions and her victims.
5. "Florida: Median Household Income: 2011" *United Health Foundation* 2011. Web. http://www.americashealthrankings.org/FL/Median_Income/2011
6. Figure from the 2010 National Intimate Partner and Sexual Violence Survey. Reported by the *Florida Council Against Sexual Violence*. 2009. Web. http://www.fcasv.org/information/sexual-assault-statistics
7. For television examples see the many incarnations of *Law & Order*, the ABC drama *Body of Proof*, or TNT's *Rizzoli and Isles*. Patricia Cornwell's Kay Scarpetta is perhaps one of the first and most famous examples of the female medical examiner in the realm of fiction.
8. Even though the two films by British documentarian Nick Broomfield, *The Selling of a Serial Killer* (1992) and *Aileen: The Life and Death of a Serial Killer* (2003), present Wuornos in a sympathetic light, they also forward the thesis that Wuornos suffered from untreated mental illness. The central social criticism of the later film, which includes her last on-camera interview, is on Florida's willingness to execute a woman who Broomfield argues is obviously incompetent.
9. The monologue is taken almost verbatim from the transcript of Wuornos's testimony at her trial for the murder of Richard Mallory.

10. Individuals can watch the January 24, 1989 interview that Bundy gave Focus on the Family head James Dobson at the organization's *Pure Intimacy* website http://www.pureintimacy.org/piArticles/A000000433.cfm

Works Cited

Brecht, Bertolt. "The Street Scene." *Brecht on Theatre*, ed. and trans. Willett, John. New York: Hill and Wang, 1964 : 120-129. Print.

Draper, Robert. "The Lost Girls of Rocky Mount." *GQ, Gentlemen's Quarterly*. June, 2010. Online

Dubail, Jean. "Prostitute Suspected in 7 Deaths, Middle-Age Men Were Targets." *Sun-Sentinel* [Ft. Lauderdale, FL] January18, 1991: 21A. Print.

Kennedy, Dolores. *On a Killing Day: The Strange Story of Aileen Wuornos*. New York: Bonus, 1992. Print.

Kleiman, Kelly. Review of *Self Defense or, the death of some salesmen*, Rivendell Theatre Ensemble at the Steppenwolf Theater Garage. Chicago : *AisleSay*. n.d. Online.

Kreitzer, Carson. *Self Defense or, the death of some salesmen*. New York, Playscripts. 2004. Print.

Lombroso, Cesare and Guglielmo Ferrero. *Criminal Woman, the Prostitute and the Normal Woman*. Trans. Rafter, Nicole Hahn and Mary Gibson. Durham, NC: Duke University Press, 2004. Print.

Long, Phil. "Official doesn't want suspect to profit." *The Tampa Tribune*. February 4. 1991: 4. Print.

McNulty, Charles. "Love's Laborers Lost." *The Village Voice*. January 16, 2003: 69. *LexisNexis*. Online.

Morris, Bob. "Howls Mustn't Silence Tanner's Prayers." *Orlando Sentinel*. January 27, 1989. Online.

Nytheatre.com. "Carson Kreitzer & Randy White: *Self Defense*." May 23, 2002. The New York Theatre Experience, Inc., 2003. Online.

Odendahl, Julie Anne. *Bodies of Evidence: Portraits of Post-Feminine Performance*. Diss. University of North Carolina Chapel Hill, 2003. Print.

Ozieblo, Barbara. "The Victim and the Audience's Pleasure: An Exploration of Carson Krietzer's *Self Defense* and Stefanie Zadravec's *Honey Brown Eyes*." *Performing Gender Violence: Plays by Contemporary American Women Dramatists*, eds. Ozieblo, Barbara and Noelia Hernando-Real. New York: Palgrave Macmillan, 2012 : 155-172. Print.

Chapter 12.

The Trial as Framework in Emily Mann's *Mrs. Packard*

Lisa Hagen

"You are sane, Elizabeth. Keep saying that to yourself over and over: 'I am sane, I am sane.'

Let it become a little ditty in your head: 'I am sane'"

(Mann 37).

"The jury trial has been a drama for centuries...All come with dependable plots and surprise endings that might be expected of any long-running production. All proceed according to rules of engagement that suspend reality even as they simulate it: combining the restraint of a packed elevator with the tension of a showdown, the etiquette of the courtroom creates a world where witnesses are corkscrewed by courtesy and whispers echo like screams. The colorful cast, packed with familiar heroes and

villains, is also universal--and at the center stage sits the defendant, whose role is perhaps the most stylized of all"
(Kadri 277-278).

Many well-known plays written by women explore the legal trial as a way of activating discussions of gendered taboo as well as gendered oppression. Plays like Sophie Treadwell's *Machinal* and Maureen Dallas Watkins' *Chicago* focus on the staged trial, allowing the audience to sit in on the process itself. The accused murderesses' gender is a lynch-pin in the nature of the transgressions levied against them. Just recently, in 2012, a group established a historical exercise to re-try Mary Todd Lincoln for insanity, of which she was convicted in 1865 (Pfeiffer), hoping to ascertain whether a contemporary lens will change the verdict. In these cases the audience serves as a jury, applying their own value systems to re-try the woman on stage every time the play (or trial) is performed. This essay examines the play *Mrs. Packard* by Emily Mann (2009), which uses historical records to dramatize the asylum incarceration and trial of Elizabeth Parsons Ware Packard in the late 19th century. Packard had spoken openly, in the church led by her husband as pastor, of religious views that contrasted with those of her strict Calvinist husband. Although Elizabeth had received a seminary education (Carlisle 44), her views were tantamount to a crime in her husband's eyes. She had spoken her views plainly while running a Bible study class, and some have suggested that she was allowed to run the class specifically in order to "expose" what her husband considered insanity (Carlisle 45). It is known that the class's participation went from six to 46 people, and that two of those class members were doctors eventually present when she was removed to the Jacksonville Insane Asylum.

When Elizabeth was taken away, her husband Theo had to break into her room with an ax, bringing in the two doctors. Elizabeth describes it this way:

> The trio approached my bed, and each doctor felt my pulse, and without asking a single question both pronounced me insane. So it

seems that in the estimation of these two M. D.'s, Dr. Merrick and Newkirk, insanity is indicated by the action of the pulse instead of the mind! (Packard, *Marital Power* 4).

She was literally carried away as her children and the town members watched. The law that allowed her husband to commit her meant that, unlike other people committed to an asylum, she was given no initial trial. Elizabeth was tried only by her husband and the members of the community he enlisted to evaluate her. Carlisle writes that this law was "[i]ntended to shield married women from public humiliation in a court proceeding, [but] instead gave husbands a means for legal subjugation of unsubmissive wives" (46-47). Elizabeth was diagnosed as "morally insane," which was medically understood at the time not to affect intellectual function. In essence this diagnosis applied to people with full mental functioning who would not be distinguishable to any outsider as insane (Carlisle 50). It thus provided the perfect label for social and cultural radicals, because it could hardly be refuted.

When Elizabeth was eventually released from the asylum, Theo confined her in their home. Not knowing this was against the law, he ensured her right to a jury trial. Elizabeth was then released from the system of justice in which her husband was the only judge, and allowed to defend herself in court. Her husband's primary point was that her insistence on interpreting the Bible liberally (and even "mystically"), as well as her rejection of his spiritual and domestic guidance, qualified her as insane (Frost-Knappman and Cullen-DuPont 292). Her attorney countered: "Elizabeth refused to believe 'the Calvinist doctrine of man's total depravity, and that God has preordained some to be saved, others to be damned. She stands fully on the platform of man's free agency and accountability to God for his actions" (Stephen Moore qtd. in Frost-Knappman and Cullen-DuPont 293). Interestingly, much of the evidence of the case had been gathered in the private sphere: one doctor used as his basis for diagnosis and testimony an interview he did with Elizabeth before her confinement while pretending to be a travelling salesman

(Frost-Knappman and Cullen-DuPont 293). Much of the testimony focused far more on Elizabeth's failure or success in performing traditional female social roles, than on her religious thoughts. One witness testified that when Theo refused to help Elizabeth weed the garden, "[s]he was angry and excited and showed ill-will" (Frost-Knappman and Cullen-DuPont 294). Clearly, the trial focused on the parameters of femininity and "proper" domestic behavior, on either side of the argument: indeed, some testimony in her favor deemed her sane because she cleaned the house upon returning home, and acted generally as the "mistress of the house" (294-295).

The case of Elizabeth Packard as well as Emily Mann's play about the case, feature a vibrant discourse on the gendered nature of Elizabeth's "crime": madness. The very perception of madness is a gendered one; hence, naming it and the Mad Woman as taboo means that those women are themselves taboo – and this comes across within the legal process. Unlike the murderesses of *Chicago* and *Machinal*, Elizabeth Packard was accused of a transgression based on perceptions of "correct" gendered behavior rather than a heinous crime. Gender is an especially conscious construct here, because it forms the basis of her crime. Dissent would not have been illegal if she had been a man. In the book *The Female Offender*, written in 1895, we can see some of the specific ways madness was gendered. For example, the text mentions that the female hysteric shows a distinct erotic component in her hysteria, which comes out of "a spirit of adventure, or a desire for unknown emotions" (Lombroso and Ferrero 224). Because women were paternalized by the systems of law and marriage, their desire to transcend any of those normative narratives could then be read as madness. For men, who held much greater freedom in these arenas, a desire for adventure or new emotions would certainly not be called mad. Furthermore, women were expected to be submissive and serve others rather than themselves. Therefore, women who privileged themselves were also seen as insane:

[T]heir disposition is profoundly egotistical, and their absorbing preoccupation with themselves makes them love scandal and a public sensation. They are excessively impressionable, consequently easily moved to choler, ferocity, to sudden and unreasonable likes and dislikes. Their will is always unstable; they take delight in evil-speaking, and if they cannot draw public attention by baseless trials and scandalous forms of revenge, they embitter the life of those around them by continual quarrels and disputes" (Lombroso and Ferrero 219).

Again, it is difficult for men to be accused of madness on the same grounds, because the socio-cultural systems that define them do not place the same restrictions of behavior upon them.

This bias also had a profound effect on women because of the social perceptions of women's sphere of influence. Criminality and insanity were believed at the time to be primarily caused by influences of the parents and home life, rather than a blood inheritance or natural predilection (Blake 664). This was especially true of mothers, and women in general were seen as having a strong influence on the moral center of society ("The Heathen" 8). In an 1871 newspaper article about the conviction of a female criminal, the author writes:

While the bulk of women are, morally, decidedly better than the bulk of mankind, thoroughly bad women are decidedly worse than the worst of bad men; and it is even more essential that they should be restrained and punished than that the rigors of the law should be enforced against male criminals ("Conviction of Mrs. Fair" 4).

Paternalism was also rampant within the legal system. For most of the 19th century, married women could not sign contracts, claim the wages they earned, own property, keep property they owned before marriage, or even take custody of children after a divorce (Kirp, Yudof and Franks 31). This state of being was succinctly summarized by the women who signed the 1848 Seneca Falls Declaration of Sentiments, who wrote that "the married woman found herself 'in the eye of the law, civilly dead'" (Kirp, Yudof and Franks 31). This paternalism ostensibly operated to protect women, but it also reinforced invented social norms. In as much as it created a "stable social order" (32), it also reified systems that were sexist and oppressive. Elizabeth Packard was a victim of these protective laws. When she was first forcibly taken to the asylum, without a trial (something provided for in the law), she writes about it this way: "

> I had no chance of *self defence* whatever...I objected, and protested against being imprisoned *without any trial*. But to no purpose. My husband insisted upon it that I had no protection in the law, but himself, and that he was doing by me just as the laws of the State allowed him to do (Packard *Marital Power* 4).

Here Elizabeth recognizes the very crux of this situation: the law assumed that women should also want these laws in effect because women should want the normative morality system they uphold to be solidified. Otherwise, the woman was insane (Kirp, Yudof and Franks 33). This benevolently biased landscape meant that dissent equaled insanity, because consent was rational. Therefore, any change was extremely difficult to obtain within a legal system that privileged rational reasoning. Women were bound: in much of society's eyes, they could not actually "rationally" reason against the social order.

Mrs. Packard, the Play

Emily Mann's historically based play, *Mrs. Packard*, uses two systems of trial: the distanced and impersonal legal process and the personal and passionate struggle of the central character in a "non-trial." It is interesting to note the relationship of documentary theatre to evidence and trials. Forsyth and Megson outline the ways that a documentary piece is firmly rooted in the giving of evidence, which can be "testimony, orature and anecdote" (3). Mann herself also calls her plays testimonies. In both cases, there is a reference to the act of a trial: presenting evidence to a jury to reach a conclusion on a subject, although, as in the jury

The Trial as Framework in Emily Mann's *Mrs. Packard* 265

trial, there is a sense of shaping (not exactly reality). In documentary theatre, Reinelt notes that this shaping has "a measure of efficacy; it is a way of knowing" (23). Indeed, using Elizabeth's own words and using the archival material she has left behind, Mann has invited a sense of "realness" to the table – we are therefore reenacting the traumas, errors, and painful events of a real person's life, repeating them the way trauma is turned over and repeated, performing the terrifying mistakes of the past in a more "real" way than a purely fictional play. So what does this do for the audience? As in the case of the Mary Todd Lincoln re-trial, the audience is given the opportunity to re-cast the role of judgment in the case; in other words, the audience re-plays the original juries (both figurative and literal) in order to reclaim, learn from, and potentially undo the collective trauma of trials from the past.

The play uses the remembered formal trial as a framework for the action in which Mann deftly makes use of the trial trope to contextualize the interpersonal events of the play that ultimately do present evidence, witness, and arguments. For example, Elizabeth must present her arguments, gather testimony, and prove her innocence in her dis-empowered position as a patient in the asylum even as we see moments of the formal trial in which others (who are given legitimized positions on a stand) condemn or defend her. Notably, she is absent from the formal trial for most of the play, and that absence from the legal process speaks loudly as Elizabeth struggles against the unfair conditions of her confinement. The set design of the original production highlighted these separate spheres, placing the formal testimony on an "elevated catwalk" (Zinman). Another review describes the "steely gray, cavernous, two-tiered setting, hauntingly lighted by Jeff Croiter, [which] offers parallel universes for telling Elizabeth's story" (Seigel). In both cases the reviewers note the two universes represented on stage (the trial and the asylum). Through subtle shifts, the play employs the trial system to describe *both* spaces. As in many other plays that contain a trial, the audience becomes the de facto jury. In this case, that audience-jury sits in judgment of both the official and unofficial trials—in the courtroom and the Fifth Ward —to which Elizabeth is subjected.

To understand the structure of the trial and the non-trial, it is important to discuss how they operate as chronological events. Elizabeth's experience begins in a simulacrum, a parody of the jury trial. In this system Theo, the town, and then Dr. McFarland try to find her guilty of insanity. Later, she is given a formal "hearing" with the Trustees that presents a much different system, a more legitimate one. She is returned to the non-trial setting as Theo imprisons her at home, and finally the story concludes as she is given a formal trial with a judge and jury. Elizabeth is thus pulled back and forth between the parallel systems. The play, rather than present these sequentially as listed above, nests the non-trial actions (at her home and the asylum) *within* the frame of the final trial. This serves to highlight the difference in power and ability between the two systems. Furthermore, the structural layout of the trial and simulacrum-trial acts in a single way upon the audience-jury. Carlisle writes that Elizabeth Packard's ideas "exemplify the tension between modern and traditional thought in mid-nineteenth century America" (43), and the two worlds shown in the play exhibit a similar tension.

The legitimate trial process which frames the action can be seen as distanced and impersonal. However, it is also the biggest source of privilege and power for Elizabeth. In fact, in her historical writings, she focuses continually on the people who are willing to testify under oath to the true nature of the situation, thus clearly recognizing the singular power of the trial. However, the heart of the play occurs during the "non-trial" of her time in the asylum. Although she is passionate about her beliefs and her sanity, she is essentially powerless in that simulacrum, unable to reach beyond the oppressive social structures that surround her. The legitimate legal trial functioned in a perhaps unexpected way. The legal system was traditionally a source of disempowerment and infantilization for women. In this case, however (and paternalism set aside), the play explores the power Elizabeth is eventually able to wrest when allowed to speak in an official capacity, in a space where her testimony has efficacy.

The Judge and trial begin the play, setting up the encompassing framework and parallel arc to the non-trial of her experiences in the asylum. The Judge charges the "jury of twelve men" (Mann 7) to listen to the case. In this moment, Mann sets up the audience-jury as a totally different force than the trial-jury. However, the action instantly shifts into Elizabeth's arrival at the asylum, beginning the depiction of the non-trial, which is essentially held within the framework of the jury trial. During interviews with the doctor, McFarland, and her husband Theo, the doctor "presides" over the arguments between Elizabeth and her husband. McFarland has a certain power in the situation that a judge might have; and, critically, Elizabeth has no real power here. It is Theo and McFarland who directly negotiate her imprisonment, whether or not Elizabeth is allowed to speak. Ultimately, McFarland interprets the evidence of in/sanity as presented by both Elizabeth and Theo, and it is Theo's damning assertions about Elizabeth's "mad" mother and her (Elizabeth's) previous commitment to an asylum that hold sway. Elizabeth counters, and McFarland delivers a decision. Because the audience has just been led into this scene by the Judge's charge to the jury, we clearly continue to play that role in this flawed refraction of the justice system. In this scene, it is Theo who delivers the sentence: "you may think your own thoughts, Elizabeth, when you are thinking right; and once you are thinking right, you may return home" (Mann 17).[1]

In this scene and others we begin to see that the non-trial is characterized by several important features. First, it has shifting and unstable procedures that cater to and favor the most socially powerful figure. Further, the participants need to use tactics (rather than truth) to succeed: Elizabeth quickly realizes that rationally recounting her truth as a testimony will do her no good with McFarland. She tries tactics like flirting and pretending to be weak in order to get a favorable judgment. This system is also defined by the generalized inefficacy of the least powerful figure's testimony, as there is no jury, no impartiality. This is especially underlined when the non-trial scene is quickly juxtaposed with a figure giving evidence in the jury trial—a scene in which all testimony "counts." The simulacrum-trial allows for outright manipulation: in one interview between McFarland and Elizabeth, he lays his hands on her in an erotic way, as "treatment." She responds passionately and he kisses her forehead after a "long moment of profound mutual attraction" (Mann 25). To her confusion, he replies: "Merely a kiss of charity, my dear" (Mann 25). The interview concludes without Elizabeth being able to make any headway towards her freedom, because the corrupted interview allows for manipulation based on physical touch and emotions. In this system, much of the testimony can be dismissed by the person in power. After Elizabeth tells McFarland her points of view on religion in Act I (which is what got her into trouble in the first place), he quickly dismisses it all as "irrelevant" (Mann 27), forcing her to address only what he (and Theo) see as the issue: her "obstinance." Finally, the "sentences" given do not adhere to any legal system, but only to the implied social system. Late in Act I, McFarland delivers this ultimatum to Elizabeth: "...you will submit to sign an affidavit to honor and obey your husband in all things—that you will be his unconditional help-mate and support in his church, in his home, and in his bed. Sign this paper, and I shall send you home, *cured.* Agreed?" (Mann 39). Although Elizabeth gives a final plea to the doctor, and although she tries to negotiate this sentence, it is of no use in this system.

As an audience-jury, we quickly see that we are witnessing a fixed system against which Elizabeth will have little luck. When asked if she likes the asylum, she replies "No, I am afraid nothing 'agrees with me' here. None of this 'agrees with me'" (Mann 11). This is where the framing system becomes so critical. As the scenes in the asylum are frequently intercut with short pieces of testimony from the jury trial, we are continually framing the past with the future. There are no scene breaks, in fact, besides that testimony. At this point, all the jury trial testimony is *against* Mrs. Packard, declaring her insane. At the same time that the audience surely sees the faults in the sometimes-flimsy testimony, it also serves to create an arc for the framing device, as the severity of the jury trial testimony reflects our perceptions of the non-trial. At this moment in the play, the simultaneous scenes begin, as we hear testimony from the jury trial, and see scenes from her incarceration. By running the scenes in parallel, the framing device comments even more strongly on the actions taking place in the asylum, where Elizabeth is judged as well. In one example, a witness in the trial describes a scene at dinner where Elizabeth had spoken strongly of religion, which led her to feel Elizabeth was insane. At the same time, Elizabeth sits eating a meal at the asylum; as the witness gives testimony about a dinner scene that calls Elizabeth insane, we see Elizabeth existing in the result of those judgments. This is powerful for a contemporary audience because we still put women on social trial: it illuminates a time when being judged socially was just as binding and damaging as being judged in court.

The key connection between the trial and the non-trial is Elizabeth's writing. The written word, and the privilege of writing, is a means of expression that connects Elizabeth to the world of the formal trial and its inherent efficacy and legitimacy. It is the written documents she fights to produce during her time at the asylum that form the basis of her success at trial. In the beginning of her volume (eventually published) about her ordeal, the historical Elizabeth wrote: "In presenting this volume before the public, *I—the first person singular*—assume the entire responsibility of the statements and opinions it contains... It contains many singular thoughts and expressions, and is, thereby, a transcript of my own individuality upon paper. It has always been my fortune...rather *mis*fortune...to be a pioneer...therefore, I am called crazy, or insane, by those...that...cannot see the reasonableness of the positions and opinions I assume to advocate and defend...Truth is my argument—truth is my only weapon—truth is my only defense—truth is my only refuge" (Packard *Great Disclosure* 7-8). It is clear how important the act of writing out her arguments is to Elizabeth—not a given, but a great privilege. It is an important symbol in the play when she occupies a universe in which she holds so little freedom.

In the play, Elizabeth is first given a pen halfway through Act I, by Dr. McFarland. He offers it to her as a gift, a benefit of his feelings for her, and it allows her to construct a new kind of testimony: a more permanent one that may be read by more people than just him. Here the manipulative interviews can be undermined by her ability to write down her thoughts. As Elizabeth feverishly transcribes her beliefs, what has happened to her, and her wishes, the play switches to yet another parallel scene of jury trial testimony. As the testimony from a doctor who examined her is given, the audience jury sees her writing out her own perception of her thoughts, underlining the idea that in both cases (the trial and the non-trial) we have yet to hear Elizabeth testify on her own behalf in a context where she holds some power. Later in Act I, she begins to use her writing privilege to record the atrocities of the asylum, calling the document her "reproof" which she will give McFarland to "study" (Mann 47). However, the first time she attempts to use her writing to get what she wants and needs (by showing McFarland how unethically the patients are being treated) it has absolutely no efficacy within the non-trial system. The power figure, McFarland, not only rejects this writing, but takes away the privilege of writing altogether, as he is the only judge. When she tries to testify directly against the offenders, she is also rebuffed; her verbal accusations are made meaningless.

In Act II, Elizabeth is denied any sort of trial: she is locked in the ward for violent maniacs, not allowed any possessions (much less pen and paper), and shut away from all interaction that may help her. At this point, however, the jury trial testimony is getting flimsier, the framing device is serving to let the audience know there is a change coming in the action of the play, and sure enough, Elizabeth finds a way, in the locked ward, to hide pen and paper and continue her writing. It is very clear how much power this writing has for Elizabeth, because McFarland is furious when he discovers that she is still writing, and goes to extreme measures to stop her. He undermines it ("This scribbling only confirms to me your complete and total madness!" [Mann 68]), and threatens to fire any employee that helps her. The non-trial that has served his power position so completely now begins to break down; it no longer functions to protect him and oppress her. He eventually resorts to putting her in isolation to contain the threat. As the jury trial continues, the testimony becoming more insistent on Elizabeth's sanity, it is juxtaposed in parallel scenes with the abject brutality acted upon her in the asylum. The audience jury experiences new testimony just as we are witness to her powerlessness within another system.

After her husband Theo visits her in the asylum, eventually robbing her of all hope of leaving and putting her in a state of extreme disempowerment, the most powerful testimony of the jury trial is delivered. A Doctor testifies:

> I have earned advanced degrees in both theology and medicine...Mrs. Packard's explanation of woman representing the Holy Ghost, and man representing the male attributes of the Father, and that the Son is the fruit of the Father and the Holy Ghost is a very ancient theological dogma, sir, and entertained by many of our most eminent and learned men. It is by no means a mark of lunacy...I did not agree with all of her thoughts, but I do not call people insane because they differ from me, nor even from the majority of people...You might as well with as much propriety call Galileo mad, or Newton, or Jesus, or Luther, or Morse who electrified the world...With Mrs. Packard, there is lacking every indication of insanity that is laid down in the books. I pronounce her a *sane* woman, and wish we had a *nation* of such women (Mann 85-86).

It is after this witness that Elizabeth receives her first opportunity to provide testimony in a system where her words hold some power to free her. She negotiates a meeting with the Trustees of the asylum, who overrule Dr. McFarland. As she speaks her mind, it is juxtaposed with even more supportive testimony from the jury trial. She delivers a statement to the trustees in her defense that uses narrative and evidence to make her case. They perceive her words very differently than do Theo and McFarland, flipping the power by setting Elizabeth free and forcing her husband to take her home. Theo, in fact, is not allowed to speak in this context, primarily because it is Elizabeth's words that have the power in this new system. This pivotal scene that begins the move towards the jury trial brings the audience fully into the framing device.

After this point, Theo brings Elizabeth home but imprisons her in the house, locking her back into the previous system in which her powerlessness stems from the denial of her point of view, refusal of permission to write or communicate, and her husband's sole power to judge her actions. However, she is able to sneak out a letter to tell a friend of her situation, and her writing saves her. Theo's actions (imprisoning her in the house) are illegal, and she earns the right to speak in front of a judge and jury. Elizabeth is able to read a prepared written statement, and the power of her ability to write is fully realized when she is able to deliver it within the context of the court. Favorini writes that for Mann, "...letting her characters speak in their own words is also a way of hearing and recognizing minority voices" (165). At this moment within the play, and for the audience, Elizabeth's voice is fully heard. "Packard, a woman who appeared destined for quiet disappearance, instead was allowed to fight for her freedom. A jury of twelve men was asked to decide whether she was mad despite the fact that hers was not a criminal case" (Carlson 21).

The formal trial system is characterized, in this play, by the following aspects: first, there is a sense of legal responsibility, and (some) laws that protect Elizabeth. There is a power figure charged with being unbiased, and a system in which her words have efficacy. Finally, it is a system in which the verdict has material power (to free her). It is critical to note that all these harbingers of power and efficacy could easily have worked *against* Elizabeth Packard. Her case was extraordinary, and many more must have fallen victim to a paternalistic legal system. In her case, a verdict against her would have legitimized her husband's power. In the real trial, the verdict was delivered after only seven minutes of deliberation. After her husband, the doctor, and many other men trapped her in an ersatz trial, she was eventually freed by an all-male jury. Afterwards, her story took an even sadder turn, as she lost her home and had no right to keep her children. In that case it was her husband that the law protected. Elizabeth never divorced Theo, but went on to become a powerful figure in the struggle to extend legal protection to married women and those living in asylums.

When the judge and jury's verdict pronounce Elizabeth "sane" it becomes an official recognition of the quiet, personal talisman she has repeated throughout the play, in her moments of most keen disempowerment: "'I am sane, I am sane.' Make it a little ditty in my head. 'I am sane...'" (Mann 48). Women who were confined in insane asylums during this time were seen as needing no protection, because the inherent goodness of their protectors was assumed (Himelhoch and Shaffer 345). This assumption effectively plunged them into a system of judgment in which their protestations held no power. Elizabeth Packard was an extraordinary woman who found a way to climb out of that system and deliver her message within a formal trial, where although she was still ultimately an object of condescension, she did earn her freedom.

Notes

1. It should be noted that the world of the non-trial (marriage, motherhood, social interaction) were not a "choice" for Elizabeth, per se. For women at the time these systems were all but compulsory. In the first Act Elizabeth tells McFarland that she might never have married if she had known what would come of it, which he calls "a calamitous choice for you to have made...a passionate woman like you!" (Mann 26). A woman of Elizabeth's intelligence and verve would be protected by the institution of marriage if her husband were tolerant, but ruined by it with a husband like Theo. It damages her partially because the criminals who were considered most dangerous were those who were wives ("Conviction of Mrs. Fair" 4).

Works Cited

Blake, E. Vale. "Spontaneous and Imitative Crime." *The Popular Science Monthly*, September 1879: 664. Print.

Carlisle, Linda V. "'New Notions and Wild Vagaries': Elizabeth Packard's Quest for Personal Liberty." *Journal of the Illinois State Historical Society.* 93:1 (Spring, 2000): 43-66. Print.

Carlson, A. Cheree. *The Crimes of Womanhood: Defining Femininity in a Court of Law.* Urbana: University of Illinois Press, 2009. Print.

Favorini, Attilio. "History, Memory and Trauma in the Documentary Plays of Emily Mann." *Get Real: Documentary Theatre Past and Present*, eds. Forsyth, Alison and Chris Megson. New York: Palgrave Macmillan, 2009. Print.

Forsyth, Alison and Chris Megson. "Introduction." *Get Real: Documentary Theatre Past and Present,* eds. Forsyth, Alison and Chris Megson. Palgrave: New York, 2009. Print.

Frost-Knappman, Elizabeth and Kathryn Cullen-DuPont. *Women's Rights on Trial: 101 Historic Trials from Anne Hutchinson to the Virginia Military Institute Cadets.* Detroit: Gale Research (New England Publishing Associates, Inc.): 1997. Print.

Himelhoch, Myra Samuels and Aruthur H. Shaffer. "Elizabeth Packard: Nineteenth-Century Crusader for the Rights of Mental Patients." *Journal of American Studies* 13:3 (December, 1979): 343-375. Print.

Kadri, Sadakat. *The Trial: A History, from Socrates to O.J. Simpson.* New York: Random House, 2005. Print.

Kirp, David L., Mark G. Yudof, and Marlene Strong Franks. *Gender Justice.* Chicago: The University of Chicago Press, 1986. Print.

Lombroso, Caesar and William Ferrero. *The Female Offender.* New York: D. Appleton and Company, 1895. Print.

Mann, Emily. *Mrs. Packard.* New York: Theatre Communications Group, 2009. Print.

Packard, Elizabeth Parsons Ware. *Marital Power Exemplified in Mrs. Packard's Trial, and Self-Defence from the Charge of Insanity; or Three*

Years' Imprisonment for Religious Belief, by the Arbitrary Will of a Husband, with An Appeal to the Government to so Change the Laws as to afford Legal Protection to Married Women. Chicago: Clarke & Company, Publishers, 1870. Print.

--------. *Great Disclosure of Spiritual Wickedness!! In High Places. With An Appeal to the Government to Protect the Inalienable Rights of Married Women.* New York: Arno Press, 1974 (orig 1865). Print.

Pfeiffer, Eric. "Mary Todd Lincoln to be retried for insanity." *Yahoo! News* September 6, 2012. Online.

Reinelt, Janelle. "The Promise of Documentary." *Get Real: Documentary Theatre Past and Present*, eds. Forsyth, Alison and Chris Megson. Palgrave: New York, 2009. Print.

Siegel, Naomi. "Daring to Disagree, and Sent to an Asylum." *New York Times* May 27, 2007. Online.

"The Conviction of Mrs. Fair." *The Evening Telegraph* [Philadelphia, PA] April 28, 1871: 4. Print.

"The Heathen." *The Evening Telegraph* [Philadelphia, PA] December 17, 1868: 8. Print.

Zinman, Toby. "Mrs. Packard." *Variety* May 14, 2007. Online.

Chapter 13.

Race on Trial

The Battle against Segregation in Naomi Wallace's *And I and Silence*

Rovie Herrera Medalle

Judgment in various forms constitutes gender policing. Women may be accused and judged not only not only in formal legal trials but also through the operation of social institutions such as government agencies, the educational system, the economic system and its labor markets, religion, and the family. Contemporary theater serves as an instrument to illuminate these forms of judgment and sanctioning, and to claim for women fair treatment in both law courts and other adversarial arenas. Naomi Wallace's play *And I and Silence* (2011) deals with the life of two young women who were judged by the American legal system in their past and subjected to harsh societal judgment in following release from prison. One of the two is African American and the other is white. In the segregated social environment of the United States in 1959, the decision of these two women to live together comes to be seen as a more serious issue than the crime that sent them to prison. Thus, the two characters undergo a form of trial through continuing accusation and discrimination.

The 1950s are commonly associated with prosperity, technological progress, traditional family values and the beginning of social movements for equal rights. This image of the era, however, obscures its regressive elements. While many women had worked outside their homes during the course of World War II, most of them returned to their former unpaid labor as housewives when men took the majority of the jobs after the war. During the postwar years some women began to return to paid work, but they had to put up with inferior conditions and were generally relegated to jobs that were considered appropriate for them, such as nurse or secretary. They usually earned less than men, and they were supervised and controlled by the men in charge. Nevertheless, by the end of the decade, as Carlise notes, "females made up more than one-third of the workforce, and more than half of all working women were married" (23). Other barriers to equality were more difficult to challenge: racism toward African Americans was deeply ingrained in the United States at the time, and segregation was the law in southern states. Many African Americans suffered abuse and rejection. At the same time, the Civil Rights Movement arose during the late 1950s, with figures such as Rosa Parks, who initiated a bus boycott in Montgomery, Alabama, and Martin Luther King Jr., who founded the Southern Christian Leadership Conference (SCLC) and began a campaign for voting rights (see Hudak).

Segregation, where it was practiced, affected all domains. Accordingly, prisons followed the so-called Jim Crow laws, which mandated "separate but equal" facilities for blacks and whites (see Johnson). Women in prison were separated but decidedly *not* equal. Prison entails considerable risks and hard conditions, and being a woman imprisoned involves even harder conditions; but being an African American woman imprisoned in the 1950s implied a dreadful situation. Prison mirrors society, and black women were discriminated against on several levels—on the one hand, by the prison administration that punished them both as criminals and as black women; and on the other hand, by the white prisoners who could feel empowered by the assumption of superiority. Bonding between a white and an African American woman in prison seems almost impossible, because a system of privileges promoted by the penal institution augmented other factors to create distance between the two racial groups. In spite of these barriers, a few women were able to view their "neighbors" in jail without prejudice, establish friendships, and even fall in love, as *And I and Silence* portrays.

Wallace's play *And I and Silence* explores the life of two women: Jamie, an African American of twenty six, and Dee, white and twenty-five years old. They met in prison in the past. In the present, nine years later, they seek to survive in segregated America where they both endure sexual abuse and humiliation. They have left prison and have not committed additional offenses, but are continually judged by the force of opinion in their surrounding society for what is considered abnormal behavior. Negative judgment is supported by images such as the alien woman, the other, the prostitute, the lesbian, and the black woman. In *And I and Silence* Wallace grants the characters agency to a certain extent because both protagonists commit suicide; but theirs is a tragic story, as this is their only way to escape judgment and gain freedom.

The timeline of Naomi Wallace's play *And I and Silence* encompasses two periods: the past, at the very beginning of the decade in 1950, and the present, at the very end in 1959. The action in *And I and Silence* goes backwards and forwards in time intertwining past and present, with two sets of actors playing the teenage girls in prison and the women who have served their time and gained release. In the past Dee is fascinated by the figure of Jamie and approaches her in order to be friends. The women have to carry on their encounters in secrecy, as contact between black and white prisoners is strictly forbidden. Together, sixteen-year-old Dee and seventeen-year-old Jamie, forge a plan for a future together after they are released from prison. The structure of the play allows the spectator to witness their hopes and dreams in the initial phase of their relationship, just as these are crumbling as a consequence of the judgment they face in segregated society. The action develops in a parallel structure, with one scene from the past and one scene from the present following a chronological order, until they collide in the last scene in which past and present are presented simultaneously. In this last scene Wallace shows the deterioration the protagonists undergo from their last meeting in jail until they decide to commit suicide. Their journey from entrapment in prison to freedom after prison becomes futile; at the end they realize that they are trapped in a society that rejects and punishes them, making a happy ending impossible. Dee says "We were happy when we were inside. Sometimes."(42) Excluding the abuse in prison, they acknowledge that their life behind bars provided them more freedom than does their life under the prevailing social conditions of the freedom presented to them after release.

The sense of entrapment and the symbol of prison is a recurrent motif in Wallace's plays. Claudia Barnett points out that Wallace "questions definitions of crime and punishment in our gender and class-oriented society. She does so in such a physical manner in order to appeal to the audience members, who sympathetically align themselves with the prisoners" (149) Space in many of Wallace's plays functions as a prison; for example, in *One Flea Spare* (1995), the characters are confined in a house as a consequence of the Plague. *Things of Dry Hours* (2007) is set inside the house as well; *Birdy* (1997) takes place in a mental asylum; *Slaughter City* (1996) gives a sense of imprisonment where the workers spend countless hours at their posts; and part of *The Trestle at Pope Lick Creek* (1998) takes place in a prison. Even the young boys in *War Boys* (1993) are behind a fence; though they are on the "right" side of the conflict, they are also prisoners of their fears and their quest for identity. Nevertheless, *And I and Silence* has a stronger sense of confinement because the moments of relief take place inside prison, and the scenes outside prison emphasize the lack of freedom. Jamie and Dee are physically confined in the past and physically confined as well as psychologically harmed, as a consequence of isolation, in the present. This play may serve as a reply to Wallace's critics, such as Kushner, who describes her as "outrageously optimistic" (qtd.in Garner), since we cannot glimpse any hope at the end of *And I and Silence*.

Wallace understands the structure of the prison in terms of Jeremy Bentham's panopticon. Both in and out of prison, Dee and Jamie live in a panopticon, watched by the spectators. Foucault develops the association of theater with the gaze and turns prison into a metaphorical theatre when he states, in *Discipline and Punish*: "They are like so many cages, so many small theatres, in which each actor is alone, perfectly individualized and constantly visible" (200). Unfortunately for Dee and Jamie, they live in a cage, alone, exposed, and vulnerable not only before the presumably empathetic audience but also before the judgmental society of the 1950s. Furthermore, many of the institutions the two women encounter outside prison function in the same way and oppress women, as Foucault suggests when he poses the question: "Is it surprising that prisons resemble factories, schools, barracks, hospitals, which all resemble prisons?" (228). Institutions of society confine and control the individual throughout life.

In spite of prison's restrictions, Jamie and Dee create a microcosm in jail where they feel safe. Their friendship grows strong in prison but becomes even more solid outside the prison walls as a consequence of their isolation. While in jail, they day-dreamed about marrying men of the same family in order to live, the four of them, together; but now they fall in love with each other. Their relationship does not present sexual desire until scene nine, although, it is not clear if they were repressing feelings beyond friendship in earlier scenes. In scene seven, for example, Dee declares: "I dream I fucked my mother." (41) While this dream may allude to lesbian desire or incest, it connects most closely with the crime for which she was imprisoned: she killed her father who abused and murdered her mother. Dee's dream, as she says "had nothin' to do with fuckin'" (*ibid*); instead it reveals a wish for communion with her mother. She wants to be inside her mother to feel the protection of the womb, as she states, "More than I did then, I miss her now" (*ibid*). In her precarious situation, she needs the security that only a mother provides. Dee needs someone to defend her in the trial she faces, but in this trial the women do not have the right to a defense. Jamie and Dee can only support each other, since no one else is willing to help them.

Within their love relationship, Dee takes the initiative and Jamie is passive. Wallace does not develop or explain their relationship thoroughly because, as she asserts, in her plays questions are more important than answers (Wallace introduction 427). The relationship among the protagonists is similar to the one that Sara and Callie have in Diana Son's *Stop Kiss* (2000). Although they have relationships with men, their circumstances lead them to sexual awakening towards their friend. For Dee and Jamie, male figures represent violence, abuse, and oppression; in addition to her father the murderer, Dee deals with Monkfish the guard and her employers. In order to release the tension of the dramatic story, Wallace includes some comic moments such as when Dee narrates how Monkfish takes her juice every day and she pisses in her cup in revenge. Nonetheless, if we look closely at those moments we will find that they disguise the infinite sorrow inside prison. Once they are outside prison both women suffer predatory treatment from their bosses. They comment on what they call "the line" on abusive treatment, and the spectator realizes that even without crossing "the line" they have to put up with deplorable conduct from the employers.

> **Dee** You let them touch you.
>
> **Jamie** Only on top of my dress. Not ever under it.
>
> **Dee** They squeezed you.
>
> **Jamie** Under the cloth I was safe.
>
> **Dee** They rub you.
>
> **Jamie** They didn't even touch my skin. And with the money I got, we ate for weeks. (57)

Dee confesses she suffers sexual abuse. She explains that she had no choice because she was afraid of being fired. At this point in the play they are in a critical situation that involves poverty and starvation. Traumatized by the abuse, she states: "my mouth. It's gone" (57). On some occasions Wallace uses surrealism, symbolism and metaphorical language to subdue the violence of the action, but she is also aware of the importance of these stories, and she combines this figurative language with raw language to expose the violence. Dee explains: "When he came into my mouth, he boxed my ears. Didn't mean to, he said, it just felt so damn good. I got off my knees" (58). As we have seen, the male figure is a negative one, men in the play function as detainers: they want to keep women in custody; they control women and objectify them, hurt them, rape them, and in multiple ways take advantage of them. These male figures emphasize the issue of gender, which combines with race to create the ongoing trial the women endure. They suffer abuse because they are women and they work as subordinates of men.

A recurrent technique in Wallace's plays is the (re) enactment of violence by the characters. In the sexual abuse episode, Jamie wants Dee to show her how it happened; Jamie acts as the boss and introduces her hand in Dee's mouth reenacting the sexual abuse. Wallace is a Brechtian playright who uses both the *gestus* and historicization. *And I and Silence* is set in the past to make us think about the present and confront racism in contemporary society. The play provides a clear example of dialectics where the different social classes and races are in tension; Jamie is in control of the situation, she is the master even though she is the one who is considered inferior by a racist society. In scene three Dee gives Jamie a walking stick, which is a symbol of high status. She suggests that Jamie could hit her with the stick if they play charades as they did in prison; Jamie's mother, Betty, was a servant, and the girls pretended to work as servants during their meetings in the cell. They said they invented this game in order to practice for the future, and the later scenes do, after all, indicate that they have very little chance of better jobs. Wallace also uses the Brechtian resource of songs; though these songs are not political, they serve the purpose of repeatedly reviving the energy of the performance.

Although they have each other, Jamie and Dee are lonely in prison; Dee lost her family and so did Jamie. Betty, Jamie's mother, was found drowned in her bucket. Though Jamie explains, "she had blackouts" (28), her death arouses suspicion: a racist boss may have murdered her or tried to abuse her. In addition, her death is tainted by a petty injustice: the master and mistress subtracted from wages owed because Betty only worked half of the week. Since there was no compassion for two orphan black children at the time, Jamie's brother Marcel was forced to rob and was killed violently. Jamie explains: "He had a piece of wood in his pocket, made it look like a gun. We went into that grocery store together. Man in the store had a real gun. Shot Marcel in the neck" (27). Violence generates more violence in the play: other members of Jamie's family are involved in violent deaths with racist undertones. Jamie serves her time in prison for being an accessory to Marcel's attempted robbery.

After their release, employment serves as a form of continuing trial, since their time in prison, Dee's social class, and Jamie's race hinder their access to better jobs. Wallace explores racial issues and tension between classes similarly in *Things of Dry Hours*, which is set in Alabama in 1930. Cali the African American woman exerts her power upon Corbin the white man in an exchange of roles, where Cali reenacts the abuse she suffers from the white folks of the town. In both cases the playwright gives the power to the black woman who in a symbolic and temporary way takes control, challenging the patriarchal white authority. In the case of *And I and Silence*, when Jamie and Dee challenge those authorities that judge them and set the law, they are metaphorically found to be in contempt of the court. Barbara Ozieblo explains how in *War Boys*, a play with three male characters, Wallace uses this technique in a different way: "The spoken or enacted monologues serve to distance the events and to draw attention away from the women while giving them a voice and presence they are denied by society." (71-2) In *War Boys* the dramatist gives voice to the absent women, whose presence is denied by society, just as in *And I and Silence* and *Things of Dry Hours* she gives power and control to the African American women who suffer discrimination and powerlessness within the society of the time. Wallace's technique, which I will call the flow of persona, serves as a useful tool in theater to balance biased treatment and to give voice to those who were silenced. In *And I and Silence* the (re)enactment functions as a plea on behalf of equality and a form of evidence in their trial.

Wallace's use of language is complex, not only combining figurative and raw language but also introducing a special language in *And I and Silence*. Bearing in mind that the playwright is well known, apart from her political discourse, for portraying male characters, *And I and Silence* is her first play in which the only characters are women who speak about womanhood. She also writes about African American women in some plays, but they interact with men, as in *Things of Dry Hours* or *Slaughter City*. Clearly, this play is the product of a decision to give the stage exclusively to women. It is structured so as to synchronize the women in many moments, not only in their language but also in their movements, as Wallace's stage directions specify for scene one, in which the women cleanse themselves and their dresses. The characters also sing together in some scenes and complete each other's rhymes and sentences. The purpose of all this synchronicity is to show that even though they are of different races and contrasting backgrounds, with Jamie from the country and Dee from the city, they connect in fundamental ways.

Race is also represented through the special language mentioned above. Wallace uses a language of contrast, with references to black and white, light and darkness throughout the play. The exaggerated dimensions implied in these oppositions are not by chance: Wallace wants the audience to realize that society—even contemporary society—still has to work on race issues. Some scenes, such as the ones in which the guards display irrational behavior towards black prisoners, show the inhumanity that Wallace wants to denounce with her play. African American citizens in the fifties endured such behavior, and some of them demonstrated their courage in standing against racist institutions. In the play, what calls Dee's attention to Jamie is her courage and readiness to confront the guards, as in the following exchange:

> **Young Dee** I saw old Mr Crackle the guard knock a bowl of hot chilli right out of your hands. [..] Hit the floor, splash.
>
> **Young Jamie** I picked the bowl up. [...]
>
> **Young Dee** Me. I would have let it lay. Eight times he knocked that bowl outta your hands. I counted. And you picked it up eight times till Mr Crackle gave in. That's the kind of friend I want. (13-14)

The scene above represents the pacific civil rights movement of the time and its role models' way of dealing with the trials imposed by the racist society. Humiliation and mistreatment are not used as a justification for violence or force. The major problem of segregation in the play is not only segregation but also the fear of being punished as a consequence of breaking this segregation. In *And I and Silence* Jamie takes on the worst part of segregated America: guards humiliate her, employers abuse her, and the most difficult part is to cope with the hatred she faces in her everyday life. She states: "Guts in my hair is nothing. Bottle 'cross my back is nothing. I walk the street alone to work I never know what's flying through the air. Pisspot from the second floor. Dog shit. People cursin' me, white people, your people, stick out a leg and trip me" (43). Jamie at this point blames Dee, because she has a sense of community. In the environment of segregation, either you belong to the black community or the white community, and Dee has to be part of one. Thus, Dee is also a collateral victim of segregation. In scene five the women want to go on a double-date with Russell and his cousin Charlie, both African American. They are forced to arrange the meeting in their house because they believe that to go out involves a risk. Even though staying in the house provides greater safety, the house functions as a prison where the two women are confined.

The connection and intimacy between Jamie and Dee, strictly forbidden by society and law, constitutes the basis for their most severe trial. When they decide to ignore the established order, which compels separation between them, the situation becomes dangerous. As they acknowledge:

Dee We can't sit together. We can't walk together anymore.

Jamie We can walk together.

Dee Then why don't we?

Jamie You know why.

Dee Sure. 'Cause folks on the street see us together, everyone thinks you're my maid [...] so we say that really you're not my servant [...] so we tell [...] the truth: That we are both servants. That we're friends. (42-43)

Dee and Jamie's relationship is complicated by many factors: their friendship scandalizes the community, their love relationship is unacceptable, and their poverty generates more prejudice. Lesbianism in women's prisons has been the object of a number of studies. Margaret Otis is, for example, in a 1913 study, explores the same sex relationships of women from different races that take place in prison. Otis describes, with the naivety and unself-consciousness of the time, the encounters between different races in jail, similar to the ones portrayed in *And I and Silence*:

> In one institution in particular the difficulty seemed so great and the disadvantage of the intimacy between the girls so apparent that segregation was resorted to. The colored girls were transferred to a separate cottage a short distance from the other buildings. The girls were given to understand that it was a serious breach of rules for them to get together, and the white girls were absolutely forbidden to have anything to do with the colored. Yet this separation did not have wholly the desired effect. The motive of "the forbidden fruit" was added. The separation seemed to enhance the value of the loved one, and that she was to a degree inaccessible, added to her charms. (113)

Otis claims in her article that women define sex by opposition (women/men) and in the case of women's prison the opposition is represented through race (black/white). Though she ascribes the attraction to hwat can be viewed as a form of racism, Otis recognized the genuine love between women who established relationships in jail: she asserts, "Sometimes the love is very real and seems almost e[n]nobling" (115).

The society of the 1950s, however, was neither ready to explore it nor interested in its potential; women such as Dee and Jamie were silenced and erased from the records. When Dee confesses that she loves Jamie, Jamie rejects her, finding it too complicated. At the beginning, she even doubts Dee's reasons for approaching her. Dee may be attracted by the unknown in the first place, and that is why Jamie is reluctant to have contact with Dee, who can be seen as a colonizer who tries to bribe her with honey drops. Nevertheless, Dee persists and eventually wins Jamie's love. Even though, as a white woman, she always had the option to break off the relationship with Jamie and to live what was considered a "normal" or "appropriate" life, she remains with her. Nevertheless, Jamie and Dee are aware of the perils of their situation, and know they have to hide their love from society's eyes because their relationship will add more charges against them in the trial they are undergoing.

Though Jamie and Dee think, dream, and act throughout the play, their lives are controlled by the trial that is ongoing. Jamie and Dee leave prison, only to find themselves trapped in their house—a prison by another name—but also in a society that does not accept their friendship. Male figures in the play represent the white patriarchy that oppresses women. Accusers are fluid and appear in different forms, such as prison guards, employers, lovers, and the common people. The accusers/abusers, who include Russell, Charlie, the guards, Dee's father, and the employers, take advantage of the women's situation in different ways. Rather than conforming to the rules and avoiding confrontation, the women challenge the rules mandating segregation. As a consequence of this association, which is seen as illicit, society is a living organism, with its biased judge and jury, judges and punishes them. They are unable to muster a defense, and throughout the play no one helps them. Confined, isolated, and starving, they are pushed to the edge by their physical and psychological suffering. Ultimately, Dee and Jamie find that segregation is more powerful than their will to stay together and their hope of attaining their dreams. Their sentence is death; nevertheless, they pronounce it on themselves in their own determination to end their suffering. At the end of the play, Jamie and Dee steal a knife and commit suicide together. Although they have agency, they are able to exercise it only within the tragic confines of their segregated society.

Through the trial of these two women, Wallace reminds us that not even seventy years ago African American suffered extreme forms of abuse in the USA. *And I and Silence* shows the ongoing social trial to which African American women were subjected, as they were raped actually and metaphorically by those in control. It shows that the love of Dee, who is white but only one woman and herself handicapped by her working-class background and prison record, fails to overcome racism and segregation. The only form of hope offered in the play lies outside it, in the historical record. In the 1960s, the Civil Rights Movement mounted a systematic campaign against segregation that enlisted thousands of volunteers of different races, sexes, and backgrounds. This movement was successful in ending segregation and made strides in overcoming racial discrimination. In presenting this story, Wallace reminds us of the atrocities of the past and cautions us to be aware of the continuing need for justice in American society.

Works Cited

Barnett, Claudia. "Physical Prisons: Naomi Wallace's Drama of Captivity." *Captive Audience: Prison and Captivity in Contemporary Theater*, ed. Fahy, Thomas and Kimball King. New York: Routledge, 2003: 147-165. Print.

Brecht, Bertolt. Brecht on Theatre: *The Development of an Aesthetic*, ed. and trans. Willet, John. New York: Hill and Wang, 1964. Print.

Carlise, Rodney P. *Handbook to Life in America: Postwar America, 1950 to 1969.* New York: Facts On File, 2009. Print.

Foucault, Michel. *Discipline and Punish: The Birth of the Prison.* Trans. Sheridan, Alan. New York: Vintage Books, 1977. Print.

Gardner, Lyn. "Enemy within." *The Guardian* February 6, 2007. Online

Hudak, Heather C. *African American History: Civil Rights Movement.* New York: Weigl Publishers, 2009. Print.

Johnson, Kimberly. *Reforming Jim Crow: Southern Politics and State in the Age Before Brown.* Oxford: Oxford University Press, 2010. Print.

Otis, Margaret. "A Perversion not Commonly Noted." *The Journal of Abnormal Psychology* 8 (June-July, 1913): 113-116. Print.

Ozieblo, Barbara. ""Pornography of Violence": Strategies of Representation in Plays by Naomi Wallace, Stefanie Zadravec, and Lynn Nottage." *Journal of American Drama and Theatre* 23. 1 (Winter, 2011): 67-79. Print.

Son, Diana. *Stop Kiss.* New York: Dramatists Play Service, 2000. Print.

Wallace, Naomi. *And I and Silence.* London: Faber and Faber, 2011. Print.

--------. "Author's Introduction." In the Heart of America. *Staging Gay Lives: An Anthology of Contemporary Gay Theater*, ed. Clum. John M. Boulder, CO: Westview Press,1996: 426-427. Print.

--------. *Birdy.* London: Faber and Faber, 1997. Print.

--------. *In the Heart of America and Other Plays.* New York: Theatre Communications Group, 2001. Print.

--------. *One Flea Spare. In the Heart of America and Other Plays.* New York: Theatre Communications Group, 2001. Print.

--------. *Slaughter City*. In the Heart of America and Other Plays. New York: Theatre Communications Group, 2001. Print.

--------. *The Trestle at Pope Lick Creek*. In the Heart of America and Other Plays. New York: Theatre Communications Group, 2001. Print.

--------. *The War Boys*. In the Heart of America and Other Plays. New York: Theatre Communications Group, 2001. Print.

--------. *Things of Dry Hours*. London: Faber and Faber, 2007. Print

CHAPTER 14.

THE DEATH OF ASHLEY SMITH

ENGENDERING SOCIAL AWARENESS THROUGH THEATRE

Amanda Lockitch

INTRODUCTION

Emerging Canadian playwright Leah Jane Esau has long been drawn to current events. Esau calls her Montreal-based theatre company, Les Nouvelles, (The News), and her plays have been inspired by real occurrences that made headlines across Canada and around the world. She is particularly haunted by stories of youths who transgress and their treatment within our social, legal, and correctional institutions. In 2010, her second year in the three-year playwriting program at the National Theatre School of Canada (NTS), Esau was assigned to write and perform a short solo piece. She had discovered a *Youtube* video of newly released documentary footage that depicts the final moments of 19-year-old Ashley Smith's life in a Canadian federal prison on 19 October 2007.[1] The video shows Smith's self-strangulation with a ligature tied around her neck and the blurred-out faces of the guards who filmed the incident, waiting too long outside her cell to save her life. Following procedures laid out for them regarding Inmate Smith by the Correctional Service of Canada (CSC), through the warden and deputy warden at the Grand Valley Institution in Kitchener, Ontario, the guards did not remove her ligature or attempt to revive Smith until she had stopped breathing (UCCO "A Rush" 39). The video is shocking and difficult to watch; yet it has brought awareness to Smith's case and by extension to the under-examined lives of prisoners in Canada, especially ones with mental illnesses that prison guards are ill-equipped to handle. It has prompted further investigation from a variety of perspectives.

Smith's life in federal prison had been a daily trial. Her early anti-social behavior escalated once she was in custody, and she accumulated charges for disobedience and violent attacks on personnel, which led to more time inside and her eventual transfer into federal prison. She suffered illegal transfers between prisons, forced injections, and extremely long periods of solitary confinement. Having been imprisoned for the minor offense of throwing crab apples at a postman, Smith nevertheless found herself powerless to gain release or mitigation of her punishment.

Entries made by Smith in her journal reveal her sense of otherness and isolation. Her own actions puzzle her; at the same time, her incarceration labels her as bad and confirms her difference from the population outside prison. The double imprisonment of being trapped in a foreign body while that body is confined in a foreign environment is presented in the two plays I discuss below which feature Smith's story as their subject. The first is the abovementioned solo piece by Esau for National Theatre School. Esau uses the concept of the beached whale, an oceanic creature stuck on dry land, to speak about Smith's plight. The second is a new work by Judith Thompson in which she equates her character Glory (Ashley) to a crocodile desperate to return to the swamp. When these two playwrights put Smith on trial, her identity no longer appears as fully human; yet it calls for the type of empathy we feel for creatures of nature caught up in the human world. We empathize with the beached

The Death of Ashley Smith

whale and question its final act, and we become agitated along with the wild animal being corralled and controlled by humans. The animal other provides a mechanism through which to view Smith's otherness and grapple with the events of Ashley Smith's life and death.

ASHLEY SMITH ON TRIAL: (MIS)MANAGEMENT IN CANADIAN FEDERAL CUSTODY

According to the timeline of her life provided by *The Fifth Estate*, Ashley Smith was born 29 January 1988 in New Brunswick and adopted five days later by Coralee Smith ("Timeline"). By all accounts she had a normal childhood, but became unruly in her teenage years. She had trouble in school, and in 2003 she ended up at the New Brunswick Youth Centre (NBYC), where a one-month sentence for throwing crab apples at a postal worker turned into nearly three years. Most of her time there was spent in the segregated "Therapeutic Quiet" unit, where she was confined for twenty-three hours a day ("Timeline"). On 24 October 2006, just nine months after her eighteenth birthday, Smith was given an "adult sentence for criminal charges laid while she was still a youth at NBYC. ... 348 days" added to the 1,455 days already served. Because the sentence was more than two years, she [was] "ordered to serve the remainder of her sentence in a federal institution" where she lived until the time of her death in 2007 ("Timeline"). All of the charges that led to Smith being moved to federal custody occurred while she was in the care of NBYC.

Julian Falkner, the lawyer representing Smith's family, argues that CSC tortured Ashley Smith through the use of chemical restraints and illegal transfers ("Behind the Wall"). While the current inquest is set to determine whether her death was suicide or an accident, CSC settled out of court with Coralee Smith in 2011 on an eleven million dollar wrongful death suit ("Ashley"). Smith had been diagnosed early on with ADHD, borderline personality disorder, and narcissistic personality traits, but the counselling and medication she received did not help. Self-harm was the most prevalent and distressing of her behaviours. She began to self-strangulate and would choke herself until she became unconscious. Her intentions in doing so were unclear—whether to end her life or to obtain momentary euphoria and then pass out. Prison officials argue that Smith believed someone would always cut off the ligature in time to save her, especially as she was under constant surveillance. One diagnosis of Smith was that her self-harm was attention seeking, and while it may have initially been the case of a young woman stuck in solitary confinement looking for any kind of human contact, Smith never received help for her behaviours. Correctional Investigator Howard Sapers says that Smith never had a "comprehensive mental health plan" in place; her "management plan became much more security focused" ("Behind the Wall"). Her need for any kind of attention from others, even negative attention due to self-inflicted harm, led to segregation, which led to more self-harm, a cycle only broken by her violent death.

Smith was initially transferred into adult prison because it was felt that there were "programs available in the adult correctional institution that would help her including anger management. But ... it was never mentioned that in order for a woman ... [to] be a part of these programs 'she had to present an appropriate behaviour'" ("Timeline"). Smith's violent acting out rendered her ineligible for the programs. In solitary, Smith was kept away from the main population and with the most violent offenders in the women's prisons. Howard Sapers, the Correctional Investigator of Canada, outlined the individual and system failures that led to Smith's death in *A Preventable Death* (2008). Inappropriate transfers, use of force, and a failed grievance system are some of the categories he investigates in trying to understand "Ms. Smith's overly restrictive and dehumanizing conditions of confinement" (Sapers). Another perspective comes from a 2010 report to the Office of the Correctional Investigator from Dr. Paul Beaudry about specific events at the Joliette Institution in Quebec, where they had "never had an inmate so problematic as [Smith] in the 10 year history of [the] institution" ("Rush" 23):

The Death of Ashley Smith

The desk in the cell had to be removed to stop [Smith] from gaining access to the cell camera, which had been destroyed and obscured several times. The wall coverings for cables, lights and electrical current had to be sealed. She ripped up a piece of Velcro that held her window curtain in place and used it to choke herself. Even while menstruating, we couldn't give her tampons because she would wrap the fibres around her neck. She would have to show us a used tampon in order to get another one. She succeeded in removing security screws from the cell furniture with her fingers, and used the screws to self-harm. (23)

The Correctional Service of Canada moved Smith to four different provinces in the time she spent in their custody. From the Nova Institution for Women in Nova Scotia, to two institutions in Quebec, a psychiatric hospital in Saskatoon, and a number of hospitals and prisons in Ontario, Smith was transferred a total of seventeen times in eleven months. According to Howard Sapers, this was against the law. Although Smith had asked repeatedly for "an outside investigation to be done" at various points in her incarceration, even after a representative of the Canadian Association of Elizabeth Fry Societies helped her file a complaint at asking for her legal "entitlement to basics, such as blanket, mattress, pen, hygiene products ... [the] complaint [was] not read until after her death" ("Timeline"). By the end of her life, Smith was given forced injections of chemical restraints used to immobilize her. While systems seem to be in place to deal with violent and challenging inmates, it is unclear why they were unable to stop Smith's suffering. In his psychiatric report Dr. Beaudry quotes article 30 of Commissioner's Directive 844 ("Use of Restraint Equipment for Health Purposes"), which "states that a 'psychiatrist, psychologist or physician must assess the inmate's mental health status within two hours of the application of restraints." This directive is dated May 27, 2008, and [Beaudry is] not able to determine whether it was in effect when the incidents of July 22, 2007, occurred. During these incidents the on-call psychiatrist did not go on site to assess Ms. Smith's mental status, although she was kept in physical restraints for just under 12 hours and received large doses of medication. Perhaps Smith's death brought about some of these changes in policy, but it seems reasonable to expect that a doctor would personally see a prisoner that has been in restraints for a full day without being ordered to do so. The difficulties caused by Smith do not mitigate the necessity of finding justice in the aftermath of her death.

While Smith's death was terrible and (thankfully) out of the ordinary, it points to the need for awareness of the trials of high-risk populations inside prisons. As mental health issues and overcrowding become more prevalent within our prisons, we must take a closer look at how we care for our most violently ill. There is a particular concern about female offenders and self-harm. If these women are too violent to live in the more socialized housing of female prisons like GVI, can they do any better in psychiatric facilities? In prison their harm to others and self-harm is curtailed by force. In a psychiatric hospital, what other means are there but restraint if medication is not warranted or is refused? How do we negotiate the difference between care and corrections?

CORRECTION SERVICES CANADA ON TRIAL: THE *FIFTH ESTATE* REPORT

The CBC's *Fifth Estate* obtained the video footage later seen by Esau on *Youtube* through an extensive legal battle. This video clip provided the central, shocking revelation of Hana Gartner's documentary *Out of Control* (first aired January 8. 2010). In this, along with her follow-up *Behind the Wall* (first aired November 12, 2010), Gartner probed the death of Ashley Smith while in protective custody. She investigated "just how kids with mental health and behavioural problems are treated behind bars in this country" by questioning how this young woman died while seven guards stood outside filming the incident ("Out of Control"). Gartner felt so strongly that the people of Canada had the right to see this footage that she spent over two years fighting CSC in court. Her reports exposed the resistance of CSC to releasing documents and video that raised questions about their handling of this young female offender. Hana Gartner won the 2010 Michener Award for Journalism for breaking the Ashley Smith story. Accepting this award was her last act as a journalist before she retired from the CBC and *The Fifth Estate*. The legal battles surrounding Smith's death are ongoing, but from what Gartner and others managed to make public, we can piece together some of the circumstances surrounding Smith's death while incarcerated.

THE MONODRAMA

Moved by the footage of this tragic and horrifying death, Esau was impelled to write a piece in reaction to it. Her 15-minute monodrama, *The Death of Ashley Smith*, is delivered by Rachel, a fictional young guard on suicide watch the day Smith choked to death. Esau sets Rachel in conversation with an unseen psychiatrist performing an evaluation of her current mental state in the aftermath of Smith's death. Fearing that she will lose her job because she followed the orders of her superiors, Rachel also questions her responsibility in Smith's death. Though Esau's play puts the corrections system on trial, its representative, the young guard Rachel, does not evoke an immediately harsh response. On the contrary, Rachel is a sympathetic character despite her involvement in Smith's incarceration and death and the ways she reflects on the experience. Rachel says she is not traumatized by this frightening event and seems more worried about her own life than the loss of Smith's. She makes hurtful and ignorant comments in the course of the play, including the comparison of Smith to a beached whale. Yet, Rachel is also a young woman doing a very difficult job and is justifiably worried about her own safety. She comments that Smith's size was threatening, as were her displays of violence towards members of the prison staff. In truth, Smith had over 800 incident reports ("Out of Control"), which Esau suggests with stacks of paper on the set's desk. Not only Esau but also the Canadian legal system found the situation of the guards sympathetic. The real guards who were at Smith's death were initially fired and charged, but ultimately found not guilty. The problems that led to her strangulation did not rest with the frontline staff of the prison, but in the orders given regarding the protocol of her treatment.

After its initial development at NTS, Esau's play was presented in 2011 at Theatre Passe Muraille in Toronto, as part of Protestival, an evening of protest-themed theatre ("Protestival!"). The most shocking moment of Esau's play occurs in her inclusion of an edited version of Smith's excruciating death video. For Esau, the play hinges on having that video seen by the public. Honouring the plea that Coralee Smith, Ashley's mother, made to Hana Gartner, the theatre audience is made to witness Ashley's final breath: "I want [the video] out in the public eye, I want all videos released, I want all personal documentation released. I feel that this has to be public" ("Behind the Wall"). This witnessing is Esau's *raison d'etre* for the play. Even with the ongoing inquest, many Canadians have yet to learn the details of Ashley Smith's death. As the buzz after Protestival about Smith's story and the 500,000[2] *Youtube* hits of the Fifth Estate footage indicate, people are shocked by this event and want to know how something of this magnitude could occur. How could this horrifying event have happened and how do we prevent similar occurrences in future? Smith's death has become part of our social discourse surrounding the treatment of marginalized prison populations including youth, the mentally ill, and women.

Prior to its presentation in Protestival, Esau asked me to read *The Death of Ashley Smith* with the aim of helping her to develop it into a full-length play, and then directing it as a co-production between Les Nouvelles and my Vancouver-based company, Meta.for Theatre Society Meta).[3] The idea was to expand her existing monodrama from a solo show into a play for three women.

WATCHING GLORY DIE BY JUDITH THOMPSON

Before embarking on its primary purpose of tracing the choices made in Esau's play, this paper must acknowledge that it is not the only drama in the works to deal with Smith's tragic end. The event has also been dramatized by one of Canada's most established playwrights, Governor General Award winner, Judith Thompson. *Watching Glory Die*, a new play in development by Thompson, presents her version of the Ashley Smith story. While it is currently unpublished and unproduced, Thompson conducted a workshop reading of the play in May, 2012 at the Factory Theatre in Toronto, where it was to have its first production in the 2012/13 season.[4] Performed by a single actress, Thompson's three characters are "bound by a tragic death" (Ouzounian). *Watching Glory Die* presents an incarcerated teen (Glory), her mother (Rosalee), and a mature female guard (Gail).[5] Thompson's play not only puts the legal system on trial through the character of Gail, but also questions how we rear and care for children who have impulses toward violence and self-destruction. It questions the fundamental motivations for violence and universalizes internal struggles that we all face to greater and lesser degrees – fear of our own otherness, anxieties surrounding our abilities, loneliness and isolation. While Thompson's play profoundly differs in dramatic style from Esau's work-in-progress, both plays rely on documentary evidence to substantiate the speech of their three female characters.

In contrast to Esau, who does not present a character based on Ashley, Thompson creates Glory to speak for Ashley. The name Glory forms a double entendre: it is the character's name, but at the same time, the idea of 'watching glory die' speaks to Canada as a nation and its lack of observation and/or intervention on behalf of prisoners who suffer from mental health issues. If we stand by and watch glory die, we allow the system to dictate the most convenient way of dealing with especially troubled offenders, putting our correctional officers at risk, and failing to give appropriate help to those (oftentimes youth and women) in dire need. Thompson often uses a fictionalized version of Smith's real words.

For example, in this excerpt from a journal entry written by Smith on 4 September 2006 while still in the youth facility in New Brunswick, one gets an idea about her state of mind, her feelings of hopelessness regarding her own self-destructive acts, and her rising fear of being sent to an adult prison. This journal entry reveals the ever-renewed daily trial faced by Ashley Smith in the correctional system:

> If I die then I will never have to worry about upsetting my Mom again... Most people are scared to die. It can't be any worse then (*sic*) living a life like mine. Being dead I think would just suit me fine. I wonder when the best time to do it would be. ... I will call my Mom before bed and have one more chat. Somehow I have to let her know that none of this is her fault. I don't know why I'm like I am but I know she didn't do it to me. People say there is nothing wrong with me. ... When I use (*sic*) to try to hang myself I was just messing around trying to make them care and pay attention. Now it's different. ... It's no longer a joke. ... Maybe I will use a brand new pair of socks. Fresh for me. ... I want to die. I went to court yesterday and I though (*sic*) he was going to send me to adult! Time is running out. My chances are getting fewer and fewer. ... I'm done trying. ("Timeline")

Thompson uses this entry as a way for her character Glory to speak in Smith's voice and give onstage life to the young woman's struggles and fears:

> Before I go back to the swamp, I need to explain to my mother about why this is the only way. But they won't let me use the phone, so I just gotta say it, and hope that through some kind of magic, she is hearing me. / Mom, I want you to know first that absolutely none of this is your fault, I don't know why I am like this but I know for sure that you did not do it to me. You were a perfect mother, the best any girl could hope for. I tried to be good for you but things just kept happening and I just can't explain why. And then once I got in here, I just kept messing up and making things worse and now I am in so deep I wont never get out unless I get myself out in the only way I know how. I am really not scared to die, Mom, because it can't be worse than

living this life. They think I just do things for attention but they do not know what goes on inside my head. ...If I could get a pair of socks. / A nice pair of clean socks. / I could shove them down my throat. (Thompson 13-14)

That her mother might hear her words through "some kind of magic" is a poetic way to contextualize Glory's speech and frame the play as a story. That the officers "wont give [Glory] pencils cause they think [she] could stab herself" gives Glory reason to "just tell all [her] thoughts out loud all day every day" (Thompson 1). In *Watching Glory Die*, Judith Thompson distances herself from the stylistic milieu and, with the creative freedom of the dramatist, uses non-realistic elements, such as playing with time: when Glory speaks, it is on the eve of her death, but for Rosalee and Gail, Glory has already died.

In Thompson's play, Glory's birth mother is a crocodile who falls in love with a man fishing for cod. When Glory cracks her way out of her egg, her crocodile mother sees she looks human and deserts her. Of her entrance into human society, Glory says, "And so then after, this human Rosalee ... she found me, ... she picked me up and she kissed my head and I was hers and she was mine. For thirteen years, till I was arrested for shoving people on the street" (Thompson 1). Although Glory has a good relationship with her mother, she struggles with being human. Like Joan McLeod's "monster in the shape of a girl," (MacLeod) Glory feels alien, and this feeling is intensified by her incarceration:

Just lately? Since I been in here? I'm feelin her. / My Crocodile Mother. / her crocodile eyes behind my eyes. / the scaly skin behind my skin / I can feel her knife sharp teeth / and her GIANT tail inside me. Flapping when I am pissed off / The crocodile part of me ramming ramming against the girl part of me / Just tryin to get out. / And I'm reassuring her, you will, dude, don't worry, you will! ... I just cannot...make myself SMALL the way they wanted me to / Small and quiet. / Why? Why can't I do that? (Thompson 28)

Thompson uses the metaphor of a crocodile returning to its swamp to reference Smith's death. While her official cause of death was "self initiated asphyxiation" the question of whether or not Smith meant to kill herself is the subject of an ongoing inquest. In Thompson's play, the guard Gail describes Smith's death:

> They call that hypoxic. / Cause it means there is no oxygen getting to the face. / The veins are...blocked by the ligature. / Her face...was like that moment / When dusk/ Turns to night... where I live/ In the country. No streetlights, no city lights, / You can see this and that shape of a tree, a barn, / And then only the outlines / And then almost nothing / It was that. / When we went in. / The almost nothing. (Thompson 22).

This passage provides an eloquent and visceral explanation of what is a ghastly nightmare to watch on the video screen. To turn the purple face of asphyxiation into the "almost nothing" helps us process and grieve a national trauma. It turns horror into art and speaks to the humanity of the audience.

In Thompson's play, Glory's return to the swamp marks the passing of her human form. Glory states that since they will never release her from prison, there is "only one other way to get out" (2). Glory wants to return to the swamp because she cannot control the crocodile inside her; it wants to bite and fling its tail and hurt people. It is something other than human, and "if [she] can just get back to the swamp, with all the other crocodiles, [she] can get the word to [Rosalee], that [she is] fine, [she is] free. *GLORY begins ripping the ligatures again and wrapping around her throat*" (21). This inner creature embodies our own otherness. We all do things we should not do. We all have a voice of censure in our heads.

Like Esau, Judith Thompson tells Smith's story as a wake-up call for Canadians, using facts from Smith's case. Rosalee, who sees Glory's time in prison as torture and advocates fiercely for women like her daughter, who are at risk, communicates one of the shocking facts uncovered in the documentary:

The Death of Ashley Smith

> They have moved her ... / seventeen times / In the last YEAR. / SEVENTEEN TIMES IN THE LAST YEAR. / And do you know why? / Do you want to know why? / Because they wanted to keep her in isolation without a report. / ... They knew they were breaking all the laws of how you treat ...inmates...young inmates, and they wanted to keep doin what they were doin they wanted to keep torturing my daughter ... . (13/23/24)

In another example, Hana Gartner's *Behind the Wall* revealed that on 1 September 2007 Ashley Smith was pepper sprayed eleven times. Esau and Thompson both reference that event:

> Rachel: That day there was an incident every ten minutes. We pepper sprayed her 11 times that day. *11 times.* / Started that morning. Wouldn't give back her food tray. (Esau 2)

> Glory: And they pepper sprayed me eleven times in one day. / ELEVEN times. /'give a little, get a little' that's what the Gail kept saying, what does that mean / Give a little, get a little. I just don't get that, do you? Maybe if I had understood that, things would be different I wouldn't have to do what I am going to do tomorrow. (Thompson 16)

It is interesting that the representatives of the CSC in both plays are female. Female prison guards work within a male dominated arena, and most of the decision makers in the correctional services are men. Yet both playwrights write the guards as female, which has the effect of heightening their empathetic reading by the audience. Not only do these women struggle to survive an aggressive work environment, as women they may also sympathise with their prisoner more than the average male. Unlike Esau's very young female guard, Thompson's Gail is in her middle years with children of her own. Gail comes from a family of correctional officers. She tells the story of an inmate who tricked her brother into smuggling drugs into the prison and threatened to expose him. Her brother killed himself, and through this we understand that the prison is a harsh reality on both sides of the bars. For both Rachel and Gail, the stresses of the job and the very real risk officers' face on a daily basis contribute to creating empathy. We do not envy the guard's position and cannot really blame her for following orders. According to Hana Gartner's research, CSC "has an annual operating budget of nearly three billion dollars; less than two percent is spent on mental health care for inmates"("Behind the Wall"). Thompson's Gail asks the audience, "Do you not think they shoulda taken her to a facility? Where they know how to take CARE of these people? WHAT WAS SHE DOING IN A JAIL?" (14). For her part, Gail, has limited ability to advocate. As she says:

> I can't quit, this is the only job I have ever done, ... / I been doin this since I was eighteen years old. / My whole family is in corrections. / That is our tradition. / This uniform. / The penitentiary. / We are not / Just security guards. / Like someone who stands in front of your condo, lets you in and out. We are not goons with keys. / You need training for this. / You need college training. Gun training. CPR (although we never actually get that) / serious training in the rules, the protocol of a penitentiary / You cant fool around with these people. These are serious criminals. ... Its only the other c.os of the world / Who get it. / Nobody else / Gets it. So nobody else has the right / To have / An opinion / About what happened / To Glory Smith. ... 'Criminal negligence causing death' / Are you kidding me? / That is like calling us murderers. / Murderers. / For doing our job, / For obeying our orders. (9/10/14)

Watching Glory Die is still in development. Therefore, in the unpublished text there are notes and reminders to Thompson written by herself such as "new writing about the naming of Glory or bringing her home or something," or calling for a "full re-write" of one of Rosalee's monologues. Different fonts, sections of capitalized dialogue, and multiple colours of ink are used in this working draft. For now, at the very end of the play the "last line or gesture" belonging to Glory is yet "to be discovered" (24). Whether Thompson will make that discovery on the page or as the first actress brings the part to life next year remains to be seen.

THE DEATH OF ASHLEY SMITH BY LEAH JANE ESAU

The Death of Ashley Smith begins with the soundscape of a carnival and the voiceover speech of a mother frantically looking for her daughter, Ashley. The image engendered of a child lost among throngs of families, bright colours, explosive sounds and smells, is frightening. The rising lights reveal Rachel, in uniform, sitting in an interrogation room behind "thousands of pages. These are Ashley Smith's files" (Esau *Death* 1). Rachel is worried that she will lose her job and is particularly concerned about how her father will react if she does. Currently on suspension, she is only making one third of her salary, an injustice to her considering she had been "bitten, punched, [and] urinated on" during some of Smith's "800 [reported] incidents" (2). Rachel says, "I'm suspended 'cause of her. I should get a medal" (2). Rachel introduces the central metaphor of the play when she compares Ashley to a whale "so dumb she's swam outta water and beached herself"(2).

Rachel represents the four real correctional officers who felt they were scapegoated by upper management for Smith's death. The charge of criminal negligence causing death was ultimately dropped for these arrested officers (Dalton). Among them was Blaine Phibbs, who becomes the basis for Esau's un-staged character, Jason, another guard and Rachel's romantic interest. According to the Union of Canadian Correctional Officers (UCCO), "Phibbs drew pictures of Smith's hometown to put in the window of her barren cell" ("Documents"). In Esau's play, Jason is shown to have gone out of his way for Smith in a similar fashion: "Jason drew the pictures, and put them up in her cell, even though he wasn't supposed to go in there. That's what solitary means. He almost got fired for doing shit like that" (*Death* 4-5). Esau's Jason has a degree in criminology, and Rachel works hard to impress him in front of the other guards. Rachel may be worn-down from working with Smith (the real guards and nurses felt the strain of the additional resources Smith required), but she is also drawn as a reasonably intelligent, productive member of society. In her short career as a correctional officer, Rachel has had to put up with older male guards demeaning her due to age and lack of work experience. She hints at the sexism and poor treatment inherent in her male-dominated job:

> Jason respects me even though I'm young. / Not like those other assholes. I'm like, I'm 22, I know what I'm doing, ok, ... [I'm] handling shit just fine, and just 'cause you're 50 doesn't mean you know more than me. 'Cause they don't. / They were all there when it happened, and they didn't do anything different than me: we did the same thing. (3)

What the guards did was film Smith's asphyxiation as part of the protocol involved with her self-harm and "use-of-force" directives (UCCO "A Rush" 31). They did not attempt to physically remove her ligature for over thirty minutes. Her last gasping breath is audible on the video ("Behind the Wall"). Once Smith became unconscious, a guard's intervention would not be classified as a use-of-force[6] incident and therefore would not require national reporting. On October 9, 2007, a use-of-force "training session" was held at Grand Valley Institution specifically pertaining to Smith. At this session, "guards were instructed when Ashley was applying ligatures not to enter her cell if she [was] still breathing" ("Timeline").

There is a great deal of documented evidence of Smith's destructive tendencies and the punitive measures that were taken to restrain her. Esau's Rachel depicts Ashley as violent and unmanageable:

> She was dangerous. Who knows what would've happened if she got out. 75 days [in prison] turned into four years. ... Sentence is extended: 30 days for refusing to be strip searched / 30 days for hitting staff / 10 days for refusal to hand over food tray / 30 days for spitting at staff / 30 days for kicking staff in groin / – it goes on, and on, and on. You know most of 'em figure it out: you hit me, that's assault, and when you go back to court, the judge is gonna keep you in jail longer. ... She never really figured that out. (3)

In fact, the majority of Smith's criminal charges were incurred while she was in custody. Aside from the 800 documented incidents from her years at New Brunswick Youth Centre (NBYC), she had 150 reported incidents of self-harm. There were days near the end of her life when she would self-strangulate "sometimes six or seven times a day. The choking became so severe that facial blood vessels burst, leaving her face permanently discolored. She lost sight in one eye and suffered nosebleeds" ("Timeline"). In the conclusion of a January 2010 report for the Correctional Investigator's office, psychiatrist Dr. Paul Beaudry explained:

> Ms. Smith suffered from very complex problems characterized by a combination of antisocial personality disorder and borderline personality traits. . . . [P]ersonality disorders are not considered to be medical conditions for which there are specific and effective treatments, ... [and] self-destructive acts and repeated assaults can severely test even the most experienced of workers ... the line separating interventions intended as therapeutic from correctional interventions can become rather blurred. (36)

If prisoners with mental health issues are deemed "not conducive to treatment" the guards can do little more than to use restraints to maintain order. They are left asking themselves how they are supposed to deal with people who are so badly in need of help, not punishment. Rachel admits that her training is inadequate: "You wanna know how they train us for 'mental health?' It's a two-hour course. We take it online" (Esau 5).[7]

The lack of substantial training for dealing with inmates with mental health issues becomes a source of empathy between Rachel and the audience; we acknowledge that as a society we bear responsibility for the on-the-job safety and well-being of our corrections officers, as much as for the safety and wellbeing of our inmates. *A Rush to Judgment: A report of the death in custody of Ashley Smith, an inmate at Grand Valley Institution for Women* by UCCO cites Montreal coroner Dr. Paul Dionne's statement that "correctional staff are neither trained nor equipped to deal with [the] challenge" of what has become "long-term warehousing of the mentally ill in the nation's prisons" (37). Rachel argues that she was just doing her job the day Smith died: "Rick came in and he said: if anyone goes in there, if anyone intervenes, then you're fired. That's what he said: fired. ... *I* didn't order her to be put in solitary confinement. *I'm* not the one who told everybody *not to intervene*. All I did was show up for work!" (Esau 5).

For Esau, "art arises from a desire to understand the crimes that are committed in our cities, a desire to investigate living conditions around us, and a desire to bring these relevant, social stories to audiences" ("About Shed"). The line between reality and creative licence is constantly negotiated in this kind of theatre; it is not wholly verbatim theatre, because characters speak lines the playwright has written as well as words actually spoken by their non-fiction counterparts. Yet, it is also not entirely a work of fiction: the power of the story comes from the newsworthiness of the event. Thus, a central dynamic in the play arises from its negotiation of the boundaries between docudrama and fiction. For example, Smith did throw apples at a postal worker, but there is no indication that they "left a bruise on his neck" or that Smith "hit him so hard he couldn't breathe" (Esau 3). As another example of blending truth and fiction, Rachel says, Ashley was "sent to the Women's unit in Saskatoon: the psych ward, and was removed two days later, 'for her own safety.' Do you know how overcrowded the psych ward is? Inmates wait months, sometime *years* to get in. They only have 12 beds for women. She missed her chance" (Esau 4). In reality, the only time Smith was at Saskatoon's Regional Psychiatric Centre (RPC), a "psychiatric hospital with the country's only therapeutic healing program designed specifically for women offenders," she was there for almost four months ("Behind the Wall"). Ultimately, Smith was removed because correctional supervisor John Tarala beat her. Although he was charged at the time, he was later found not guilty of assault ("Sask."). While at RPC Smith befriended nurse Sindee Tchorzewski who bravely spoke out against Tarala and made such an impression on Smith that five months later Smith wrote Tchorzewski a letter saying how much she misses her and that she wishes she was "still back at RPC" because she would "do things different" (Smith). RPC had over 200 patients at the time of Gartner's report, but there were only 12 beds for women offenders.

Esau's fundamental reason for writing the play is to make sure that Smith's story is exposed and continues to be a point of discussion amongst politically and socially engaged Canadians. Esau says of her earlier play *Shed*, which dealt with a 2006 incident in which several Winnipeg children, aged eight to eleven, locked a 14-year-old companion into a playground shed and lit it on fire, that it "in no way means to be a documentary or creative non-fiction: it is a work of fiction, inspired by a news article" ("About Shed"); but *The Death of Ashley Smith* creates a greater struggle with that stylistic line. It is one of the reasons that Esau is hesitant to employ the character of Coralee Smith, although in an expansion of the play it would be important to hear the voice of Ashley's mother, in order to understand her confusion and disempowerment. She could not help her daughter with her internal struggle to "fit" into society, nor could she help her once she was caught in the legal system. Esau has made a specific choice not to speak in the voice of Ashley Smith herself. Although there are journal excerpts available through news reports that show Smith's state of mind at various points of her internment, Esau does not want to fictionalize what Smith may or may not have been thinking and feeling in the months and minutes before her death. Smith's real words are presented, yet they come through other characters. Someone else is always mediating our experience of her.

While Thompson uses the sound effect of a ligature ripping between scenes to indicate Smith's dreadful end, Esau shows a minute of Smith's actual death. Esau's script carries a cautionary warning for potential readers or producers regarding her use of the video: "this video contains a graphic prison recording of 19 year old Ashley Smith, choking herself to death, while prison guards watch and film" (Esau 1). What are the ethical ramifications of using the real footage of Smith's death as the climax of the drama? Is she obligated to warn her viewing public? There were no warnings posted at Protestival, and afterwards one person approached

Esau to question her on the use of the video, ultimately agreeing that it was important for her to have seen it. Esau welcomes this kind of disquietude. Shifting the audience's focus from the live action of the stage to a screen should logically increase aesthetic distance; however, the video of Smith is so compelling it is impossible not to become viscerally engaged. Nevertheless, showing the video clip raises the question of whether the viewing is exploitive and voyeuristic, or whether it simply fulfills Coralee Smith's wish for the public to become aware of (and outraged by) the treatment of Ashley and other young offenders with mental health issues in our federal penitentiaries. In Gartner's *Out of Control*, Coralee Smith tells us, "Canada should know. . . .There are young people in jail for minor infractions, for mental conditions, not being treated and held for five, six, seven, eight years." According to newspaper reporter Diana Zlomislic, "Nearly five years after Smith's death, Canadian prisons are still relying on segregation, force and chemical restraints to manage mentally ill inmates" (Zlomislic). At the end of the monodrama, the voice of the mother calls out three times: "Has anyone see my daughter?" At this point, however, the sounds of the carnival are replaced by a single, slowing beat on a heart rate monitor. In this clever use of sound design, Esau juxtaposes the fairly common experience of losing a child for a time in a public space, to the wholly disorienting and sickening tragedy of losing Ashley Smith to a correctional system that failed to help her.

When Esau and I began discussions about how to expand her play, we both saw it as a series of monologues to be performed by three women. Using a structure reminiscent of Judith Thompson's *Palace of the End*, each monologue stands alone. In our case, they afford different perspectives on the event of Smith's death. Each monologue contains its own character and story arc, but the three together provide a broader picture of the whole tragedy. The story builds one monologue at a time as each subsequent character provides additional information. For me, the first monologue belongs to Coralee Smith demanding that Canadians learn the truth of why and how her daughter died the way she did. The second character is a psychiatrist (or nurse) who assesses Smith after her death through her records and questions her (lack of) treatment. The final monologue is by Rachel, the young guard who wonders how she will recover from this event. The soundscape of the mother trying to find her daughter at the beginning and the end remain, as does the footage of Smith's death. Additional sound effects taking place between the monologues supplement the carnival and heart rate monitor. This structure differs from Thompson's *Watching Glory Die*, in which the text, performed by a solo actor, is interwoven and builds on both its character and story arc each time we rotate between the characters of Glory, Rosalee, and Gail. By contrast, Esau's use of the actual footage unsettles the audience and even prompts outrage. Its intent is to drive you home to continue to research the story.

At one point in Esau's play Rachel says, "Can you tell them I'm ready to go back to work? I'm not traumatized by what happened" (4), and yet Esau has clearly drawn a woman in conflict. Scapegoated by her superiors ("We wait / We wait half an hour / We were just ... we were just doing what we were told" [6]), uncertain of her future ("Jason says he's ... gonna go back to his hometown and start a coffee shop. / I can't get fired, I can't" [6]), and regretful of the decisions she made the day Smith died ("I should'da, I should'da maybe, like gone in and checked on her, even though they would'da fired me – 'cause now they're gonna fire me anyways! I can feel it" [6]), Rachel displays a high level of anxiety, fear, and anger. I too felt a high level of anxiety, fear, and anger after seeing *The Death of Ashley Smith* at Protestival, much of which I attribute to (re)watching the video of Smith's death. This play should make us panic. Ashley Smith's negligent treatment could have happened to any Canadian citizen caught in similar circumstances.

At present, Esau believes the success of this piece is due to its brevity. For her, the whole point is to have the video seen, to have the reports by Gartner continue to reach the broader Canadian population, and to not let Ashley Smith's story become yesterday's news. Through its inclusion in theatre festivals, Esau's play ensures this video clip at least will reach a diverse yet publicly engaged audience, and will perhaps move those audiences to go to their computers to see the whole story for themselves. Esau also questions whether the strength of the piece lies in its single perspective. In this case, she would have to expand the play with only the character of Rachel on stage. Perhaps the piece as it is already fulfils its function. It asks us to continue an inquiry into the Canadian penal system and to go beyond this one horrible event. Once I began to learn about Ashley's plight, it became very difficult not to want to find everything that was written about it including the reports from mental health professionals and the Union of Correctional Services. It has raised my awareness of other instances of legal injustices occurring in our prisons in relation to the marginalized populations. Since the inquest into Smith's death is ongoing, Esau has put the project on hold for the time being. New evidence will inevitably bring new ideas and new dialogue. As we are discovering, there is so much more to this story and therefor so much more to process. For now, her short but powerful play can make its rounds as part of larger festivals and continue to reach audiences across Canada and abroad.

Conclusion

The importance of Ashley Smith's story is made clear by the number of trials people have waged since her death. The ongoing inquest puts the CSC on trial daily. That two Canadian playwrights, one at the beginning of her career and one firmly ensconced as a leader and mentor, had such intense reactions to her death that it prompted creative output shows both the anomalous nature of this event and its frightful reality. Both authors heard a need in Coralee Smith to have the Canadian public know about her daughter's death. The life and death of Ashley Smith belongs within Canadian consciousness and public discourse. With these two new Canadian plays, Smith's case can urge us to become more informed about our prisons and the people inside them. It is remarkable to me that I have been able to read Thompson's text in its working stage and

I look forward to its premiere. The staging of both of these productions will continue to bring attention to stories like Ashley Smith's. Through the powerful medium of theatre can we engender social awareness and discussion. Only through our awareness can we make a difference.

Notes

1. The *Youtube* video is an excerpt from Hana Gartner's *Out of Control*.
2. That particular clip now has over 857, 000 views.
3. Esau and I met when I was co-convening the Festival of Original Theatre (FOOT) at the University of Toronto and she was assigned as a production assistant. Festival of Original Theatre (FOOT) Conference: Exquisite Corpses, Bloody Bodies: Murder, Myth and Representations of Violence on Stage and Screen (University of Toronto Centre for Drama, Theatre and Performance Studies. 2009).
4. Artistic director and Factory Theatre founder Ken Gass was fired by the theatre's board of directors in June, 2012. He has since begun the Canadian Rep Theatre and is directing and producing Thompson's work at the Cultch in Vancouver in April –May 2014.
5. Since this text is a work-in-progress, all page numbering is my own.
6. There were an inordinately high number of use-of-force reports regarding Inmate Smith because she was not a docile prisoner. She was often non-compliant and her destruction of cells and self-harm were part of the reason for her long-term residence in segregation.
7. This fact comes from Gartner's *Behind the Wall*.

Works Cited

"Ashley Smith family settles $11M suit." CBC Canada, May 4, 2011. Online.

Beaudry, Paul. *Ms. Ashley Smith: Psychiatric opinion based on record review.* CBC News. January, 2010. Online.

Dalton, Melinda. "Charges dropped against Grand Valley prison Guards." *The Star* December 8, 2008. Online

Esau, Leah Jane. "About Shed." Online.

--------. *Curriculum vitae.* Online.

--------. *The Death of Ashley Smith.* Unpublished ms.

Gartner, Hana. "Out of Control." CBC: *The Fifth Estate.* January 8, 2010. Television.

--------. "Behind the Wall." CBC: *The Fifth Estate*: November 12, 2010. Television.

MacLeod, Joan. *Shape of a Girl/Jewel.* Vancouver: Talonbooks, 2002. Print.

Ouzounian, Richard. "Factory Theatre, Acting Up Stage announce their new season." *Toronto Online* April 3, 2012. Online.

"Protestival!" BlogTO. July 28, 2011. Online.

Sapers, Howard. *A Preventable Death.* Office of the Correctional Investigator. June 20, 2008. Online.

"Sask. Guard cleared in Ashley Smith assault case." CBC News, January 21, 2010. Online.

Smith, Ashley. "Letter to Sindee Tchorzewski at RPC." August 8, 2007. Online.

"Timeline for Ashley Smith." CBC: *The Fifth Estate.* Online

Union of Canadian Correctional Officers (UCCO). *A new national strategy for high-risk women.* Autumn, 2005. Print.

--------. *A Rush to Judgment: A report on the death in custody of Ashley Smith, an inmate at the Grand Valley Institution for Women.* October, 2008. Print.

------. Documents/UCCO-SACC/Ontario/documents/ Archives, 2008. Online.

"Winnipeg teen survives bullies' shed fire." CBC News: Manitoba. October 16, 2006. Online.

Zlomislic, Diana. "Mentally ill female prisoners treated cruelly, inhumanely, report finds." *The Star* May 9, 2012. Online.

Index

abortion, 3, 169
acting conventions, 55
Adler, Alfred, 234
adultery, 7, 114, 118, 125, 129, 141, 143, 152, 164, 189
Aeschylus
  Eumenides, 27
Africa, 230
agency, 51–54, 69, 72, 102, 261, 279, 289
agōn, 15, 26
Althusser, Louis, 13–14, 208
Anderson, Maxwell, 138, 142–143, 148, 150
  Joan of Lorraine, 19
  Mary of Scotland, 137, 139–141
Anne of Denmark, 106
Anouilh, Jean
  Lark, The, 19
Aristotle, 5, 160–161, 165–166, 202
Athens, 15, 28
audience, 2, 8, 15–17, 19–20, 38, 52, 54, 57–58, 60, 78, 80, 82–83, 87, 89, 94, 101, 103, 106, 116, 119, 126, 131, 140, 150–151, 158, 165, 171, 177, 202–203, 211, 215, 225, 241, 243–249, 251–252, 254, 260, 265–272, 280–281, 285, 300, 304–306, 309, 312–314

Babington plot, 137–139
Bad Companions, 199
Barker, John Nelson
  Superstition, 18
beauty, 12, 70–71, 73–75, 77, 84–85,

beauty (*continued*), 88, 121, 164
blinding, 29, 34, 37
Bloomer girls, 181
Boleyn, Anne, 7
Bolt, Robert, 138, 142–144, 148, 150
  Vivat! Vivat Regina!, 137, 139, 141
Bothwell, James, 138, 140–142, 148–150
Brecht, Bertolt, 6, 144, 171–172, 232, 283
  Caucasian Chalk Circle, 18–19
  Good Person of Szechwan, The, 19
  St. Joan of the Stockyards, 19
  "Street Scene", 286
Bryans, Joan, 113, 125–131
  By Some Divine Mistake, 8, 10, 12, 114, 124
Buddhism, 51
Bundy, Ted, 244, 253–255, 257

Catholicism, 122–124, 138–140, 142–143, 145–146, 148, 150–152, 154
charis, 41
China, 6, 8, 18, 45–47, 50–61
Chinese music theatre, 6, 8, 45
Churchill, Caryl
  Vinegar Tom, 7, 9, 11–12, 14, 157–159, 166–173
civil dispute, 70
Civil Rights Movement, 278, 286, 289

Clarke, Mary Carr
   Sarah Maria Cornell; or, the Fall River Murder, 18
class, 1–2, 6–7, 59, 122, 127, 131, 166, 170, 183, 187, 198, 260, 280, 284, 289
Communicado Theatre Company, 145
Confucius, 45, 48–53, 57–60
corruption, 13, 48, 70, 76, 78, 80–81, 84, 96, 100, 105
costume, 33–34, 42, 143, 152, 166, 180, 282
court hearing, 79
crime, 7, 9, 12, 19, 48, 67, 87, 94–95, 103, 108, 113–114, 116, 138, 157, 162, 208, 226–227, 229, 233, 235, 242, 244, 246, 248, 252–255, 260, 262, 277, 280–281
cross-dressing, 91, 103–104
cross-gender acting, 55, 61

dao, 46, 51, 56, 61
Darnley, Henry, Lord, 10, 138, 140–142, 148–150
Daviot, Gordon, 141
death row, 177, 254
Dekker, Thomas (with John Ford and William Rowley)
   The Witch of Edmonton, 157
Dickinson, Emily, 213
Dionysus, 41
divorce, 3, 125, 263
domesticity, 180–181

Elizabeth I, Queen of England, 10, 137, 142, 146
Elizabethan period, 113–114, 117
England, 7, 11, 103, 122, 125, 128, 133, 137–139, 141–142, 144–147,

England (*continued*), 149, 151, 157–159, 169, 182, 201, 206
Esau, Leah Jane, 293–294, 298, 301, 304–305, 308–310, 312, 314, 316
   Death of Ashley Smith, The, 9, 12, 16, 299–300, 307, 311, 313
   Shed, 311
ethics, 46, 49, 51–53, 56, 183, 223–225, 229, 233–236
Euripides, 26, 28, 35, 38, 74, 116, 225
   Hecuba, 7, 10, 14, 25, 41
evidence, 4, 76–77, 79, 84, 87, 101, 160, 163, 168, 173, 177, 187, 191, 207, 215, 240–241, 250, 261, 264–265, 267–268, 272, 285, 301, 308, 314
execution, 48–50, 54, 56, 124, 138–140, 142, 145, 149–150, 152, 160, 164, 173, 189, 229, 232, 241–243, 249–250, 253

family, 6, 11, 14, 50, 68, 72, 89, 99, 120, 147, 161, 165, 182, 190, 192, 201–202, 208–209, 214, 223, 226–229, 232–234, 244–245, 247–249, 257, 277–278, 281, 283–284, 295, 305–306
femininity, 10–11, 91, 103, 105–107, 115, 145, 182, 186, 224, 241, 262
feminism, 201–202, 208
Fifth Estate, 295, 298–299
flapper, 177–178, 180, 182–183, 185, 189, 194, 196–197, 201
Ford, John, 141, 157
Foucault, Paul-Michel, 281
Fraser, Antonia, 138, 152–153
Freud, Sigmund, 229

GQ Magazine, 249

Index

Gaillaire-Bourega, Fatima
   You Have Come Back, 19
Gartner, Hana, 299–300, 306, 311, 313
   Out of Control (television documentary), 298, 312, 316
   Behind the Wall (television documentary), 298, 305, 316
gender, 1–7, 9–10, 12–17, 19–20, 25, 28–31, 33–40, 42, 53, 55–57, 61, 70–71, 78, 89–90, 93–95, 104, 107, 113–117, 119, 121, 123, 129–130, 132, 146, 153, 158–159, 162, 166–167, 170–172, 178, 180, 186, 191, 195–196, 199, 208, 223–224, 260, 262, 277, 280, 283
gendered space, 33, 36, 39
gendered transgression, 260
Genet, Jean
   Maids, The, 19
Gentile, Donna, 246–247
ghost, 46–48, 51–52, 54, 152, 226, 228, 271
Gilligan, Carol, 115, 224–225
Glaspell, Susan, 184
   Trifles, 19
Green, Debbie Tucker
   Stoning Mary, 8, 10, 14, 225, 229–235
Guan Hanquing
   Riverside Pavilion, The, 59
   Snow in Midsummer, 8, 12–14, 45–48, 53, 55, 57–59, 61
Gunderson, Laura
   Emilie the Marquise du Chatelet Defends Her Life Tonight, 20

Hall, Edith, 15, 29, 158–159
Hammett, Dashiell, 199–200
HERE Arts Center, 243

Hellman, Lillian, 200–201, 217
   The Children's Hour, 8, 11, 13–14, 199, 202–204, 208, 215
Hermann, Gottfried, 38, 42
Homer, 41
homosexuality, 160, 215
homosocial relationships, 103
honor, 73, 75, 100, 209
Hu Zhiyu
   "Preface for the Poem for Madam Song," 46

impartiality, 28, 268
insanity, 260–261, 263–264, 266, 271

Jacobean stage, 106
James I of England, 18, 20, 106
   Daemonologie, 102
Jazz Age, 180, 182
Jenkins, Tricia, 244
Joan of Arc, 13–14, 19, 114, 120–123, 129–133
Jonson, Ben, 102
   Masque of Blackness, 106
jury, 3, 19, 127, 173, 178, 190, 193–194, 200, 205, 215, 251, 259–261, 264–273, 288
   audience as jury, 15–17
justice, 6, 15, 30, 35, 40, 50–51, 53–54, 58, 68, 87, 90–94, 97–99, 101, 104–105, 107, 115, 121, 128, 149, 158, 195, 204–205, 208, 216, 223–224, 229, 233–234, 246, 253–254, 261, 267, 289, 298

Kesselman, Wendy
   My Sister in This House, 19
Knox, John, 141, 145, 147, 150

Knox, John (*continued*)
   First Blast of the Trumpet Against the Monstrous Regiment of Women, The, 143
Kohlberg, Lawrence, 224
Kreitzer, Carson, 11, 14, 16, 240–241, 243–245, 248, 250, 252–256
   Self Defense, or the death of some salesmen, 8–9, 239
Kushner, Tony, 280

language, 202
Last Resort Bar, the, 36, 239, 244, 246
law, 3, 5, 7–8, 10, 14, 18, 46–50, 58, 69, 88, 94, 99–101, 106–107, 114–115, 131, 138, 192, 203–204, 216, 229, 240, 242, 247–248, 254, 256, 261–264, 273, 277–278, 284, 286, 297
Leicester, Robert Dudley, earl of, 138, 140, 142
lesbianism, 200, 207–208, 210, 213, 215, 250, 287
Li Qianfu
   Circle of Chalk, 18
Lochhead, Liz, 141–143, 146, 148–152
   Mary Queen of Scots Got Her Head Chopped Off, 12, 137–139, 144–145, 147, 153
Lombroso, Caesar, 239–240, 262–263

madness, 119, 148, 262–263, 271
Malleus Maleficarum, 170–171, 173
Mann, Emily, 11, 262, 265, 267–268, 270–274
   Mrs. Packard, 8, 259–260, 264

married women, 194, 261, 263, 273
Mary of Scotland (film 1936), 137, 139–141
Mary, Queen of Scots (film 1971), 12, 137–139, 144–145, 147, 152–153
McCarthy, Joseph, 171
McCulloch, Margery Palmer, 147, 153
Mei Lanfang, 19
Miller, Arthur
   "Are You Now or Were You Ever," 160
   Crucible, The, 7–8, 13–15, 157–166, 170–173
   Death of a Salesman, The, 162, 256
   "Tragedy and the Common Man," 160, 162
misogyny, 30, 34, 39, 104, 143, 145, 150, 202, 213
Monstrous Regiment, 143, 159, 166
motherhood, 194, 274
Mulgrew, Gerry, 145–147

National Theatre of Scotland, 145
new woman, 180–181
Nicholson, Taraha Shenice, 248
No Humans Involved (NHI), 246–248, 252, 255
Noah, Mordecai M.
   She Would Be a Soldier, 18

Obolensky, Masha
   Not Enough Air, 20

Packard, Elizabeth, 8, 11, 259–262, 264, 266, 268–269, 271–273
Palmer, Richard H., 141
paternalism, 263–264, 266

Patmore, Coventry, 9
patriarchy, 4–6, 12–16, 51, 58, 72, 88, 159, 162, 171–172, 181, 183, 191, 194, 203–204, 229, 234–235, 284
Peking Opera, 19
Plato, 103, 148
plunder, 30, 32
Pralle, Arlene, 244
Presbyterian, 147
prison, 11–12, 16, 21, 117, 130, 149, 189, 228, 232, 241, 250, 253, 277–284, 286–289, 293–294, 296, 298–300, 302, 304–305, 308, 311
prostitution, 3, 11, 72, 121, 239–240, 248, 250
Protestantism, 138, 145–148
psychoanalysis, 224
Pussy Riot, 4, 21

Ragen, Naomi
   Women's Minyan, 19
rape, 67–68, 78, 87, 90–93, 105, 244, 249, 251–252, 254, 283
Rattenbury, Alma Pakenham, 114, 124
Rickman, Alan
   My Name Is Rachel Corrie, 19
Rivendell Theatre Ensemble, 251
Rizzio, David, 142–143, 148–149
Roman legend, 68

saint, 7, 13, 19, 113–114, 120, 122–123, 131, 146
Salem, MA, 159–160, 164, 173
separate spheres, 265
sexuality, 70, 85, 90, 141–143, 147–148, 170, 172, 199, 206, 208–210, 212, 214, 239
Schiller, Friedrich, 133, 138, 142, 145, 150

Schiller, Friedrich (*continued*)
   Mary Stuart, 137, 139–140, 152
Scotland, 8, 137–154, 200–201
Scottish nationalism, 145
segregation, 277–278, 286–289, 296, 312, 316
Shakespeare, William, 70, 74, 85, 113, 118, 120, 131, 133, 203
   Antony and Cleopatra, 105
   Hamlet, 18, 82
   Henry VI, 114
   King Lear, 18, 100
   Macbeth, 157
   Much Ado About Nothing, 18
   "Rape of Lucrece, The," 92
   Taming of the Shrew, The, 18
   Titus Andronicus, 68
   Troilus and Cressida, 8, 11–12, 15, 67–69, 71, 77, 82
   Winter's Tale, The, 7–8, 10, 13–14, 114, 117, 119, 129–130
Shaw, George Bernard
   Saint Joan, 7, 13, 19, 114, 120, 131
Sima Guan
   Precepts on Family Life, 50
Simon, Bennett, 223, 225, 227–228, 233–234
Smith, Ashley (Inquest), 9, 12, 16, 293, 295, 298–302, 305, 307, 309, 311–315
Smith, Coralee, 295, 300, 311–312, 314
Snyder, Ruth, 20, 187–195
sob sister, 178, 183–185, 189–191, 196
social norms, 4, 123, 210, 264
Son, Diana, 253–254, 271, 282
Sophocles, 116
   Antigone, 18

Sophocles (*continued*)
   Oedipus Rex, 16
speakeasy, 198
speech, 5, 14, 25, 27, 34, 42, 71, 75, 79, 128, 142–143, 146, 149–151, 153, 163, 169, 172, 185, 191, 203–204, 207, 213, 215, 227, 243, 263, 267, 272, 284–285, 294, 301–302, 304, 310–312
Spenser, Edmund, 143, 148
Stephenson, Shelagh, 235
   Five Kinds of Silence, 8, 10, 12, 225–229, 231, 234

Tanner, John, 240, 253–255
Taoism, 51
testimony, 79–80, 89, 91, 164, 192, 252, 254, 256, 261–262, 264–265, 267–271
Thatcher, Margaret, 146
Thompson, Judith, 17, 294, 302, 304–305, 311–312, 314, 316
   Watching Glory Die, 9, 12, 16, 301, 303, 306, 313
tragedy, 2, 5, 12, 14, 28, 34, 38, 40–42, 87, 90, 104, 108, 116, 120, 139, 160, 162, 165–166, 191, 223, 225, 227, 233–234, 312
Treadwell, Sophie, 184, 189–190
   Machinal, 9–10, 12, 20, 177–178, 183, 191–194, 196, 198, 260, 262
trial
   formal trial, 70, 265–266, 269, 272–273
   simulacrum-trial, 266, 268
   social trial, 269, 289
Trojan war, 25, 30–31, 41–42, 69, 71, 73–74, 83–84
true woman, 181

Tucker Green, Debbie
   Stoning Mary, 8, 10, 14, 225, 229–235

unruly woman, 1–2, 4–5, 15, 76

von Rŭte of Bern, Han, 18
verdict, 118, 125, 127–128, 130, 145, 206, 211–213, 215–216, 260, 272–273
Vine, Katharine
   My Name Is Rachel Corrie, 19
Virgin Mary, 147
virtue, 13, 49–50, 52, 68, 70, 114, 116, 120, 161, 163, 180

Wallace, Naomi, 281–282
   And I and Silence, 9, 11, 14, 277, 279–280, 283–287, 289
   Birdy, 280
   One Flea Spare, 280
   Slaughter City, 280, 285
   Things of Dry Hours, 280, 284–285
   Trestle at Pope Lick Creek, The, 280
   War Boys, 280, 284
war, 7, 15, 25, 30–32, 34, 38–39, 68–70, 72–73, 75–77, 80, 83–84, 106, 125, 133, 178–181, 196, 198, 233, 278, 280, 284
Watkins, Maureen Dallas
   Chicago, 19, 260, 262
Webster, John, 88–90, 94, 102, 107
   Appius and Virginia, 91
   Devil's Law-Case, The, 99, 106
   Duchess of Malfi, The, 93
   White Devil, The, 8, 10, 12, 87, 92, 101, 103
whore, 72, 76, 80, 82–85, 87–90, 92,

whore (*continued*), 96–97, 104–105, 107, 142–143, 147, 153, 163, 167
witchcraft, 7, 11, 102, 157–159, 161–162, 167–168, 170–171, 173
woman's suffrage, 179
women journalists, 183, 185–186, 196
Woolf, Virginia, 9, 223, 229
World War I, 178–181, 196
writing, 2, 8–9, 15, 18, 46, 50, 59, 116–117, 122, 151, 153, 166,

writing (*continued*), 177–178, 186, 225, 232, 260, 262, 269, 272, 302, 306, 310, 314

xiqu, 45–46, 51, 53–57

Yu Tang Chun the Courtesan, 19
Yuan Dynasty, 18, 45, 58, 60

Ziegler, Anna
  Photograph 51, 20

www.ingramcontent.com/pod-product-compliance
Lightning Source LLC
Chambersburg PA
CBHW050837230426
43667CB00012B/2042